Educational Vocational Guidance and Counselling

Educational Vocational Guidance and Counselling

Principles, Techniques and Programmes

Rashmi Agrawal

SHIPRA

(2021, 2017, 2013, 2007, First Published 2006)

ISBN: 978: 81-7541-306-1

2025 Impression

Educational Vocational Guidance and Counselling
Principles, Techniques and Programmes

Published by:

SHIPRA PUBLICATIONS
LG 18-19, Pankaj Central Market,
I.P. Ext., Patparganj, Delhi 110092, India
+91 11 47322068; 96500 28065, 9810522367
info@shiprapublication.com
www.shiprapublication.com

Preface

One rainy day I was driving on the road when from a distance I saw a small boy 5 or 6 years' old riding a big bicycle. A big stone came in his way and he fell tumbling down. The big bicycle was on him and he was trying unsuccessfully to take the bicycle off from him. The boy started crying. Several vehicles by passed but none stopped. On reaching the spot, I stopped my car. I helped the child to stand up. To my utter surprise, a number of people gathered and started accusing me of being responsible for the accident. The boy came to my rescue and said 'I fell myself, she has helped me'. Some people may think that the lesson from this incident is that we should not help people in need. I don't agree.

I remember one more experience from the days when I was working with street children. I was interacting with a group of 6 or 7 children who were rag pickers. I saw them fighting over small scrap items. They were also stealing some items from each other's bags to get a few more coins. I talked to the children, shared their problems, experiences and aspirations and had a cup of tea together. After my interaction with them, thinking that I have taken a lot of their time during which they could have earned, I tried to give them some money. The child whom I first offered the money refused to take and said "I don't want money but just tell me when will you come back *didi*. Nobody sits and talks with us like this."

Even after so many years, these words still strike an emotional chord in me.

Such experiences strengthen our faith in the inherent goodness of human nature and in the principle that everybody is nice. But all of us require help to choose a right direction at a right time. This is the baseline of guidance and counselling.

There are numerous concepts of guidance, theories, principles and techniques, which a practitioner must know but small gestures of care and concern like a pat on the back, a soft smile or a gentle touch can do wonders to a person in distress. This requires no theories and no techniques and, in a real sense, is counselling.

Problems come in everybody's life. These may come at any stage of life—it can be childhood, adolescence, adulthood or old age. People sometimes can face the problems on their own, some times they have family or friends to guide them. But at some time or the other they require professional help. The need for such professional help is increasing day by day as people feel alone in the nuclear families, frustrated with or without jobs, stressed due to pressures of studies and societal demands, tensed due to competition and fast changing life styles and patterns. Children have no time to play and grow naturally, pressures on adolescents and adults are too many and the elderly have no place to go and no one to share their grievances with. Professional help is essential in all such and many more situations, which only a trained person who understands 'what guidance is' can give.

This book covers a wide spectrum of topics such as the concepts, need, principles and types of guidance and counselling, the processes involved, the importance of career information and techniques of collecting, collating and dissemination of the same, need for psychological testing and types of tests, non-testing techniques of guidance, resources available for guidance and how to utilize them, preparation of action plans etc. All these topics are dealt with in a theoretical perspective as well as practical setting. Lot of examples given in the book, which have been based on personal experiences of the author, would provide in-depth knowledge of the subject to the readers and a guideline to those who want to be practitioners in the field. The book also provides information on the issues guidance personnel must pay attention to, such as, emerging fields of employment, importance of self-employment and skill development in the changing labour markets, specific problems of women in the field of education and employment etc.

In this book, most often the words like 'he' or 'his' have been used which should not be taken to mean specific gender. Here 'he' or 'his' have been used to cover both males and females.

I would like to thank all those who had faith in me and came to share their problems with me all these years. These experiences have helped me in writing this book with a practical approach.

I am grateful to Mr. D. Kumar, Director, Shipra Publications whose trust in my writings continues unabated.

Rashmi Agrawal

Contents

List of Tables

List of Figures

The Basic Concepts

Career Information	: A description of inter-relationships of chains of positions held or likely to be held by an individual in his working span
Individual Guidance	: One to one interaction
Group Guidance	: Multi-channel interaction
Vocational Guidance	: A process intended to help people cope with problems relating to occupation choices, plans and adjustments.
Interview	: Face to face conversation directed to a definite purpose.
Psychological Test	: A sample of one's behaviour and performance through which generalisation is done.
Career Talks	: Pre-planned presentation of information to a group.
Projective Techniques	: An indirect way to assess the personality by presenting stimuli.
Employment Market Information	: Information on level, trends and employment different industries and occupations.
Vocational Adjustment	: Outcome of handling vocational development problems
Vocational Development	: A process concerned with all aspects of vocational career.
Vocational Maturity	: The degree of vocational development at a given point as compared to the peer group of same age.
Vocational Maturity Quotient (V.M.Q.)	: Ratio of vocational age to chronological age.
Vocational Success	: One's vocational achievements.
Indirect Source of Information	: Direct contact with the source is not there
Direct Source of Information	: Contacts with persons concerned.
Counselling	: A face to face interaction in which growth takes place.
Reliability	: A test should be able to measure its purpose
Objectivity	: A test should not have personal bias effect.
Standardisation	: Comparability of test scores to the peer group of same age and education level.
Attitude	: Values.
Achievements Test	: Knowledge acquired by learning, training or experience.
Rapport Formation	: To establish an informal psychological climate
Career Pattern	: Changes in the socio-economic level of the jobs held during one's working life.

1

Guidance—The Concept and Objectives

Today's world is a fast changing world. Due to massive industrialization, technological upgradation and globalisation, distances are rapidly shrinking. People are no longer contented to be confined to one locality or even one country. Tremendous opportunities for education, technical knowledge and vocations are available to each and all according to one's own abilities and choices. But how would one know where the same are available, whether one is suited to a particular opportunity or a particular opportunity suits him and how to approach to avail of the opportunity? There are other situations in which similar questions arise. A person is doing a business. He meets with heavy losses in the venture. He does not know where to go and how to deal with the situation? A girl wants to join fine arts but her family is insisting that she goes in for a course in Law. In another situation a person is over-worked. He is frustrated. He has started taking drugs. Yet another situation could be in which an individual is not able to concentrate on his studies due to various family, personal or emotional problems. The answers to all such and similar questions lie in the concept of guidance.

What is Guidance?

Guidance has been defined as 'a continuous process of helping the individual develop to a maximum of his capacity in the direction most beneficial to himself and to society.'

This definition implies that:

- Guidance is a continuous process, which means that it is required from 'cradle to grave': A person needs guidance throughout his or her life
- Guidance helps individual. It means that every individual is important. It, thus, recognises individual differences. It should also be understood here that guidance is only to help people in a manner which is voluntary and not by force. Guidance indicates various directions to the person but does not direct which particular direction one must choose.

- Further, the individual has to develop himself to the maximum of his capacity. This part of the definition refers to the potential and capability of individual. In other words, guidance helps the individual in discovering himself – his abilities, interests, weaknesses etc. and act accordingly.
- Lastly, development of the individual is in the direction, which is most useful for him as well as for the society, which means that his capacities may be utilised in beneficial channels.

These underlying aspects of guidance have been brought out by various exponents of guidance in the following definitions.

Jones, focusing upon individual stated "Guidance involves personal help given by someone... It does not solve problems for the individual but helps him to solve them. The focus of guidance is the individual, not the problem, its purpose is to promote the growth of the individual in self-direction."

Ruth Strang, defining guidance, emphasised it as a "process of helping every individual, through his own efforts, to discover and develop his potentialities for his personal happiness and social usefulness."

Crow and Crow's definition of guidance also indicated as to who should provide guidance. In their opinion "Guidance is assistance made available by personally qualified and adequately trained men or women to an individual of any age to help him manage his own life activities, develop his own point of view, make his own decisions and carry his own burdens."

Humpureys and Traxler, emphasised the concept of guidance as a continuous process, and said, "At any level, guidance implies that the individual attains self-direction ...Guidance of the younger or less mature individual, of course, calls for closer direction than does guidance of the older or more mature individual. The term guidance, moreover, aptly applies to working with an individual all along the lines from early childhood into adulthood." This definition also indicates the extent to which direction may be given by the guidance worker to the client at various levels of life span.

Mathewson's definition of guidance refers to the developmental aspect of guidance: "Guidance is a continuous and pervasive process as a favourable directional influence upon appropriate social behaviour, personal effectiveness in every day affairs, academic competence and progress and assimilation of right values and attitudes." In his opinion, guidance is not only remedial, but is developmental as well.

It may be noted that all the definitions agree that the person who is providing guidance does not take any decisions for the person who seeks guidance. The guidance worker has only to assist the guidance seeker in taking his own decisions.

Need for Guidance

As already stated, guidance is required at every stage of a person's life. But the question is why a person needs guidance at all? Here are some examples which would highlight the need for guidance:

- Sir C.V. Raman, the well-known scientist, started his career in the field of audits and accounts and then switched over to physics. Thus, he had ultimately chosen the career through trial and error in which he attained great heights. Such trials and errors could waste a lot of time, energy and money. To avoid this, guidance is necessary at a proper stage.
- Tarun's friend joined MBBS course. He thought that 'since his friend is going to become a doctor, I should also be the same.' So he also appeared for the entrance exam and got through. After one year of the course, when he was sent for practicals to a hospital and saw a dead body with blood all over, he fainted and dropped forever the idea of becoming a doctor. He was in the streets again with all confusion as to what to do? If he could analyse his personality earlier with the help of guidance this situation could have been avoided. Guidance helps in choosing a career according to one's potential and personality
- Sumit passed his graduation in general subjects with good grades. Due to family constraints he wanted to take up a job. When he started trying for a job in the job-market there were no takers for him, and there was 'no vacancy' for him everywhere as he had no technical qualification. Proper guidance in time would have enabled him to know the demand for various skills in the market and to pursue a course with job potential.
- Joint family system in India, like most other countries, is cracking up. Earlier the seniors in the family used to be there as a support system for the younger ones, guiding them in times of crisis. Now with nuclear families, guidance from professionals is required as a support system.
- With the rapid diversification in the educational streams, the technical arenas, and the world of work, it is almost impossible for a person without a professional level guidance, to acquire and understand the vast information about various aspects of careers, and then make a choice from the available alternatives.
- In a school system, there are children with extra-ordinary talents and, on the other hand, there are children who are slow achievers.

Both types of groups of children need extra and special care. A teacher in the classroom should know their special needs. Specialised guidance services can help to tackle such problems. At school or college levels there could be several other problems such as adjustment with school, teachers or peers, maintenance of proper discipline, family problems that may be affecting an individual's psycho-social development. All such problems require guidance at proper time.

- In the area of work, people face problems of inadequate communication skills, lack of team spirit, job stress, non-adjustment with the type, process or duration of work, non-adjustment with the work environment, low salaries etc. Guidance is needed to help people in all such situations.
- There can be social needs also. Individuals are supposed to develop right kinds of attitudes towards themselves, family and society. They should know their social responsibilities and should develop desirable habits. There could also be a mismatch between individual aspirations and social demands that may create frustration and tensions. At family level there could be sibling rivalry. Appropriate guidance helps the individuals in dealing with all such issues.
- Most youngsters in school left to themselves would aspire to become engineers or doctors. But the society needs people in a variety of occupations. Economic development programmes require engineers, craftsmen, social scientists, administrators and so on. It is not in the interest of the society or government or even the individuals that the educational system over-produces manpower in one field while there are shortages in the others. Guidance can help in channeling youth into different vocations required by society.
- In the modern day world, increasing competition between employers due to globalisation and economic liberalisation is often leading to reduction in workforce in the firms. The workers thus retrenched, many of whom are in their middle ages and possess skills/experience no longer needed, would need help and guidance in learning new skills and finding alternative avenues of jobs/ self-employment.
- Some of us are good in technical fields. However, for success in life, it is not enough to possess expertise in a particular field. In these days, multiple skills are increasingly becoming the need of the hour. Moreover, soft skills – communication skills, inter-personal relations, ability to work in a team, decision-making, etc. have become more

essential. Development of one's personality to acquire the soft skills requires guidance services.

- Guidance also deals with personal – emotional problems. To quote a few, such problems could be lack of decision-making abilities, lack of leadership qualities, shyness, extreme aggression or sensitivity, lack of self-confidence or high self-esteem, inability to cope with emotional stress, etc.

Table 1.1: Need for Guidance: A Summary Table

Educational Needs	*Vocational Needs*	*Personal Needs*	*Social Needs*
• Choice of education streams	• Choice of vocations	• Overall dev. of the individual	• Planning development and utilisation of manpower
• Choice of training courses	• Matching of self with the vocations	• Facing new challenges	• Bringing weaker sections to main stream
• Self assessment and matching with the courses	• Vocational development	• Coping with problems	• Encourage women to enter into labour market
• Learning skills	• Self-employment motivation	• Better adjustment with self and environment	• Develop desirable behaviour in people
• Time management	• Adjustment with vocation	• Understand, accept and realisation of self	• Development of individual to develop the society.
• Dealing with handicaps	• Minimize wastage in choice of career	• Right attitudes towards self, work and society	• Eradication of evils like child labour, drug abuse
• Adjustments with school environment	• Mid-career retirement planning.	• Development of soft skills	• Population control
	• Change of vocations		

Objectives of Guidance

The major objectives of guidance are:

- To help individual to understand and accept the positive and negative aspects of his personality, interests, aptitudes, attitudes etc.

- Develop one's potential to the maximum through assisting him in exploring his self as well as the environment.
- Provide a wide choice and opportunities available for him and pre-requisites for availing such opportunities
- Help in making own decisions in the light of relative advantages and disadvantages of different alternatives to choose from
- Help in preparing an action plan for following up his decisions with appropriate action
- Help make adjustment in the new life situation
- Make one accept the responsibility for his own decisions
- Enable to accept the failures and success and move forward with them
- Help in making further decisions in the light of success and failures, if required.
- Help in facing the challenges of life and manage tensions by realising and accepting the facts
- Enable the individual learn the life skill techniques to cope with the problems of daily life and be useful to the society.
- Help in solving social and personal problems and be able to adjust with oneself and the environment.

Principles of Guidance

- Guidance serves developmental and adjustment needs of all.
- Guidance is a continuous process.
- Trained personnel should provide guidance services.
- Guidance services should be well planned.
- Guidance should be need-based, and according to the specific individual/target groups and environment. No uniform guidance programme can be implemented universally.
- It should focus on the overall development of the individual.
- A well-planned and effective guidance programme makes the education more relevant.
- Orientation of teachers, principals, community agencies and other support services are necessary to make the guidance programme effective
- Guidance recognises individual's rights, capabilities and weaknesses to help one taking decisions.
- Individual differences are recognised in guidance.
- The guidance worker has to be impartial and unbiased to be a role model.
- Guidance helps one in making decisions oneself but does not force a decision. Thus it develops insight in the individual.

Scope of Guidance

Initially guidance started with the concept of vocational guidance, which aimed at helping the students in their educational and vocational planning. Such guidance had relevance primarily to school settings and perhaps at the entry stages of employment. This had a very narrow scope. But as the societies developed and expanded many more situations other than vocational issues cropped up where the need for professional guidance emerged, and its scope expanded vertically and horizontally. Its responsibility now, is not restricted only to making a choice of career but also how to adjust in it, to excel in a job, and to attain maximum levels of job satisfaction and job success, and to meet with the changing demands of the work situation? Life styles have to be adjusted according to the needs of the ever changing demands of the occupations. For example, the rapidly growing phenomenon of Business Process Outsourcing in many spheres has resulted in many workers staying in offices and away from home at nights, causing stresses in the family life. Continuous upgradation of skills possessed is required to keep pace with changing technologies. On the other hand, complexities of life are increasing. Be it the financial matters, competition, adjustments at home with marital life, adjustments with children, coping with retirement blues, maintaining status in the society, contributing to the society and the nation, developing social skills—in all these spheres guidance is increasingly finding relevance.

Culture and traditions are fast changing. As society opens up so are the problems. There are problems relating to sexual development. Parents are still shy in discussing and dealing with the sex related problems of children. Adolescence brings with it a whole gamut of problems – smoking, alcoholism, drug addiction are influencing the young minds. Parents as well as individuals need help on all these issues. It may be said that scope of guidance is extremely large and sky is the limit.

Guidance and Education

Do education and guidance mean the same process or are they different? The answer to this depends on the meanings one attaches to education and guidance. The concept of guidance is easier of the two. As discussed earlier, it involves advice given to individuals to enable them to make decisions on various aspects of life (including choice of career) as, for example, on what the person wants to do; how best what he/she wants to do can be achieved; what would be the result of his/her action; what are the alternative courses of action and their relative merits, etc.?

On the other hand, the term education is capable of varying interpretations. It can be interpreted as development within an individual the process that enables him/her to adapt to the physical and social environment in which he/she is placed in a mutually beneficial way. This involves acquiring knowledge and skills that are in tune with the individual's abilities and aspirations, and habits and behaviour that are in tune with society's needs and expectations. In this sense, education is essentially related to an individual, and is an individual process. It can take place as a response to specific phenomena or situations. One can learn merely by observing, or simply by inspiration or as reaction to external stimuli. Even though *Ekalavya* used an idol of *Guru Drona* for guidance and drew inspiration from it, his learning of archery was practically the result of this own effort and without any external guidance. Thus, if education is considered as a process of change within an individual unaffected by the presence or absence of an external agent, it cannot be termed as guidance.

Education can also be interpreted (in a narrow sense) to mean 'instruction'. This brings in an external agent – the teacher or trainer. The interaction that takes place between the individual and the teacher need not always take the form of guidance. Instruction usually implies a situation where a decision on what to learn has already been made by the individual and a decision on what to teach has already been made by the teacher. The individual has elected a field of learning on his own, and the teacher has a pre-determined range of knowledge or skills to impart in that field, irrespective of the individual's circumstances, abilities and aptitudes and capacity to absorb the additional knowledge or skills. The teacher plays no role in advising the individual as to whether the chosen field is appropriate to the individual's abilities, aptitudes and achievements, nor does he take note of the individual's aspirations. However, within this narrow chosen area, he may guide the individual on the road to success. Thus, education viewed as instruction, does not qualify to be termed guidance. Though much education even today is in the form of instruction, the traditional form of education as instruction has been gradually yielding place to a more flexible system in which the process of guidance and counselling plays a more effective part.

One could also view education in a broader framework as a function of the society (as against the earlier interpretation as a process within an individual) in which the society makes a conscious effort "to guide and direct the growth of its members so that they will be able to live lives that will be individually satisfying and socially active". This view tries to strike a balance between those who hold the view that education is an individual affair and that society has no role in it and those who hold the opposing view that social efficiency is more important than development of the individual. Here again two situations are possible. The society may merely determine what is to be taught and create facilities for such teaching but does not help the individual in making appropriate choices of what to learn and how best to learn. Or, the society may recognise the role of individual and create opportunities for the individual to make a choice and assist him/her in making such a choice. It is only in this broadest sense of education, where the function of the individual is recognised within the framework of societal demand that education and guidance come close to each other.

As mentioned earlier, education can take place without guidance through efforts on the part of the individual. To that extent the concept of education is wider than that implied in guidance. In a world that is becoming more and more complex due to technological advances, the scope for individual learning without guidance is becoming narrower and narrower each day. Wrinkle and Gilchrist view the relationship of education and guidance as "Teaching without guidance cannot be good teaching and guidance without good teaching is incomplete." With this approach guidance and education are interlinked.

Fig. 1.1: Guidance at a Glance

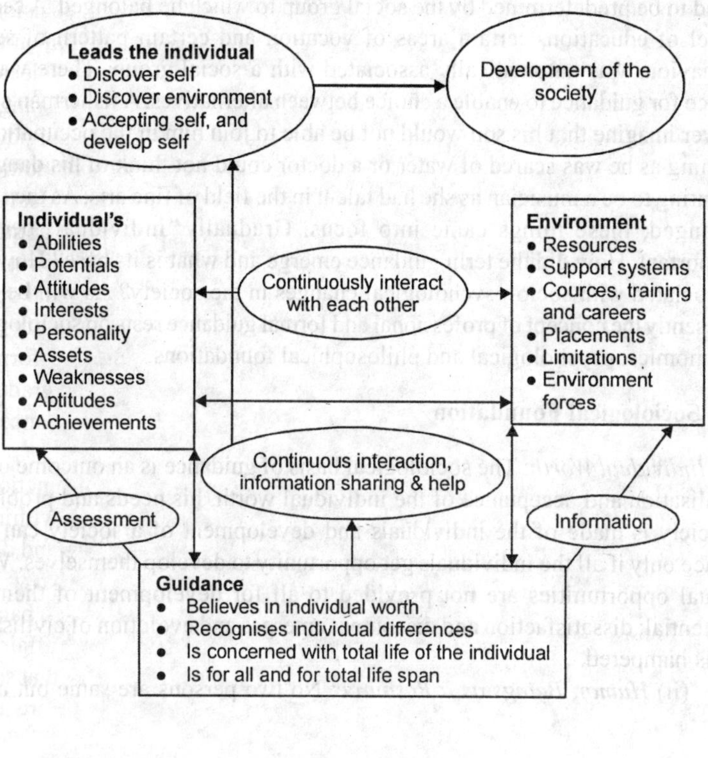

2

Foundations of Guidance

Guidance is a commonly used word, and is used in terms of informal guidance and also as formal guidance. Two friends discussing over some issue where some kind of advice takes place is also guidance. Advice from elders, parents and teachers is also termed as guidance. These are some examples of informal guidance. But as discussed elsewhere, there is a constantly growing need for imparting professional guidance – a need that emerged due to changes in the socio-economic, cultural and psych-social fabric of the societies. In the past, a person's vocation, behaviour, education, and almost every aspect of life used to be predetermined by the social group to which he belonged. A certain level of education, certain areas of vocation and certain pattern of social behaviour was automatically associated with a social group. There was no place for guidance to enable a choice between alternatives. A fisherman could never imagine that his son would not be able to join him in the occupation of fishing as he was scared of water or a doctor could not think of his daughter wanting to be a musician as she had talent in the field of fine arts. As the times changed, these things came into focus. Gradually 'individual' became important. How did the term guidance emerge and what is its base? How is it associated with socio-psychological changes in the society? As will be seen presently the concept of professional and formal guidance rests on sociological, economics, psychological and philosophical foundations.

(a) Sociological Foundation

(i) *Individual Worth*: The sociological basis of guidance is an outcome of the realisation and acceptance of the individual worth, his needs and problems. Society is made of the individuals and development of a society can take place only if all the individuals get opportunity to develop themselves. When equal opportunities are not provided to all for development of their full potential; dissatisfaction and discontent emerges and evolution of civilisation gets hampered.

(ii) *Human Beings as a Resource*: No two persons are same but at the same time everyone is endowed with some or the other talent which needs to be identified and facilitated to be developed. If that is not done, people would be a liability on the nations than being an asset. The importance of human beings as resources for a country has to be realised and an atmosphere has to be provided where each one can develop his abilities and potentials to the maximum. The socially useful population becomes an important resource for any nation. This concept is also the foundation of guidance, as guidance can develop people as a resource.

(iii) *Demands of the Society from the People*: Society collectively needs and demands from its people positive attitudes, desirable behaviours, sense of responsibility towards the society, and ability to cope with the changing expectations of today's world. Today's world is fast changing and society's demands are becoming complex. Maintaining unity among people, facing the global challenges and technological development, struggling against evils like fighting terrorism, drug addiction, surviving in environment of competition in the world of work and complexities of daily life—all these are to be achieved with harmony, life skill techniques and a positive approach. Guidance addresses these situations.

The complexities of modern life have made life simplistic on the one hand and have created manifold problems on the other. The individual is confused. Opportunities are vast but the competition is tough. What to do and what not to do—individual remains in a dilemma. How to deal with peers, teachers, parents, neighbours etc. are some of the areas and social issues where guidance is relevant.

(iv) *Individuals with Special Needs*: In every society there are people who require extra attention and care. There are old people, there are infants, there are people with some handicap, some are specially gifted children, some belong to single parenthood, and some children are coming from problem and or violent homes. Obviously their needs for assistance differ and society cannot afford to ignore their needs. Professional guidance services can deal with such people with special needs.

(v) *Women and their Problems*: Women constitute about half of the total population. Overcoming the social handicaps they faced in the past, they not only are joining diverse educational streams but also diverse occupational fields. A number of problems are emerging with this changed scenario of rising participation of women in economic activities. Women performing the dual roles of looking after the home and children, and work outside the home, face a lot of strain and stress and need assistance. Moreover, in the modern labour market, where the presence of women is increasingly conspicuous—new relationships, new adjustments, new needs, new societal expectations have emerged. Guidance plays a special role in keeping societal harmony and progress in the right direction.

(b) Economic Foundation

(i) *Specialisation and Multi-skilling*: Another issue that makes guidance relevant is the demand for specialised skills and even multiple skills in the society. There are fields, which require specialisation for doing a particular activity. For example, in the profession of medicine one doctor specialises in giving anesthesia to the patients during the course of operations, the other is ENT specialist and so on.. In some areas of work there is a demand for multi-skilled people. This is, in fact, the trend in recent times. For example, a person who is handling photocopying work, should also be able to handle phones, PBX, Fax and other electronic equipments in an office and almost everyone needs skills in using computers apart from the skills in his own specialised field. New occupational areas are also emerging like herbal plantations, biotechnology etc. that require trained people. Who can do what is the basic question. How to match occupations with people? Guidance can address these and other related issues.

(ii) *Placements*: There may be people possessing requisite skills, and there may be demand for such skills. Even then, there can sometimes be constraints in the labour market that prevent the coming together of this demand and supply of skills. Imagine a situation where a girl is trained on how to grow herbal plantations, which can generally be grown in hilly areas. The girl, however, has her family in the plains. She cannot move out from her native place. Now what about her getting a placement? In another situation, there may be persons with skills and no demand for them. A person, for example, has skill in providing training in yoga but there are no vacancies. There can be numerous situations relating to trained manpower. Everyone has his choices and preferences for a job, job area and job activity. Getting placement according to that preference is a challenge. How to get it? How to know about it? How can one get a right placement or how a job can get the right person? If these issues are handled properly, individuals can get job satisfaction and if individuals can succeed in their respective jobs, ultimately the society succeeds.

(iii) *Utilisation of Manpower*: The State formulates programmes for the development of economy. A variety of skills are required to man these programmes and at different places. The State also makes arrangements for the development of such skills. However, proper utilisation of the trained manpower for purposes for which it is meant can be a difficult task as the choice is in the hands of the individuals trained. An example is the need of doctors in rural areas. There may be enough doctors but they do not go to rural areas. Another example is the need for the people to join the armed forces. Guidance would enable channeling these human resources into areas where they are required.

(iv) *Job Losses*: For a variety of reasons people lose their jobs after holding them for quite a long period. With changing technology and competition, the employer may not need the skills possessed by his workers. Or he may relocate his industry to some other place or even close it leading to job losses. Such retrenchments lead to economic discomfort as well as emotional tensions. Guidance can play a vital role in helping the retrenched workers to acquire alternative skills, move to alternative places of employment or seek fresh jobs.

(c) Psychological Bases of Guidance

It has been seen, while discussing the sociological bases of guidance, that the focus is on individuals—their development in relation to the society. The psychological foundation of guidance is similarly important which emphasises the individual's abilities, interest and aptitudes, differences between one individual and the other, differences within the individual in relation to traits and skills, the personality characteristics and his adjustments with himself and environment.

(i) *Individual Differences*: People differ in their physical characteristics. The height, weight, the structure, the face, etc. make one person different from the other. People also differ in their mental capabilities. Abilities vary, attitudes, interests and aptitudes differ and so do the personalities. It is common experience that some children are very sharp in doing the calculations or playing with the numbers, while others are good in painting or music and some others doing the mechanical repairing etc. Personality-wise, some people are fond of making friends while some want to be aloof; some are outspoken while some are shy. Besides, they also differ in emotional maturity and emotional adjustments. The children of same age may show different degrees of emotional maturity in similar situations. Of the two children who fail in the examination in the same standard, one may remain calm and quiet and may analyse his reason for failure and decide to try again with more positive attitude, while the other child may burst into tears, may get bouts of depression, may think that he can never succeed and give up.

Such differences are measurable and individuals who need help can be identified and counselled appropriately.

(ii) *The Differences Within*: Individuals differ from one another in many ways. But the differences within the individual can also be seen and measured.

These differences within the individual are in terms of various traits. One individual may get 100 per cent marks in science subjects, but only 40 per cent in languages. Or he may be good in climbing a hill but not well in swimming. Guidance can help in identifying individual's strengths and weakness. Strengths may be developed to their maximum while weaknesses may be overcome through proper guidance up to a certain extent. Teachers and parents can also be helped in dealing with strengths and weaknesses of the individual. Guidance provides an insight to understand the nature of the individual in a better way. The patterns of one's traits may be matched with the requirements of the trait patterns of different occupations. The matching of the two to a greater extent may result in greater satisfaction and happiness for the individual.

(iii) *The Personality Characteristics*: Personality of an individual is another psychological base for guidance. Personality is combination of both physical and mental characteristics. Problem in one area may lead to problems in the other. If a person is not physically fit or remains sick, his behaviour would be different. He may show irritation, anger, frustration etc. On the other hand if a person is healthy, he would be energetic and show happy attitudes and behaviours. In the same situations, two individuals may show different behaviours. During the examinations some children are extremely anxious while some are calm. The guidance programme has to take the individual as a whole and identify specific personality characteristics that may help in understanding the individual and helping him to choose the right direction or modify behaviour as and when needed through intervention. Here the psychology of individual adjustment should be looked into. How a person would behave or adjust with the situations depends upon his perception of self. In order to modify the behaviour, the change in self-concept is essential. Think about a person who thinks that he can not do good in public speaking, he would like to avoid such situations where he is supposed to speak before people. To alter this situation, he has to analyse his problem and think that he can do it. Guidance worker can help in modifications of behaviours through various techniques.

The psychological understanding of a person is the foundation of guidance process.

(d) Philosophical Bases of Guidance

(i) *The Indian Culture and Indian Constitution*: The Indian culture is based on the principles of *Vasudheva Kutumbkum* which means that the whole earth is one home and all should live as if they belong to the same family. That is possible only when the values of unity, equality and respect for each other are imbibed in the daily living. There should not be any discrimination on the basis of the caste, creed and religion. Dignity of the human beings should be valued. The Indian Constitution embodies these values of respect, equality and dignity of the citizen and seeks to assure to all

(a) Justice – social, economic and political
(b) Liberty – of thought, expression, belief, faith and worship
(c) Equality – of status and of opportunity and to promote among all feeling of fraternity while assuring the dignity of the individual.

This philosophy of human dignity and equality is the foundation of guidance, where each individual is important

(ii) *The Goals of Life*: The Indian philosophy is based on the concept that the ultimate aim of life is self-understanding, self-acceptance and self-realisation. The role a '*guru*' or the 'guide' in this process of self-realisation of the individual is well recognised. Guidance helps in attaining self-realisation sooner than later.

3

Types of Guidance

The word 'guidance' symbolises the general process in which an individual unable to solve a problem or make a decision by himself receives assistance and advice from another person. The type of advice and assistance needed would vary from situation to situation. While some may need such guidance to take up a particular educational stream or vocational field, others may have to be guided in personal problems like marital life and health, and yet others in matters concerning the society, like good citizenship, community service, etc.

Myers has classified guidance into eight types with the same perspective:

1. Educational Guidance
2. Vocational Guidance
3. Recreational Guidance
4. Civic Guidance
5. Community Service Guidance
6. Social and Moral Guidance
7. Health Guidance
8. Leadership Guidance

Keeping the problems in the various spheres of life in focus, guidance, for practical purposes, may be broadly classified as educational guidance, vocational guidance and personal guidance. Guidance relating to health, recreation etc. may be treated as parts of personal guidance. In this broad framework, the educational and vocational guidance is being discussed in this chapter. Since the personal and social guidance is assuming large focus in recent years, this would be detailed in the next chapter.

(a) Educational Guidance

In the modern days a wider choice of educational streams is available for the children than before. Earlier, there were only a few subjects which everybody had to study. Now each subject has various branches, which are not known to all the students. Students also have their own choices. In earlier times, if a father was in business his child used to be in the same profession. Same was the case of doctors and lawyers. But in the changed scenario, it is not necessary for the children to follow their parent's footsteps. They have varying interests and their cultural backgrounds and traditions differ. They need to know which stream should be suitable for them according to their background and traditions. Education is also seen to be related to vocational choice and planning a career. In the vocational choice it is also imperative that people should know which educational streams are in demand for future vocations. Life is becoming complex and people have to adapt to a new life style, to the new technology and to everchanging market demands. Students may also face some other problems like under achievement, lack of concentration, lack of motivation for studies, etc. All such situations show the need for educational guidance. The number of institutions providing education in the same field has also increased along with the increase in the number of children going to school from all strata of the society. These institutions differ in the levels of prestige attached to them, in the quality of education they offer, in the cost of learning in them, the procedures for gaining admission into them and eligibility conditions. One needs to know about all these aspects before choosing an institution.

Thus, educational guidance meets the requirements of problems relating to education in the school. These could be choice of subjects, low academic achievements, lack of concentration in the classroom activities, etc. According to Myers "Educational guidance is a process concerned with bringing about between an individual pupil with his distinctive characteristics on the one hand, and differing groups of opportunities and requirements on the other, a favourable setting for the individual's development or education. If there is a single group of opportunities and requirements, as is the case with a fixed curriculum, the problem is simply one of the education by the best methods possible in a setting already determined and not of educational guidance." According to Jones, "Educational guidance is the assistance given to the pupils in their choices and adjustments with relation to schools, curriculums, courses and school life." In the opinion of Traxler, "Guidance enables each individual to understand his abilities, interests and personality traits, to develop them, to relate them to his life goals and finally to reach a state of complete and mature self-guidance as desirable citizen of a democratic social order. Guidance is thus vitally related to every aspect of the school, the curriculum, the methods of instruction, the supervision of instruction, disciplinary procedure, attendance, problems of scheduling, the extra-curricular, the health and physical fitness programme, and home and community relations."

Tolbert defines educational guidance as "the total programme or all the activities and services engaged in by an educational institution that are primarily aimed at assisting an individual to make and carry out adequate plans and to achieve satisfactory adjustment in all aspects of his daily life".

The above definitions not only define educational guidance but also indicate some of the problems that the student may face during their stay in the schools. The definitions also reflect the need for educational guidance from kindergarten stage to higher levels.

Objectives of Educational Guidance

- To help the student to achieve in adjusting himself to the school environment, the peer group and the school curriculum
- To assess the individuals through psychological tests and other non-testing techniques
- To assess the needs of the individuals for educational guidance
- To prepare a plan for rendering guidance services according to the needs
- To set up a career resource center in the school
- To help students to make a choice of subjects which may be most suitable to them according to their interests, aptitudes and personality
- To provide information regarding the courses and institutions available for higher level schooling or training
- To provide detailed information about the eligibility criteria about various courses and training programmes
- To provide information about the finances which are required for opting a particular course
- To help in monitoring the academic progress
- To help in choosing the leisure time activity according to his interest and resources
- To help in developing good study habits
- To monitor academic achievements of students and identify high and low achievers and help teachers in dealing with such students
- To assist the students with special needs
- To help parents to deal with their children specially with special needs

Principles of Educational Guidance

(a) Must be objective
(b) Individual differences must be recognised
(c) Every child has some or the other talent which can and should be identified

(d) The strategy to help the client should be based on resources and support services available to him
(e) Need of the guidance is felt by all at one or the other time.

Functions of Educational Guidance

The broad functions of educational guidance would include collection of information about various educational opportunities (their location, costs, requirements, careers, etc.) on the one hand and about the students (scholastic achievements, family backgrounds, health and financial status, etc.) on the other; preparation of education guidance material and formation of profiles; providing orientation about guidance services to parents, teachers and students; dissemination of educational information through mass media, organising class talks, etc.; administration of psychological tests; identify children requiring special guidance such as low achievers, and interacting with children, their parents and teachers to discuss their educational problems.

The specific functions of educational guidance professional are:

- To provide orientation about guidance services to students, teachers, parents and community
- To collect and disseminate educational information useful for the students
- To arrange group guidance as well as individual guidance activities
- To help the individual selection of educational streams suitable to his aptitudes and interests, personality and intelligence
- To help the individual in improving the academic achievements
- To help the child in modifying the study habits if required
- To help the child in making proper use of library
- To improve the motivation of the students in the school curriculum and activities
- Help students in preparing for competitive entrance exams.
- To identify the weak areas of the individual and help him in overcoming those
- To assess the individuals through psychological tests and other non-testing techniques
- To assess the needs of the individuals for educational guidance
- To assist children with handicaps
- To help the students in dealing with failures
- To arrange special guidance services for gifted, slow learners and children coming from backward areas
- To discuss with the teachers and parents about the problems of the child to solve them
- Prepare Cumulative Record Card

These are some of the activities a guidance worker can organise in a school. Many of these activities can also be taken up outside the school environments.

(b) Vocational Guidance

With a variety of educational streams as well as occupational opportunities available to the students, it is not always possible for them to match their abilities with the demands of occupations. For making a right vocational choice, information relating to various occupations is necessary in relation to one's achievements, abilities, aptitudes and interests.

National Vocational Guidance Association defined (1924) the concept of vocational guidance as "the giving of information, experience, and advice in regard to choosing an occupation, preparing for it, entering it, and progressing in it." The definition places emphasis on giving information, experience and advice. Another Committee of the Association revised (1937) the definition as "Vocational guidance is the process of assisting the individual to choose an occupation, prepare for it, enter upon and progress in it. It is concerned primarily with helping individuals make decisions and choices involved in planning a future and building a career." The revised definition, indicates a shift from 'giving advice' to 'assisting the individual to make a choice' on his own. Super in 1949 defined the concept as "… help people make good vocational adjustments and to facilitate the smooth functioning of the social economy through the effective use of manpower." He was of the view that every individual is endowed with some or the other abilities and if one could identify those abilities he would be able to adopt himself in different situation and activities. In his words "Vocational guidance is, therefore, a dual process of helping the individual to understand and accept himself, and of helping him to understand and adjust to society; it is both psychological and socio-economic."

Thus, vocational guidance is not only achievement but also adjustment. The definition stood revised as follows:

"Vocational guidance is the process of helping a person to develop and accept an integrated and adequate picture of himself and his role in the world of work, to test this concept against reality, and to convert it into a reality, with satisfaction to himself and benefit to society."

Myers defined the concept in the following manner:

"Vocational guidance is fundamentally an effort to conserve the priceless native capacities of youth and the costly training provided for youth in the schools. It seeks to conserve these richest of all human resources by aiding the individual to invest and use them where they will bring greatest satisfaction and success to himself and greatest benefit to society."

All these definitions, thus, emphasise the development of the individuals to the maximum extent to be successful in their chosen occupations to be satisfied and be useful to the society.

Objectives of Vocational Guidance

Jones has identified the following as the specific aims of vocational guidance:

1. To assist the student to acquire knowledge of the characteristics and functions, the duties and rewards of the group of occupations within which will probably lies his choice.
2. To enable him to find what general and specific abilities, skills, etc., are required for the group of occupations under consideration and what the qualifications of age, preparation, sex, etc., for entering them are.
3. To provide opportunity for experiences in school (try-out courses) and out of school (after-school and vocation jobs) which may give such information about conditions of work as may assist the individual to discover his own abilities and help in the development of wider interest.
4. To help the individual realise that all honest labour is worthwhile and that the most important bases for choice of an occupation are: (i) the special service that the individual can render to society, (ii) personal satisfaction in the occupation, and (iii) aptitude for the work required.
5. To assist the individual to acquire a technique of analysis of occupational information and to develop the habit of analysing such information before making a final choice.
6. To assist the individual to secure such information about himself—his abilities, general and specific, his interests and his powers as he may need for a wise choice.
7. To assist economically handicapped children above the compulsory attendance age to secure financial assistance through public or private funds, scholarships or other means so that they may have opportunities for further education in accordance with their vocational plans.
8. To assist the students to secure knowledge of the facilities offered by various educational institutions for vocational training and the requirements for admission to them, the length of training offered and the cost of attendance.
9. To help the worker to adjust himself to the occupation in which he is engaged; to assist him to understand his relationships to workers in his own related occupations and to society as a whole.
10. To enable the student to secure reliable information about the risk of alluring short cuts to fortune.

The recommendations of Education Commission set up by Government of India in 1964 indicated the aims and scope of educational vocational guidance emphasising to widen the scope of these services. These recommendations suggested the following:

(i) The aim of guidance is not just to help the students in making a right choice for a vocation but the focus should be on the overall development of the child so that he could make a good citizen of the country.

(ii) Guidance should start at primary level and continue thereafter at all stages of primary education. Help may be provided to students in solving their learning difficulties, in developing their academic excellence, and helping the students who are thinking dropping out the school systems, to develop study habits.

(iii) The purpose of guidance at secondary level should be to identify the capabilities, potentials, limitations and strengths of the individuals and help them in making realistic vocational choices.

(iv) Students who are hyperactive need extra attention. Their potentials can be developed through advising them to take up extra-curricular activities, providing specialised courses according to their talent to channelise their energies and potentials. They may be helped in a number of creative ways. On the other hand, there may be low achievers and slow learners. Help should be provided to these children to get adjusted in the normal school and, if there is a need, they should be referred to the special agencies. Special classes may be arranged for slow learners so that they could cope with the normal school programme.

(v) Children join the school stream from various strata of society. They may belong to weaker sections; they may belong to various cultures; they may be first-generation learners who have no orientation of education at home. Adjustment in the schools may be a great difficulty and they could also be potential dropouts. Such students have to be identified and provided counselling.

(vi) Guidance has a different role at college level. There is a problem of transition from school to college. Some students have to join the co-education system for the first time, which may bring in another set of problems to them. There is a future problem of lack of jobs staring at them. At this stage, it is extremely important to help them in dealing with their problems of all kinds—educational, vocational and personal. They should also be guided about the adjustment needed in the job market and how to deal with it. They should be acquainted with the process of obtaining and filling up the forms and of interviews. Information may also provided to college students about apprenticeship, training, competitive examinations and scholarships available in the country and abroad for higher education, etc.

Need for Vocational Guidance

1. *Matching individuals and demands of skills in jobs*: It is an established fact that people differ from one another in their abilities, skills and personalities. A person can be skilled in doing clerical work, which is a desk job, while the other may be good in outdoor activities like jobs relating to public dealing. People with physical strength may be suitable for security-related occupations and so on. While, thus, on the one hand, people differ in their abilities, on the other hand different jobs demand different skills. Matching of individual skills with the skills demanded by the occupations calls for vocational guidance services.
2. *Assessment of Individual*: How would one know about himself? A person may have interest in music but may not be that talented to take it as a career. What are the capabilities a person has and what are his limitations? These are to be analysed with the help of a professional guidance worker to assist the individual in assessing himself and accordingly choose the right kind of career.
3. *The World of Work*: The world of work is expanding. Jobs are available at national and international levels, through direct advertisement, through contacts, through outsourcing. What is the whole range of occupations? What options one has with him? How to choose from several alternatives? How to know about the details about the occupations? What are the terms and conditions? How the life would be after choosing a particular occupation? All these and many more issues are addressed by vocational guidance.
4. *Minimise the Mismatch*: People choose occupations often by chance or whatever is available or due to influence of parents and friends. At a later stage when they do not succeed in these jobs, they feel that the choice did not match with their capabilities. Many people in this situation either remain dissatisfied throughout life or leave the jobs for better options. Vocational guidance at a proper time may help in reducing such mismatch and also the wastage of time, money, energy and other resources.
5. *Maximum Utilisation of Human Resource*: Manpower can be developed as a resource with proper and timely guidance. Once

developed such resources need to be properly utilised. The skills of each individual may be identified and opportunities may be explored for their proper nurture. Productivity can be increased with development and utilisation of human resources. It can be a boon for the employers, society and the nation.

6. *Dealing with failures:* The present age is one of competition. It is a kind of the 'survival of the fittest' situation. Even after putting in all the effort needed to reach one's goals, failures are bound to occur. Entry into an occupation, even when a person is suitable, may present a number of barriers. These can be failures in the entry examinations, failures in competing with others in settling down in an occupation and failures in getting promotions. In dealing with failures in the occupational fields, the role of vocational guidance cannot be ignored. The role of vocational guidance is not only restricted to one's entry into the occupation but is also to help the individual in making useful contributions and to excel in life through continuous exploration and development.

Functions of Vocational Guidance Programme

1. Assessment of the individual in terms of his academic achievements, intelligence, aptitudes, interests, attitudes, personality characteristics, hobbies, habits, health and limitations.
2. Assessment of individual's immediate environment such as background of family, financial resources, expectations of the family, support systems, pressures and stresses.
3. Assessment of occupational fields – jobs available in the local area and outside, demands of skills, emerging fields of occupations, entry demands, nature and conditions of work, collection, compilation and dissemination of information.
4. Assessing suitability of the individual to the demands of the job market and vice-a-versa.
5. Helping the individual in preparing for entry into the job-market.
6. Facilitating setting up self-employment ventures if the individual so desires.
7. Counselling for adjustments in the job.
8. Follow up services – taking feedback from the clients to further help them as well as modify the programme.

What types of problems one may face and how a professional guidance worker could identify these have been discussed in the next chapter.

4

Personal and Social Guidance

Guidance movement started with vocational guidance and later it included educational guidance. But with the increase of complexities in life, the need for personal guidance has been growing. An example can be a student who is good in studies but cannot participate in extra-curricular activities; in the class, whenever he tries to speak (even when he knows the subject) he is not able to express himself well; he is suffering from lack of confidence due to which he is not able to utilise his capabilities. Another person who always thinks that he cannot do, although he is not lacking in capabilities and potentials; he has low levels of self-esteem. There is yet another student who is suffering from malnutrition and poor health, which is affecting his performance. All such types of cases require personal guidance. Individual belongs to society and society consists of individuals. On one hand, individual has to develop such skills that could contribute to the development of the society, while on the other hand, society should create an environment where the individual gets opportunity to utilise his competencies. Being a part of the society, people also have to learn coping strategies to tackle the problems they may face from time to time. Thus, personal guidance is basically concerned with the enhancement and development of life skills. A child experiences in the family, in the school and in the society; he learns from these experiences and personal and social development takes place. Personal guidance helps in the individual's development in a desired direction.

There is another aspect of social guidance. Some personal issues, when they start affecting the society, become social issues where necessity of social guidance emerges. For example, marriage is a personal issue. Who will marry whom, or if a divorce is needed, is somewhat a personal matter but marriages at early ages have negative implications for growth of healthy population, while a sharp increase in divorce rates may change the social fabric of the country, hinder the normal growth of the children, and single parenting may raise concerns for the society in terms of security, employment etc. Hence the need of social guidance, firstly to prevent such problems and secondly to deal with the problems if they emerge.

Social guidance is assuming greater importance in recent years due to various socio-economic and cultural changes in the societies. Some social issues that are of immediate attention are female feticide, issue of maintaining harmony among various groups of people with varying traditions, religions and cultures, increasing rates of crimes specially against the vulnerable groups such as women, the elderly and children, health-related problems such as AIDS, empowerment of women, etc. Social guidance in such matters requires multi-faceted approach ranging from individual guidance to group guidance, from family guidance to community guidance and interventions at family, school, community as well as national levels.

Objectives

The objectives of personal and social guidance can be summarised as below:

- To help in developing personal and social competencies
- To make the children aware of the life skill techniques.
- To assist in learning and developing life skills
- To identify personal and social aspects that are hindering the normal development of the child
- To help the students in minimising the gaps between personal aspirations and social demands.
- To help in maximising personal and social success in life.
- To help the individual to develop to his fullest competencies and be a good citizen.
- To help the people to make up a harmonious society where everybody gets opportunities to excel and all enjoy living in that society.

The personal and social guidance includes the following broad areas:

Health Guidance

The need for health guidance starts at the nursery level of school. In developing countries like India, a large number of children suffer from malnutrition and other ailments. There are also issues of hygiene and sanitation. The guidance teacher should be able to identify such children who need health guidance and should refer them to the medical facilities available either in the school or outside. The parent should also be educated in such cases. Low school achievement may also be due to ill health. Abnormal behaviours of the children in the school should not be ignored as these may be associated with health problems.

Use of tobacco, alcohol and even other drugs is becoming more common in the schools, with many students getting tempted towards such intoxicants, which would affect their health. Sex related problems is another area which needs immediate attention. On one hand, due to curiosity, students are going for unsafe sex, and on the other some smaller students are forced into sex-related activities by anti-social elements. Awareness programs are to be organised on a massive scale. The role of guidance worker here is not only to refer the diseased person to the doctor but also to create awareness on how to prevent such occurrences.

Social and Emotional Guidance

As has been discussed elsewhere not only the joint family system is cracking up but there is also an increase in the number of single parent children due to the increase in divorces. There are also families with domestic violence which hampers the normal development of the children. They may suffer from irritability, high aggression, and sibling rivalry. Children with low self-esteem may indulge in frequent fighting with peer groups or they may face other adjustment problems with the school environment. To tackle such problems counselling is essential. Some other support services in the community may also be utilised for social guidance. These agencies can be Child Guidance Centres, special cells in the hospitals, etc.

Recreational Guidance

Present generation is 'do me' generation. Recreational facilities are now available on payment. The well off students can buy such facilities, while the not so well off persons can only aspire for them. In such circumstances they always impose demands on the parents. There are varieties of recreational facilities available within reach of most.

Recreation of modern day children is getting restricted to watching television and playing games on computers. Consumerism is becoming an activity of recreation. Children keep an eye on changing fashions and go for buying whatever new comes to the market. Purchasing things is developing unhealthy competition among children. Junk foods are popular with the present day's generation. Children avoid playing with each other, socialising, and engaging in creative activity.

Recreational guidance can help a child in striking a balance between various activities. He can choose activities according to his interests, capacities and available opportunities. Playing games together with other children, creative activities alongwith others creates healthy competition and develop various mental facilities.

Ethical Guidance

Values and morals develop naturally with the process of growing up in the environment of the families and the schools, but due to several factors a need is being felt to include moral and value education at school level. Cultural invasion through mass media and liberal education have been upsetting the traditional ethical fabric of the society and new value systems and codes of conduct are evolving. There is also an increasing felt need to maintain harmony among the groups of students coming from various religious, ethical and cultural backgrounds. Hence, ethical guidance is important.

Types of Problems of Students

Before a guidance worker tries to help a student, he should be aware of the entire gamut of the student's problems, and know how to identify the specific problem of the students. A child may face more than one problem at a time and with varying frequency. The counsellor has to tackle the problems in their entirety. He cannot focus on one problem at a time leaving the others. Various experts have tried to classify the problems keeping in mind, the various areas and fields a person belongs to.

Many a time personal problems of a child are the basic cause of all of his educational and vocational problems. The student may not be able to get good grades due to his health problems, which he may or may not be aware of. The counsellor should identify if he has frequent fever, cold and cough, fatigue, visual difficulties, etc. In such cases a child should be referred to the physician. The counsellor should also identify the physically challenged students and appropriate guidance should be given to the teachers dealing with disabilities.

Finances may be another area of problems which generally students have. The counsellor should be able to provide information about the financial assistance available to them. Other personal problems may be relating to socio-psychological adjustment in the school, with the peer group, with the seniors, with the teachers, etc. This may affect the scholastic achievement of the student. The child may also be emotionally disturbed, irritating and frustrated. Sometimes the family problems, such as preference for a particular child in the family and over-or-under domination, affect the child's overall development adversely. In India, dissemination against girl children is very common. The counsellor's role is to help the child in his overall development and, therefore, he cannot ignore any of the problems a child might be experiencing. Personal problems may be identified with the help of classmates, friends, parents, teachers and other members of the community. The best source for providing information about his personal problem is the child himself.

Jones has classified the problems according to 8 such areas. These are health and physical development, home and family relationships, leisure time, personality, religious life and church affiliations, school, social problems and vocational problems. Under these 8 areas he has tried to analyse specific conditions a child may face.

1. Health and physical development conditions:
   (a) Physical defects—sight, hearing speech, deformity
   (b) Inability to excel in athletics
   (c) Lack of physical coordination
   (d) Lack of physical vigor
   (e) Malnutrition
   (f) Physical unattractiveness
   (g) Sickness
   (h) Undersize or oversize
2. Home and family relationships conditions:
   (a) Dominance of parents
   (b) Lack of control by parents
   (c) Lack of home fellowship
   (d) Broken homes—death, divorce, separation
   (e) Home duties—too few or too many
   (f) Jealousy or friction among children
   (g) Non-wholesome home conditions—physical, social, moral
   (h) Disapproving family
   (i) Lack of cooperation with school
3. Leisure time conditions:
   (a) Lack of interest in sports and games
   (b) Inability because of poor health or physical handicaps to engage in sports
   (c) Limited resources for enjoyment
   (d) Lack of interest in reading
   (e) Lack of skill in handicraft
4. Personality conditions:
   (a) Extreme sensitiveness
   (b) Shyness
   (c) Lack of aggressiveness
   (d) Strong aversions
   (e) Self-confidence or its lack
   (f) Excessive conceit, egotism
   (g) Carelessness
   (h) Inability to get along with people

(i) Delusions
(j) Lack of sportsmanship
(k) Inferiority complex
(l) Superiority complex
(m) Lack of social-mindedness
(n) Emotional instablity

5. Religious life and church affiliations conditions:
(a) Religious doubts and conflicts
(b) Extreme religious attitude of parents
(c) Conversion
(d) Excessive religious activity
(e) Apparent conflict between science and religion

6. School conditions:
(a) Budgeting time
(b) Ineffective study habits
(c) Lack of application
(d) Lack of independence
(e) Too much help given by teacher
(f) Lack of interest in schoolwork
(g) Feeling of boredom
(h) Inability to see value in certain subjects
(i) Fear of failure
(j) Unwillingness to put forth effort
(k) Dislike for teacher or for school
(l) Too long assignments
(m) Impatience with slower pupils
(n) Poor study conditions in school or at home
(o) Lack of adjustment of work to mental ability of pupil
(p) Poor preparation
(q) Too much attention to athletics or other student activities
(r) Feeling of injustice
(s) Poor orientation in general
(t) Feeling that no one takes an interest in him
(u) Poor choice of school or of subject
(v) Choice of school or college
(w) Planning work in preparation for college
(x) Truancy

7. Social (including moral and civic) conditions:
(a) Cheating, lying, stealing
(b) Lack of moral standards

(c) Manners
(d) Antisocial tendencies
(e) Racial handicaps and antipathies
(f) Insufficient social life
(g) Excessive social life
(h) Unwise use of leisure
(i) Smoking and drinking
(j) Discourtesy
(k) Rebellion against authority
(l) Intolerance of others' beliefs and opinions
(m) Choice of friends of opposite sex
(n) "Petting" and "necking"
(o) Flirting
(p) Disappointment in love
(q) Being in love
(r) Unreasonable restriction on friendship with opposite sex
(s) Sex perversions
(t) Double standards of morality
(u) Low ideals of civic responsibility
(v) Unwillingness to assume citizenship duties
(w) Inability to choose leaders wisely
(x) Unwillingness to follow chosen leaders
(y) Unwillingness to accept responsibility as a leader

8. Vocational conditions:
(a) Insistence by parents on a certain vocation
(b) Inability to choose among several vocations
(c) Unwise choice of vocation
(d) Determining fitness for a given vocation
(e) Choosing the best preparation for the vocation
(f) Lack of time or money to secure the preparation necessary for the vocation chosen.
(g) Lack of opportunities in the vocation chosen
(h) Difficulty in finding a job
(i) Difficulty in adjustment to the conditions of the job.

The list is only indicative.

Another way of identifying the problems of the people is the technique of problem checklists developed by Mooney. These problem checklists have been developed in five forms – for junior high school students, senior high school students, college students, nurses and for rural youth. In every form there are various areas and items have been listed in each area. For example, in junior high school form, there are seven areas with 210 items in each area. In college and senior high school forms, there are 11 areas with 30 problems in each. This checklist may be given to the individuals to point out their problems, which can be helpful for the counsellors to identify the problem. Froehlich and Hoyt listed six areas of the problems, which included vocational, educational, social and personal, financial, family adjustment and health. They have also tried to identify the specific problems that could be common to students in each area. Bordin did not agree with this classification given by these two experts. He was of the view that the problems should be classified in terms of adjustment to environment. Therefore, the emphasis is on environment and not on the individual. He classifies the problems of individuals as dependence, lack of information, self-conflict, choice and anxiety. There may also be students who think that they cannot classify their problems.

To sum up, following may be some common problems of the students:

1. Discrepancy between educational ambitions and abilities (If a student has made a vocational choice out of line with his abilities, he is likely to have made educational plans that are also out of line with his abilities)
2. Underachievement (This problem occurs about twice as frequently as that of overachievement)
3. Overachievement
4. Lack of educational motivation (lack of desire to work hard or do well in school)
5. Deficient study skills
6. Inefficiency in basic skills, such as reading or arithmetic or spelling

Within the social or personal adjustment area, the following specific problems are often found:

1. Feelings of inferiority or lack of self-confidence
2. Lack of the basic social skills necessary to make good social adjustments
3. Unpleasant or irritating personality traits
4. Problems requiring psychological or psychiatric assistance

Within the financial area, the following three problems are fairly common:

1. Too much outside work to permit achievement up to capacity
2. Restrictions on educational-vocational planning because of inadequate financial resources
3. Educational-vocational plans dependent upon receiving financial aid (This problem is less severe than the preceding one)

Within the area of family relationships, the following problems are common:

1. Conflicts over educational and vocational plans
2. Over dependence of girls on their families
3. Difficulties of boys in establishing independence from their families
4. Conflicts between brothers and sisters
5. Conflicts of will and personality between the adult members and the younger members of the family

Finally, within the area of physical or health problems, the following specific problems are found:

1. Frequent absence from school because of illness
2. Educational or vocational limitations imposed by physical disabilities
3. Worry about health, due to real or imagined physical ailments (This problem is found more frequently among girls than boys)
4. Physiological changes, with accompanying worries, resulting from sexual development and misinformation about sex problems

Any checklist of the problem areas may be adopted by the guidance worker, but it should be kept in mind that the problems stated by the students should be verified, because a child may give wrong information or may not be able to classify his exact problem. The causes of the problem also need to be looked into.

Functions of the Guidance Worker

(a) Functions of a guidance worker in personal and social guidance, *inter alia*, include development of life skills. Life skill guidance relates to creating a 'drug free' atmosphere in the school, spread awareness about sex education in general and AIDS in particular, and develop the skills among the students to fight temptations. The guidance worker should help the students in controlling and managing the aggression and preventing violent tendencies. Inter-personal skills, communication skills techniques and team spirit have to be developed among the students.

Another life skill is to learn grief management. Everyone faces situations of grief one time or other. It could be failure, not achieving as per the aspirations or according to the expectations of parents or society, loss of some dear one, loss of a possession. Grief is of maximum intensity at the time something unwanted occurs but declines with passage of time. The time of occurrence of the event which is the cause of sadness is of crucial importance. One has to develop the skill to deal with such grief specially during the crucial periods.

Counsellor has to help the student in developing coping strategies for such situations. Suicides by students at the time examination results are announced are becoming a common phenomenon. It indicates that such students feel a lot of mental pressure and succumb to it in the absence of necessary skill to deal with them.

Crisis management is another area where life skills are required. Crisis may occur in the school, in the community or at place of work and children should be ready to deal with crisis situations with a problem solving approach. Crisis may be in terms of natural calamities or man made calamity. Children should be made aware of such situations and should be mentally prepared to deal with them. These skills can be developed through 'role-playing' or 'simulation techniques'.

Time management is another aspect of life skills. There are children who are glued to T.V. or computers for long hours. This affects their physical and mental health negatively. They gradually become conditioned to electronic equipments. They get no time for outdoor activities like games, physical activity, studies, and socialisation which is a must for normal growth. The busy parents also ask their toddlers to sit before T.V. so that they may not disturb them. Such situations should be avoided. Children should learn how to divide their time in varying types of activities and counsellors help the students in learning that.

How to be a good social being is a very important aspect of one's life. Being a good citizen in the society includes development of socially acceptable behaviours, be of use to the society, develop social skills that could help the individual to communicate among the people in a desirable manner, maintain harmony, develop helping attitudes etc. These are developed from the very beginning. It may be observed that initially a child in infancy is very possessive of his things like toys and clothes. As he grows, he develops the skills of sharing and caring. In the single child families, where parents do not allow the child to be social with the children of the community, the child may find it difficult to develop the skill of sharing. Such children, when admitted to school, face problems of adjustments, and if not helped in time, may develop as 'self-centred' adults when they grow up.

Considering the importance of life skills, they are being introduced in the new syllabus of the schools finalised by the government recently. No doubt regular teaching of life skills in the school from the very beginning will have its desired impact on young minds.

(b) Another important function of guidance counsellor in personal and social guidance is to assess the needs of the students and help them to meet their needs. For example, the students with some physical disability may require information about facilities available for them in or outside the school. The guidance worker should have such information and refer these students to the desired destination. He can also help the school administration to make the school environment and infrastructure user friendly.

(c) The counsellor has also to organise parental guidance services to help children deal their personal and emotional problems. The role of the counsellor in parental guidance would be discussion about the child – his capacities and shortcomings and make the parents accept 'what the child is'. Parents should have realistic aspirations. In other words counsellors have to help the parents to understand and accept their child in a better way.

The guidance worker may adopt any checklist of the problem areas, but it should be kept in mind that the problems stated by the students should be verified, because a child may give wrong information or may not be able to classify his exact problem. The causes of the problem also needs to be looked into some of the problems may be identified by the guidance worker himself.

How to Identify Problems

1. Educational Field

1. For identifying education-related problems, the guidance worker should compare the educational grades in the school with intelligence levels and capacities. Through this process, he can identify the slow achievers and over achievers. A special programme for each group is desired.
2. Counsellors can help the students to deal with their time management. Some students do not get time to study all the subjects or their time table does not include any leisure time or time for extra-curricular activities. Sometimes they do not have any time even to take their meals. Guidance worker can identify these problems.
3. There are students who lack motivation for studies and are always busy in extra-curricular activities. The reasons for lack of motivation are to be observed and motivational programme may be organised by the guidance worker.
4. Constant interaction may be had with teachers to identify the problems of the students in educational area.

2. Vocational Field

By administering aptitudes and interests test, the counsellor can see whether the choice of vocation made by the student corresponds to the aptitudes or not. May be that student has no choice at all. The counsellor has to provide occupational profiles that could be suitable for him. There is a possibility that a student has more than one choice and is not able to decide which line he should choose. His aspirations may also be unrealistic. All these problems may be taken care of by the counsellor by providing factual information about the individual as well as the occupation.

Within the vocational area, three types of people are there to be identified:

1. Students with discrepancy between ambitions and abilities
2. Students with inaccurate or inadequate information about job requirements or opportunities
3. Students with complete indecision (This may be due to the student's consideration of several possible and equally attractive choices, his responses to outside pressures from family members or others, or a complete lack of occupational information)

2. Personal Problems

Personal problems may be of various kinds. The student may not be able to get good grades due to his health problems, which he may or may not be aware of. The counsellor should identify if he has frequent fever, cold and cough, fatigue, visual difficulties, etc. In such cases a child should be referred to the physician. The counsellor should also identify the physically challenged students and appropriate guidance should be given to the teachers dealing with disabilities.

Finances may be another area of problems, which generally students have. The counsellor should be able to provide information about the financial assistance available to them. Other personal problems may be relating to socio-psychological adjustment in the school, with the peer group, with the seniors, with the teachers, etc. This may affect the scholastic achievement of the student. The child may also be emotionally disturbed, irritating and frustrated. Sometimes the family problems, such as preference for a particular child in the family and over-or-under domination, affect the child's overall development adversely. In India, dissemination against girl children is very common. The counsellor's role is to help the child in his overall development and, therefore, he cannot ignore any of the problems a child might be experiencing. Personal problems may be identified with the help of classmates, friends, parents, teachers and other members of the community. The best source for providing information about his personal problem is the child himself.

5

Essential Guidance Services

It has been seen that the guidance programme consists of educational guidance, vocational guidance and personal guidance. How this can be imparted? What should be the minimum basic services that should be included in a guidance programme. In the following paragraphs the essential services, which should be rendered through guidance, have been discussed

Fig. 5.1: Essential Services of Guidance

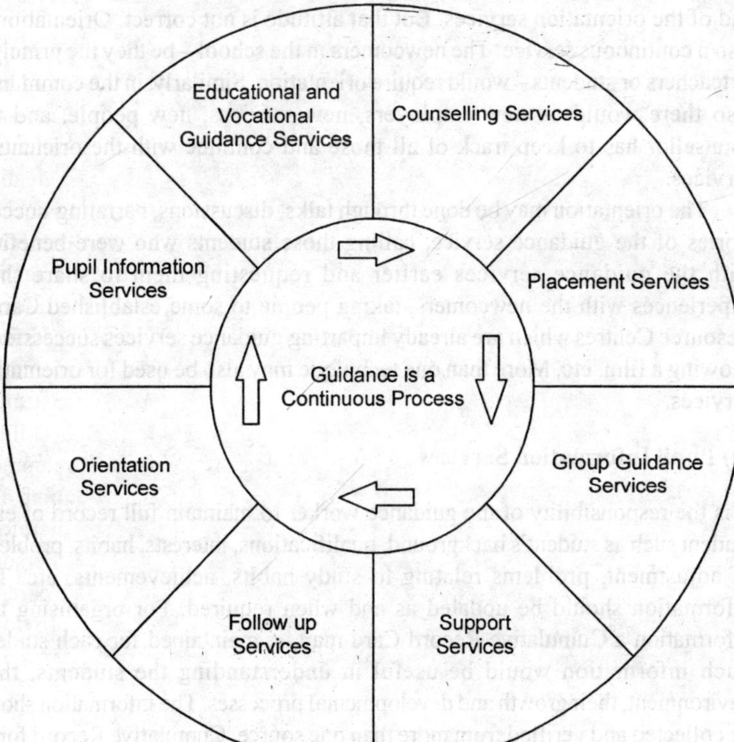

(i) Orientation Services

Orientation of guidance services is extremely essential to make the programme relevant and effective. Guidance counsellor cannot work in isolation. He needs the cooperation from parents, teachers, principal, employers and the community. He has to utilise the various resources available in the area, which can provide technical and other inputs for a guidance programme. Guidance counsellors should discuss about the guidance services, their need and importance and how the others can be helpful in making the services a success. Similarly the orientation of the target group (in case of school guidance programme, the target group would be students) is important as without the target group no programme can take place at all. Students are to be taken into confidence and the usefulness of the guidance services has to be explained. If a Career Resource Centre is in one school and the guidance counsellor has to cover other nearby schools also, he has to provide orientation services in all the schools. Many may think that once orientation has been given, it is the end of the orientation services. But that attitude is not correct. Orientation is also a continuous service. The newcomers in the school – be they the principal or teachers or students – would require orientation. Similarly, in the community also there would be new employers, new services, new people, and the counsellor has to keep track of all those and continue with the orientation services.

The orientation may be done through talks, discussions, narrating success stories of the guidance service, calling those students who were benefited with the guidance services earlier and requesting them to share their experiences with the newcomers, taking people to some established Career Resource Centres which are already imparting guidance services successfully, showing a film, etc. More than one technique may also be used for orientation services.

(ii) Pupil Information Services

It is the responsibility of the guidance worker to maintain full record of each student such as student's background, qualifications, interests, habits, problems of adjustment, problems relating to study habits, achievements, etc. The information should be updated as and when required. For organising this information a Cumulative Record Card may be maintained for each student. Such information would be useful in understanding the students, their environment, their growth and developmental processes. The information should be collected and verified from more than one source. Cumulative Record forms help in maintaining the facts about each individual over a period of time. These can be used in discussions with the teachers, parents, identifying the needs of the individuals, helping the students in educational-vocational guidance and making decisions. On the basis of this information students may be helped for modifying their behaviours in desired directions. Employers can also be helped in knowing about the potentials of the students in various areas.

A format may be developed for each student for maintaining the information depending upon the level of the education a child is at.

Sample of Cumulative Record Form

A. Personal Background

- Name Age Sex
- Name of the father Occupation
- Name of the mother Occupation
- Address
- With whom the child is living and relationship
- Other family members with their age, sex, education and activity status

Relationship	Age	Sex	Education	Activity Status
1.				
2.				
3.				
4.				
5.				

- Position among brothers/sisters 1 2 3 4 5 6 7
- Home Town: If left home-town why?
- Any information about family, the child may like to provide.

B. School Background

- Name of the School
- Class in which studying
- Subjects taken (when optional subjects are there)
- Schools earlier attended – name, period, class
- Why left earlier school
- Grades got in earlier school
- Any weak areas (subjects)
- Which subjects the student likes, which he/she does not
- Experience of the child with earlier school
- Friends in earlier schools
- Whether maintaining the relationship
- Attendance in the present school
- Performance in the academics.

C. Details of Performance in the School:

	Subjects	Performance	Grades	Problems
• Primary Level				
• Middle Level				

- 10th Standard
- +2 level

D. Information about Health:

- General Health Excellent Good Average Below Average
- Hearing
- Sight
- Malnutrition
- Any sickness
- Frequent fever or other ailments
- Any allergies
- Physical disability (if any)
- Any check-ups got done – when and what were the results?

E. Psychological Test Record:

What measured? How measured? Which Norms used for results?

1. Intelligence
2. Attitude
3. Interest
4. Aptitude
5. Personality
6. Achievement
7. Any other

F. Information collected through non-testing techniques like observations, reporting from others, teachers, incidents, etc. Record here.

Technique Who reported Information Comments

G. Hobbies and Co-curricular Activities: Indicate in order of priority

- Sports & Games
- NCC
- Theatre
- Music
- Dance
- Fine Arts & Crafts
- Science activities
- Taking leadership roles like monitor of the class, organisation of functions
- Literature/Writing
- Social service
- Travel & tours
- Reading
- T.V. watching
- Leisure time activities
- Any other

H. General Information:

- Friends' circle
- Adjustment in the school
- Discipline in the school

- Behaviour with teachers/peers
- Regularity in home work
- Financial status
- Experience (if any)
- Membership of clubs.

I. Problems

- Problems Indicated – educational, vocational, personal
- Problems Identified – educational, vocational, personal
  (State the problems in details)
- Support system available
- Support system required.

J. Any other information/remarks counsellor may like to add.

Note: This is only a sample of format, which may be amended as per need.

Summary of Cumulative Record Card

(a) Personal Identification Data
(b) Family background
(c) Health & physical growth
(d) School history
(e) Abilities
(f) Leisure time activities – Hobbies
(g) Co-curricular activities
(h) Educational vocational Plans
(i) Problem areas
(j) Report from teachers, Parents, peer group
(k) Hold any responsible position
(l) Reading habits
(m) Any job Experience
(n) Periodical follow-up
(o) Remarks by the counsellor
(p) Updating of information.

The information to fill up the format has to be collected and compiled through various sources such as school records, teachers, the child himself, the report cards, psychological tests, etc. Cumulative Record Cards for each individual may be maintained on computers also.

Features of a Good Record Card

Hahn and Mc Clean has listed the following features of a good Cumulative Record Card:

1. A comprehensive and detailed system of cumulative personnel records is indispensable for the proper functioning of the modern school.
2. The most important purpose of personnel records is to improve the instruction and guidance of each individual pupil.
3. Records are needed that will be continuous over the whole school history from the kindergarten to the junior college, and that will follow the child from school to school.
4. The personnel records for all pupils should be readily accessible to the entire faculty of the school.
5. The record system should be simple enough and well enough organised so that the essential facts about any given pupil will be brought together on one central record card or set of cards in such a way that they may be grasped through a few moments of study by busy teachers and counsellors who are not highly trained in interpreting records.
6. An attempt should be made to keep the records high in reliability and comparability by basing them as far as possible on objective data.
7. The records should be uniform in type throughout all the schools of the local system.
8. The record system should provide for a minimum of repetition of items.
9. The building of personnel records system for a given school does not begin with a consideration of records themselves; it begins with a study of the nature and purposes of the school and of the pupil.
10. If a school adopts one comprehensive cumulative record form as its basic personnel record, it should not only plan this form with meticulous attention to detail, but it should also carefully plan the forms which are to be used in collecting data which will contribute to the main record.
11. A detailed manual of directions should accompany the personnel records for the guidance of persons filling out or using the forms.
12. There is a natural and logical relationship between the information on reports made to parents and the information recorded for purpose of permanent record; this relationship should be taken into account in planning both types of forms.
13. The system of personnel records must not be static; it must be revised frequently as a school's theory of education changes.
14. It is imperative that a system of personnel records be associated with

a program of teacher education in the use of these records.

How to Use Cumulative Record Card

- For using the CRC the person has to see the interrelationship of information. One should have an insight to understand the human behaviour.
- CRC provides a sound data base which can help in understanding the student, his academic performance, his family background, his behaviour, his assets, his relationship with others etc.
- It can help in diagnosing the problem and plan remedial measures.
- It can serve as an aid for parent-teacher counselling.
- On the basis of this data base, group and individual guidance activities can be planned.
- This can serve as a tool for discussions with the employers

(iii) Educational and Occupational Guidance Services

For planning and executing career plan, a student requires various types of information. The educational information may include the various choices and opportunities open to him at various levels, the procedure for admission, courses in the streams chosen and jobs available, types of abilities required for a particular educational stream.

Occupational information that should be available with the guidance worker would be nature of work, places of work, skills required, training and experience required, places of training, demand for the jobs, career development opportunities, working conditions, pay scales, etc.

Educational and occupation information services under a guidance programme are useful not only for students but also for parents, teachers and employers. The information is vast and cannot be circumscribed. If the information is available at one place all the needy may refer it for planning and development purposes. Students would know what skills are to be developed for a particular job and from where, parents may be able to advise the children about advantages, disadvantages of particular jobs and employers would be able to match their requirements with the skills of the students. Students would know what new skills are emerging in the market.

For collecting the information, a counsellor must know the sources of information. He should be able to disseminate the information properly through various techniques and means. He should also understand the importance of career information in a guidance programme. He should not give any information if he is not certain about its correctness.

For knowing the job opportunities, skills in demand, the emerging areas, he should conduct a small survey of the area to have first hand information. Many opportunities for salary/wage employment may not be available. In that case, he should explore the possibilities of self-employment ventures and their linkages with markets and consumers.

(iv) Group Guidance Services

Under these services a number of activities may be organised to deal with the common problems of the students. Group guidance is less time consuming than dealing with the problems of the students individually. The various techniques used for group guidance and objectives of group guidance services have been discussed in the Chapter of Group guidance

(v) Counselling Services

Under the group guidance services, students who require individual attention may be identified. The school guidance programme should be able to cater to the needs of individual, as this is most important. Counselling services are, generally, for those who are under-achievers, whose academic performance declines; late comers; absentees; needing extra attention for academic achievements; dropouts from the school; have sudden problems at family front; are not able to adjust with the school environment, have adjustment problems with some teachers or classmates; who are shy; show attention getting behaviours; first generation learners; show problem behaviours or have unrealistic aspirations.

Counselling can be done only when the client has full trust in the counsellor, who should be a well-trained person. Maintaining confidentiality is the basic principle of counselling. Counselling is a time consuming process. Timings for counselling should be chosen keeping in mind the school's academic time table so that student may not miss his classes. The place of counselling should be calm and quiet, and one where the client would feel relaxed.

(vi) Support Services

Besides the above basic services, the guidance worker should be able to map the resources outside school and agencies that can help in organising guidance activities in the school. The other agencies, such as employment exchanges, the employers, the banks, may provide a lot of information input to the guidance worker. Some students may need special services in respect of health problems and others may need welfare services. A guidance worker should collect information of the institutions offering such help. The guidance worker should also have a good rapport with fellow teachers, the principals and other authorities by explaining the purpose of guidance programme so that he could get the information from the respective teachers from time to time about the students.

The guidance worker should also know the support system of individuals. In case of need he should discuss the problem of the child with family members and friends. If a child has some health problems he should be helped by referring him to the appropriate place.

(vii) Placement Services

Of late placement services are getting importance as a part of guidance programme. Placement in jobs has become a technical affair and it is the responsibility of institutions to help the students to get a right placement. Employers also need a suitable person to carry out the work. Counsellor's role in providing the placement services is not only to help the students in getting prepared, filling up the application form, preparing Curriculum Vitae, and preparing for interviews, but also to list the agencies that help in placement and also keep liaison with the employers to get the information about the types of jobs available with them, their requirements, and emerging avenues of employment. Information regarding part-time jobs, summer jobs, details of getting registration in the employment exchange, vacancy analysis, details of financial assistance available to the persons who want to start their own work, future expected vacancies, developmental plans of the area which would require manpower, new and emerging industries, etc. has to be kept easily accessible with the guidance counsellor. The placement services are not restricted to helping a student in getting a job but in the words of Stoops and Wahlquist: "The placement service should follow up placement to help students improve their services and to gain satisfaction on the job. In this sense, placement service begins with proper training and continues as long as the school can help the worker advance and readjust while working."

The counsellor should maintain sample formats of applications. Project profiles and area skill survey reports should be shared with the students. Mock sessions may be had to prepare the students for interviews. Visits to employment exchange and placement services may be arranged. For interaction with employers and credit institutions *Rozgar Melas* where employers meet the job seekers are popular methods.

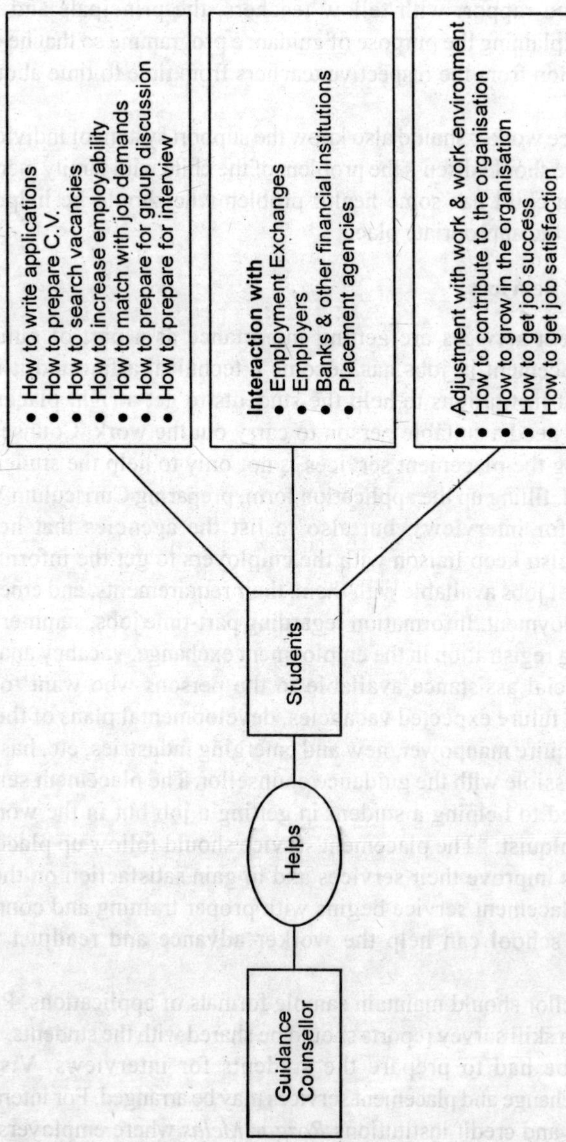

Fig. 5.2: Placement Services

(viii) Follow-up Services

Students have been helped in the school by the guidance counsellor but to what extent? What is the progress? A follow-up programme should be put in place. The basic aim of the follow-up services is to ensure that the beneficiary has settled and adjusted well in his chosen area of work or educational stream and in life. Let us look at some examples. A child has been helped in choosing the subjects at +2 level. But is he finding any difficulty during the course at +2 level? Does he need further help? Or, in case of the students who have left the school, it would be of interest to know as to how well they are doing in their post-school activities. Suppose somebody has started a self-employment venture. Follow-up is necessary to see whether he is able to sell his product in the market? Does he require further financial assistance or any further technical help? In dealing with personal problems of the students, after termination of the counselling sessions, the counsellor should see whether the client is able to cope up with new and emerging situation? Whether new developments require any modifications in the plans the students have made for themselves? What help is required to the students who are dropping out from the school. These are some of the questions the guidance personnel have to address themselves.

(ix) Evaluation Services

Any guidance programme should include evaluation as an integral part of the programme. The evaluation may be concurrent or after one year or two years as per plan. It may be conducted by the counsellor, by a Guidance Committee or by an outside agency but the activity should be included in the schedule. Follow-up services also provide some kind of evaluation of the programme. The success of the programme can only be ascertained through evaluation. Evaluation can show whether the guidance is meeting the needs of the students or not, and what modifications are required to make it more effective.

6

Group Guidance

Group: When we talk about group guidance programme, it is imperative to know what a 'group' is? According to Webster's dictionary a group is "two or more figures forming a design or a unit in a design; an assemblage of persons or things forming a separate unit, a cluster, an aggregation, an assemblage of objects having some relationship, resemblance or common characteristic." Various other scholars defined the term 'group' in a number of ways according to purpose, or the way some interaction takes place among people, or dependence upon each other etc. According to Delamator, "A comprehensive definition of 'group' can be formulated in terms of the following properties: interaction between individuals, perceptions of other members and the development of shared perceptions, the development of affective ties, and the development of interdependence of roles." This definition emphasises the existence of interaction, sharing of perceptions, ties and interdependence on each other's roles as group characteristics. From the point of view of guidance a group would consist of persons with similar problems and similar goals.

Some examples of groups that could be formed in guidance programmes are:

- A group of students of class X who want to make a choice of subjects
- A group of persons who need to be motivated to take up self-employment
- A group of job seekers who want to know about the job opportunities available after passing Class XII.
- A group of slow learners
- A group of parents with problems of aggressive children.

Types of Group: Some commonly used terms of types of groups are:

1. *T-Groups*: Training groups are referred to as T-Groups. Here group members learn through interaction among themselves. They also feel how people behave and function in groups. One's own behaviour in-group learning is also explored. The basis of T-Groups lies in the fact that people learn automatically by making relationships with each other in a group.

2. *Sensitivity Group*: It is also a kind of T-Group. But here the individual

remains in the focus and not the group. With group interaction, one develops self-insight. The basic objective is the personal development of the individual.

3. *Encounter Groups*: Encounter groups are those in which one member tries to express his inner feelings to others. He tries to open up. The intention is to free himself from some of the internal stresses and in the process change his mindset and behaviour.

4. *Mini Groups*: When the group consists of 4-5 members it is called a Mini group. Here, the possibilities of interaction with each other are more being a small group.

5. *Primary Groups and Secondary Groups*: A Primary group is that group with which the individual is associated involuntarily. The individual has no choice in being with or outside that group. An example of such primary group is 'family'. Secondary groups are those where an individual may choose to be a member such as school, society, community. These secondary groups may be formal/informal, organised/unorganised groups, social groups, small or big groups.

How to form a Group for Guidance?

Group could be of any type, but for guidance purposes a group should have a common goal. Just a collection of people may not be called a group for organising guidance activities. Selection of group members will have to depend on:

- sharing a common problem
- Volunteering to be members
- Willingness to group activities
- Homogeneity

Group Guidance

There are various techniques of providing guidance services. The services may be provided to groups or individually. The services rendered to people in groups are termed as Group Guidance.

While the individual guidance is one to one interaction the group guidance is multi-channel interaction which can happen in several ways

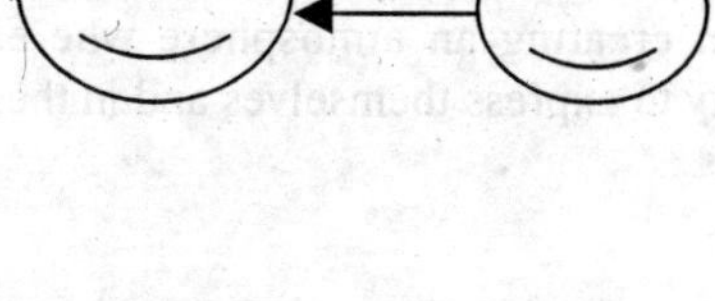

Fig. 6.1: Communication Process

Crow and Crow define group guidance as "Guidance in group situations usually is thought of as referring to those guidance services that are made available by school personnel to large or small group of pupils". According to Jones, "Group guidance is any group enterprise or activity in which the primary purpose is to assist each individual in the group to solve his problems and to make his adjustments." Froehlich observed that this phrase "encompasses the activities of the guidance programme in providing organised group services to help students acquire needed experiences for intelligent personal planning … The important point is that they are essential services which, if the guidance programme is to be successful, must be available to all the students".

In other words, if guidance is to be made available to all, it is possible only if certain activities are planned in groups. Moreover, certain activities under guidance programme do not require individualised interaction. For example, to orientate students or the teachers or the parents about the guidance programme activities can be organised under group guidance. Similarly, to provide information about educational courses or vocational fields, the same may be organised forming homogenous groups. Group guidance, in fact, also prepares foundation for individual guidance as the guidance worker may identify the individuals participating in group guidance programme that require individual attention and guidance later.

Objectives of Group Guidance

- To help people in identifying common problems, analyse them and find solutions.
- To place a wide canvass of information before people with common problems which could be useful for them to find a solution.
- To provide a platform where people with common problems could interact with each other and could be benefited by each other's perspectives, ideas and experiences.
- To help in creating an atmosphere where people could get an opportunity to express themselves and in the process could analyse themselves.

- To identify individuals who require individual guidance.
- To help in developing life-skill techniques and using their potentials through positive channels.
- To economise time—many persons are benefited at the same time.

Thus, the aim of group guidance is not only curative but also preventive because a developmental process takes place, which makes individuals self-sufficient in developing coping strategies for future problems.

Advantages of Group Guidance

1. *Therapeutic Effect*: The individual with a certain problem does not feel that he alone is sailing in troubled waters. When he is in a group, he knows that others also have similar or other kinds of problems, which consoles him automatically.
2. *Interaction with Others*: Each person can be benefited with the experiences and ideas of others. It also improves communication with others. One may find a solution to his problems during such communications.
3. *Develop Social Skills*: With group participation one develops team spirit, learns about group dynamics and analyses his own self. Interactions with people with varying attitudes, habits, backgrounds helps in development of self-confidence.

One **example** would explain how group guidance helps in developing social skills.

Sunita was a brilliant student. She excelled not only in school and college examinations but also cleared a number of competitive written tests. But at the time of interview she always failed. She was unable to communicate and felt extremely nervous. She developed phobia for interviews. During group guidance programme 'mock sessions' for interviews were arranged, where a number of students with the same problems participated. With a group of ten such participants, 5 persons were made interviewers and the other 5 interviewees. After one session, the roles were reversed. During this process Sunita learnt to communicate. When she was interviewer she became very confident. The confidence once developed could be seen when she was playing the part of interviewee. After such programme, she was finally able to compete in real life interview session also.

4. *Insight into the Problem*: During discussions among the group, one analyses the problems in his own perspective as well as in others' perspective and the probability is quite high that he gets insight into how to solve his problems. Due to communication of the problems with others, personal tensions also get released and one is able to think with a proper and positive frame of mind.

Example:

A group of four young boys failed in the Board examination of class XII. All were extremely frustrated. They participated in a Group Guidance programme of the school. Here is the communication of 4 boys (a, b, c, d) and how the process of change occurred.

(a) I belong to a very poor family. After passing XII examination I wanted to take up a job. Now I have nowhere to go. I was so tense that I even thought of committing suicide.

(b) I am also a poor person. But I don't think about committing suicide, although I don't know what to do.

(c) I belong to a rich family. My father wanted me to help him in his business but I wanted to study. All my aspirations are now over.

(d) I was not a good student from the very beginning. I told my family that I didn't want to study. But they insisted on me to take science subjects and study. When I failed, they have scolded me. I don't know how to go back home. I don't want to go home.

At this point, guidance worker discussed with them about several options which were available with them. He also discussed the life skill techniques to cope up with their frustration.

The group of four interacted among themselves. The guidance worker also talked with the parents of four boys. During such interaction 'a' asked 'c' if he could get a job with his father, 'b' got the idea of doing a technical course, 'c' thought he would re-appear in the examination and 'd' decided to change his subjects, his parents also agreed. The tension of all the four abated and they could think in a positive manner. They also helped each other in solving their problems with the help of the counsellor.

5. *Study the Behaviour of Students in Groups*: Group guidance is provided through various techniques, which pose various situations before the students. The counsellor may observe their behaviour and reactions during such group situation, which may not be possible otherwise.

6. *Collective Decisions*: Many problems are common among the students. Group guidance provides an outlet where students can discuss the problems freely. They may not come out with their problems in individual interactions. With various suggestions coming from various corners, they are able to take collective decisions. They also learn to work in teams and take decisions in-group situations.

Planning a Group Guidance Programme

Planning is extremely essential for the conduct of a Group Guidance Programme. It makes the programme focused and effective. A senior manager from a Bank visited an Employment Exchange, and stated that he had been invited to tell the participants about the loan facilities available for them to start self-employment ventures. It was understood that he was invited by the Employment Officer in charge of the Employment Exchange, who suddenly proceeded on leave without informing anybody in the office about the visit of the Manager. The next person in command collected some students who actually came for getting their names registered and told them that they would be registered only if they will listen to the lecture. Most of them were not interested but they had to attend the lecture. Most of them were only waiting for the lecture to end. It is evident that any unplanned programme would lead to disaster.

How to Plan

(a) Objectives of the Programme should be clear.
(b) Target group should be defined: In the above example target group could be those people who are in the process of starting their own ventures and want to know the details of obtaining loans.
(c) Time management: The programme should be of proper duration, neither too long nor too short. If a lecture has to be organised, time limit can be 40 minutes +15 minutes for discussion. If it is group discussion, it should be between 20 minutes to 30 minutes and 10 minutes to wrap up discussion. Too long a programme can create monotony and too short a programme may not provide desired information.
(d) Identification of Support Services: A group programme may require support of many other agencies and organisations. For example, for organising a Career Conference, help is required from the experts in the field, a place, printing of material etc.
(e) Homogeneous Group: Groups should be formed according to the objectives of a group guidance programme, which are homogeneous in character. In a class talk of 'What after XII', the students of XI and XII should be called or if the talk is on 'options for XII for students with Science' only students from Science stream should be invited.

Scope of Group Guidance Programme

As group guidance is rendered through organising group activities, it is assumed that there are certain issues that can be addressed in groups even when guidance is to help an 'individual'. The scope of group guidance is limited to only common issues. Some such issues can be as follows:

- Discussion of a single occupation in details. For example 'Details of competitive examination or entrance exam for engineering or job profile of an architect, etc.
- Discussions on occupational field visits.
- Motivational programmes, such as promoting self-employment.
- General information like interview technique, how to improve handwriting, how to develop good reading habits, etc.
- General problems of work environment and work adjustment.
- Educational planning – the options available.

It may be observed from the above that most of the activities in group guidance relate to information sharing.

Techniques of Group Guidance

A number of techniques are used in organising group guidance. The important point is that the choice of technique should be according to the objective of the programme, the target group, the availability of time, the number of participants etc. To provide the information to a large number of people, lecture method can be used. But if there are ten or 15 participants and the purpose is to know their problem, their needs, etc. a group discussion can be organised. Some of techniques that are used in group guidance are detailed below:

1. Group Discussions

Group discussions are organised in the groups of 10 to 15 persons with some common problems. It is assumed that each individual of the group has something to contribute on the given topic. For example, if the topic is 'Importance of choosing a career', the group discussion may lead to economic, social, psychological aspects of career and how it affects the life style. People may discuss about positive and negative aspects of a career.

For organising a group discussion, considerations should be

- *Setting* – where the activity is to be organised, whether the room has adequate space, lightning, whether it is free from outside noises or not and whether the setting has proper seating arrangement so that group members would be able to see each other and listen properly. It is always better to have group discussions with a round table arrangement.
- *Size* – Size of the group is important. If it is too small, many ideas may not come up or, if it is too large, many persons may not get adequate time to put through their ideas.

- *Time* – How much time should be given to discuss the topic is an important aspect to be considered. Timing should be set according to the topic and number of participants. Ideally the time of group discussion should be between 20 minutes to 40 minutes.
- *Topic* – Topic for the group discussion should be chosen very carefully considering the socio-cultural background of the participants as well as their needs. The topic should not hurt the sentiments of anybody and it should be relevant to the problems of the target group.
- To-the-Point Discussions – It should be ensured that discussions are focused and take place in the right direction and in congenial atmosphere. Ideas straying from the main focus should not be encouraged.

How to analyse Group discussions:

- *Participation* – It has to be observed how many members of the group participate and who generally remain, silent. There would be some people who are not participating or are getting interrupted by others or are shy to speak. Who is more frequently talking and with whom may also be observed. The left-outs may need special attention at later stages. The people with leadership qualities, communicative abilities, team spirits and innovative ideas may be identified.
- *Influence* – During the group discussion, leadership emerges. Who emerged as the leader in the group? Was he facilitating discussions or was he dominating? Was there more than one leader? Were there groups within the group with rivalry? Such observations should be noted.
- *Style of Influence* – Obviously some people will influence others. This style of influence may be positive or negative. Positive influence encourages others to give their ideas and communicate freely while negative influence sends others to their silent shells.
- *Decision-making Process* – It is to be observed whether any decision-making took place, and if so whether it was based on facts and ideas or was it imposed by some members of the group? Were suggestions coming to take decisions? How were ideas getting rejected? Were there good working relationships?
- Expressions – How was the communication in terms of tone, voice, pitch, gestures, etc.

Limitations of Group Discussions:

- Persons with communication problems and of introvert nature remain left out and do not come out with their ideas. They start feeling lower in self-esteem, thinking that they cannot participate in the group discussion.

- If the topic is not told in advance, group members may not have much information to share
- Rules and goal of organising the group discussion should be explained properly, as otherwise it may lead to needless arguments among the group members.

2. Career Guidance Exhibitions

It is said that one picture is worth ten thousand words. Organisation of exhibition is another technique where information can be disseminated to a large number of persons. For organising career exhibitions, display material posters and charts have to be prepared. While posters are generally intended to motivate, charts provide detailed information. Posters and charts can be prepared for all types of guidance, *i.e.,* educational, vocational and personal. For educational guidance, charts may be prepared giving details of various courses available at different stages, their admission criteria, etc. Under vocational guidance, information may be provided about various job options available after, X, XI, Graduation, by various educational streams or details about one occupation such as entry qualifications, process of entry in the job, pay scale, nature of duties, working conditions, future prospects, etc. For personal guidance, posters may be prepared about coping strategies or motivating a person to develop good study habits, or to take up self-employment or to join defence forces.

Fig. 6.2: Example of Poster

Fig. 6.3: Example of Chart I

Courses in ITI				
Course	Duration	Eligibility	Number of Seats	Job Opportunities

II
Options for School Leavers (+2)

1. Further Studies: B.A., B.Com, B.Sc., Medical, Engineering degree courses, Engg. Diploma courses, Professional courses like B.Arch., B. Nursing, B.Pharma, etc.
2. Competitive Exams for – jobs
3. Apprenticeship Training – On-the-job-training
4. Self-employment – Taking work at home, opening a shop, start crèches / school, etc
5. Direct Employment – Sales, Transport, Agriculture, Defence, Protecting services, etc
6. Informal Courses – Tailoring, designing, Interior Designing, Beautician, etc

For details please refer to Folder no...

What to consider:

- Location (Where to organise)
- Budget (How much resources are available)
- Manpower (Who would prepare posters and charts?)
- Information (What are the sources of correct, accurate and updated information?)
- Quality
  - Posters and charts should be need-based.
  - They should be attractive and display should be eye-catching
  - Series of posters containing details about one topic should be displayed together

- Visibility and clarity of writings on charts and language used should be easily understood.

Limitations:

- Posters and charts can give only limited information. If the client wants more details he may not get instantly. The posters/charts should indicate the sources of additional information.
- Motivating posters can be misleading. For example, everybody may not be able to get loans from the banks for starting self-employment.
- If proper publicity is not given about organisation of exhibition, many people may not visit.

3. Class Talks

The organisation of class talks may be extremely beneficial to provide information to a specific group of students. There can be various types of talks:

(a) *Educational Talks*: Educational talks may relate to some common education problems of a particular class. For example educational talks may include problems like 'how to memorize', or'how to prepare for examination' or' options after class VIII.' The choice of the theme would depend upon the target group.

(b) *Vocational Talks*: Vocational talks may relate to the problems relating to vocational choice or giving information about a particular occupation or entry into the occupation etc.

(c) *Motivational Talks*: This type of talks are meant to inspire students to concentrate on their studies, setting up of their goals in life, motivating them to form positive attitudes towards life, work, etc.

(d) *General talks*: General talks may not be problem specific. These can be about informing the students about guidance services in schools or the role of employment exchanges or health facilities available near the school.

Purpose of Class Talk:

- To give exposure about various aspects of educational and vocational fields
- To provide motivation in certain areas
- To provide specific information
- To develop real self – concept

Choosing a topic for the Talks:

- The nature of group – socio-economic and educational background. For example, a talk on what to do after passing XII Standard would not be useful for students of class VI or VII. Academic performance level should also be considered. The students with low academic achievements may not be interested in the topic like 'How to appear for Administrative Services'.
- Employment availability is another important point to be considered. If there is already saturation in employment in a particular occupation, there is no point in providing information on that particular occupation.
- Local needs of area should also be considered. If, in an area people are required for repairing household goods, a talk may be arranged on the openings and preparation for repairers.
- Societal traditions and norms should be taken care of. In certain societies where girls are supposed to remain in 'Purdah' topic on how to enter in 'modeling' field would be a waste.
- Topic may be chosen after discussions with the students.

Planning and Organisation of Class Talk:

(a) *Where*: The place for the talk should be the classroom or a hall auditorium. It is to be decided whether the talk would be in the school or students are to be taken outside the school. The place chosen should have proper sitting arrangement and a place for displaying posters and charts. If using the audio-visual methods, appropriate equipment and proper place to use that equipment should be available.

(b) *When*: Timings of the talk are important. A talk on "Options available after X may be useful for X class students passing out. Morning time may be better useful for the talk than the evening time.

(c) *Who*: Who would give the talk is to be decided – the guidance counsellor or some expert from outside.

(d) *Single Talk or Series of Talks*: It depends upon the topic. One talk may be sufficient, on memorisation process, but the topic of options available for XII class students and details of these options may require more than one talk. In such cases, a series of talks may be planned. For example 1. Competitive examinations after passing XII for further education. 2. Job options after XII. 3. Jobs through competitive exams after XII. 4. Courses after XII – stream wise, and so on.

(e) *Number of Participants*: The ideal number of participants for a talk is between 30 to 40 students.

(f) *Duration*: Duration should generally be between 30 to 40 minutes. After the talk, about 15 minutes time should be given for queries from the students.

(g) *Methodology*: How to deliver the talk should be decided in advance. Would it be in lecture form or question-answer form? Whether the talk would be followed by Power Point Presentations or some other audio-visual aids? It is always better to combine the talk with audio-visual material.

(h) *Preparation*: For organising a class talk, the students should be informed well in advance about the topic, about the person who has been invited to speak, the time, the place, the duration etc. so that students may be mentally prepared to attend the talk. They may be asked to keep a notebook and a pen to note the desired information. They may also be asked to be ready with their queries. The class talk should be simple in language. Delivery should be slow and to the point.

Organisation of Contents:

The contents of the talk would vary with the topic. For giving information about an occupation, the following contents may be incorporated:

1. Introduction – The Occupation
2. Importance of the Occupation
3. Nature of duties
4. Educational and Training requirements
5. Experience needed
6. Physical requirements if any
7. Personal traits needed
8. Entry into the occupation and preparation
9. Working conditions
10. Salaries and perks
11. Employers and organisations where the Occupation is found
12. Promotions and opportunities for development
13. Hazards, if any
14. Future trends of Occupation
15. Self-employment opportunities
16. Contacts for further details.

Precautions:

- Exaggerated statements should not be given. Real picture of an occupation should be provided
- So far as possible all the details must be given including negative

aspects of pursuing a course or opting an occupation. The talk should include where to get additional information

- Information should include relevant statistics including projection for future
- Ornamental language should not be used
- Information should be relevant for the target group. For example, for the rural students of a village where there is no electricity, information about computers may not be relevant
- Choose the media, which is popular in the locality like puppets in Rajasthan.

Sample of Class Talks

Name of the school:	Boys Higher Secondary School
Class & Section:	IX B
No. of students:	35
Age Range:	15-17
Date:	11 November, 2005
Time:	11 AM
Topic:	Need & importance of career planning
Medium of talk:	Hindi

Objectives

1. General:
   A. To motivate students towards educational and vocational planning.
   B. To motivate the students to plan their future careers.
   C. To help them in assessing their own strengths and weaknesses.
   D. To make them aware of the world of work.
2. Specific:
   A. To help in realising the need for educational and vocational guidance.
   B. To make them aware of the need for educational and vocational planning.
   C. To make them aware of the factors which they should consider in career planning.
   D. To help them in realising the need for thinking about their own abilities, aptitudes and interests.

Presentation

Introduction: If you want to climb on a ladder you have to go step by step. You can't reach the upper most level in one step. To reach there, you have to think how to get there. For example, if you have to arrange a party what would you do?

Expected answer: How to arrange? What to arrange? where to arrange? Arrangement of crockery, tables, etc. Thus, before achieving some goal or before trying to get something, one has to think about how to reach it. He has to consider all the aspects of the matter, and this is known as planning. Without making a plan we cannot do anything. It will, otherwise, be just like wandering in the dark. No door of success can be opened without planning.

So, today we will discuss something about the need and importance of educational and vocational planning.

Q. Narendra what do you think about yourself? What do you want to be when you grow up?

A. I want to be a doctor, or engineer or businessman.

Yes, I am happy to know that you want to do something in your life. Like you, everybody should make some plans for future. Most of you will be thinking as to what they will do when they grow up and what their friends will be when they grow up?

But attainment of goal is not a child's play. Choosing a vocation and preparing for it are such important tasks that one needs to think carefully before taking any steps in a particular direction. Your future depends upon your present planning, because what you have to study and where to study depends on what you want to be in your future. So your education depends on your vocational choice, just as your vocation generally depends on your educational preparation.

In this connection, it would be wise to put the following questions to yourself.

1. What do I know about myself? What are my interests and attainments in different school subjects?
2. Do I know what subjects I should study in college?
3. Up to what stage I should or can continue education?
4. Do I know that I am more suited for certain types of jobs than for others, if so what are they?
5. How to get a job and how to choose it?

For arriving at answers to all these questions you should know two things.

1. World of work
2. More and More knowledge about yourself.

Some important aspects of the world of work are: job opportunities in various fields, qualifications and skills needed for various jobs, training, experience required, age limits, physical conditions, hours of work shift, etc.

Q. Do you know how the jobs differ in their work requirements, attractions, etc?

Let us take the example of a pilot. There are some special physical requirements to become a pilot, such as the length of legs, eyesight, etc. To take another example, life of a businessman or a doctor is a very busy life. There are no vacations, no certainty of income in comparison with the job of a teacher.

One thing very important to mention here is that the choice of a vocation is the pivot around which the whole life moves. It affects the way of life as well as the life of the family. Choosing a vocation is also like tossing a dice. Once cast, the result is fixed.

Q. Ashok, can you tell me how a job determines the way of life?

One's status, income, circle of friendships, extra-curricular activities, prestige, etc. all depend upon the job which he is in. If you consider examples from the lives of people in different occupations you will realise more clearly how people working in different occupations adopt different ways of life. As a businessman, one has no fixed holidays and no fixed salary. He is usually interested in keeping up to date information regarding market rates and the availability of goods. His circle of friendships will be within his own group, mostly comprising businessmen.

So when you choose a vocation, you choose at the same time, a certain way of life also, and if you are careless in choosing the vocation, there will be no job satisfaction and you may face disappointment and difficulties in life. We people work for satisfaction of needs. Work is a medium for satisfying them because we get money and also mental satisfaction. So if there is any trouble or dissatisfaction in this medium, *i.e.,* work itself, life will become full of miseries.

Now we shall consider this aspect knowing more and more about yourself.

Q. Can everybody do the same type of work?

Expected Answer: No.

Yes, because there are individual differences. You ask yourself questions like: what things and activities do I like? In which subject do I do well? As you seek answers to these questions, you will gradually gain a better understanding of yourself.

First of all, physical health and strength have a close relationship with the vocational choice. You will do some jobs well and in some others you may be handicapped depending on your physical attributes.

Next, your interests and abilities play an important role in the choice of a vocation.

Q. Can you do every job with the same interest and enthusiasm?

Expected Answer: No.

Every body has his own hobbies and interests. According to such interests, people like to study science, commerce, fine arts, and some take up sports. Ideally, everybody should choose his vocation according to his own interests, as otherwise he wouldn't do the job honestly and enthusiastically.

However, interest alone is not enough. Every occupation, in order to be handled successfully, requires a certain level of general intelligence and also of specific ability. For example, for becoming a musician one should have an ear for music. Similarly, abilities to do something also differ from individual to individual. Some abilities are natural talents. Only to a certain extent abilities may be further developed, by hard work or extra attention.

I hope by now you have some idea as to how you should prepare yourself for choosing your career and also what things you should know in doing so. Though planning for a vocation is ultimately your own responsibility, you can benefit by the opinions and suggestions given by others.

If you closely observe your parents, your brothers, friends and their friends, you will realise how vast or varied the world of work is and how much planning goes into preparing for and getting a job. Haphazard choice may lead to continued frustration in life and you may feel you have missed the boat in life and be discouraged to think positively. So planning your future career by planning educationally and vocationally from the very beginning is very important.

I hope all of you will start thinking about your future from now.

Finally, if you want to ask something about the subject we have discussed your questions are welcome.

Black Board Summary: Need and importance of career planning.

1. Introduction
2. Need for planning
3. Occupation affects the way of life

Right choice, saves time, money, resources and protects from frustration.

4. Know your self
5. Know the world of work

Support with success and stories of failures—film show

Class Talk II

Name of the school: Boys Higher Secondary School
Class & Section: IX B
Date: 28.12.2005
Time: 10.30 A.M.
No. of students: 38
Medium: Hindi

Topic: Effective study habits and how to prepare for examinations.

Objectives:

1. To help the students in understanding the need and importance of effective study habits.
2. To assist the students to develop effective study habits.
3. To help the students to make effective preparations for examinations.
4. To help them to plan their studies and to study well.
5. To assist the students to make a proper use of their time.

Introduction: In my previous section, I have discussed with you about the need and importance of career plan and I have tried to correlate your whole life with your education. When your whole life depends upon your education, you should know how you should study so that you may be able to get the maximum benefit of your education. Now I take up the topic of how to develop effective study habits and how to prepare for examinations.

Q. Ajay, how many marks did you get in various subjects?

Ans:

Q. Ashok, you tell me about your marks.

Ans:

You people will be wondering why I am asking about your marks. I will soon satisfy your curiosity. Here, you see two students having different sets of marks in the same subjects. So we can conclude two things: firstly, students vary in their levels of achievement; secondly, the same student has different levels of achievement in different subjects.

Q. Some of you tell me why is it so?

Different Answers.

O.K. These differences may be because of various reasons such as –

1. Intelligence: As I have told you in the previous section, there are individual differences in intelligence, ability, memory, interests etc.
2. Hereditary factors
3. Circumstances of the individual
4. Study habits.

Q. Can you change your environment or hereditary factors?

Ans. No

Yes, there are so many factors which are beyond our capacity to influence, and change them, such as your socio-economic conditions, your level of intelligence, your personal circumstances. These are things you cannot easily change, though they are playing an effective role in your determining level of achievement. But, there are certain things that are within your capacity to change. One of them is your study habits, *i.e.,* how you plan for study, what time you study, how much time you schedule for your studies, what methods you choose for studies, etc. These are some very important factors, paying attention to which enriches your achievement. Learning is not like the water already filled in a pot. A lot of effort goes into filling the pot.

First of all we will discuss the factors which are obstacles to effective study.

Q. You tell me what are those factors.

Some Answers:

These may be,

1. *Your interests and attitudes*: I think all of you have some experience of it. The subject which you like, you read more. The teacher whom you like, you study his subjects more and more. If your achievement in a subject is good, you like to study it further. If any of these are in the negative, *i.e.,* if you do not like the subject or if you do not like the teacher or you do not perform well in it, you are likely to avoid studying the subject. So, such negative attitudes hinder the effectiveness of study.
2. *Shifting the attention*: I will make it clear through an example. Some students study while turning on the radio or T.V. Naturally, their attention gets diverted, and they can't study with full attention.
3. *Physical conditions*: Under this factor we can consider two things – firstly, physical conditions of the individuals themselves, and secondly, the environmental conditions, such as the place, light, space and air. If the atmosphere is calm and quiet, light is sufficient, you have a proper space to study, your study place is fixed, your study material is at a convenient place and you have proper temperature in the study room, you will feel enthusiastic and would not feel the fatigue. You can study very well. If these conditions are not favourable you cannot make your study effective. By the physical conditions of the student, we mean his emotional state or physical well being. If he is not feeling well is emotionally disturbed, it may produce severe

feeling of fatigue. Actually, fatigue occurs if a person tries to study against his will.

4. *Psychological factors*: Your relations within the family, the relationships that prevail between different members of your family, the system of punishments and rewards, etc., affect the study habits. If you are disturbed as a result of family circumstances, you can't study well.
5. *Schedule of time*: If you are not devoting the time properly to each subject according to requirements, you wouldn't be able to get good marks and it will cause frustration, tension and conflict.
6. *Will power and confidence*: Sometimes students lose their confidence. They think 'I cannot do it', or 'It is highly tough', or 'I can't concentrate'. Such a feeling causes lack of confidence and you can't make any adjustment with your environment and it affects your studies. After discussing the factors which have an inhibitory effect on studies, I would like to suggest to you how to deal with such factors how to defeat the obstacles and how to attain self-confidence.

There is no magic formula to make students suddenly intelligent or help them to pass their examinations with credit. For your success in examinations you have to develop good study habits.

Q.1. At what time do you study? Morning, evening, late night or early morning?

Answer:...

2. How many hours do you utilise for study at home?
3. How do you plan your studies?
4. Which subjects you read more?

For improving the study habits you should keep in mind the following suggestions.

1. You Should Plan Your Studies Well

Without planning you can't do systematic study. You should plan how much time you have to study. At what time you have to study; whether you should give equal time to each subject; how much rest you should take after studying a subject; how often should a subject be revised etc. Forgetfulness has an important effect on learning. So, you should review what you have studied. You can revise it within two days, after one week or within 15 days. Then your capacity of retention will be strong. You should do your homework by yourself.

For effective study, there are some points which you should keep in mind, while planning your studies.

1. When you will study, you should try to understand the subject material. You will not adopt the method of getting the material by heart.
2. You should try to single out the ideas and principles being presented. You should remember the main theme and the supporting ideas.
3. You should reread the portions which you do not understand.
4. You should read charts, tables and formulas carefully.
5. When you are studying, you should write out the lines on a separate paper. It will add to your memory.
6. You should take brief notes in the class that will enable you to catch the main concepts.
7. Stop occasionally when you read and try to recall what you have read.
8. You should not be disappointed if there is no stability in achievement. Take the example of a person who is learning typing. At an early stage he will progress fast and within 3 months he achieves a speed of 30 words per minute. After that, he is getting no progress. If, afterwards, the progress is slower or there is no progress he should not be disappointed. After some time, he will again progress.
9. You should plan your studies in such a way that all subjects can be covered. You should be very careful about the sequence in which you should study the subjects. Suppose you have done mathematics first, if you start numerical positions of science next you will get bored.

   Similarity of the material also reduces the ability to retain in memory. If you have studied one subject and after that you start to study another subject similar to the one. You have studied you will lose memory of the first subject. If you have studied Hindi, you can study mathematics after that, but you should not study any other literature.
10. If you also plan your time table at home you should be regular in your studies.

2. Physical and Emotional Conditions

Q. What type of atmosphere should be there for study?

Ans. …

1. You should be free from anxieties, frustrations and other type of disturbances.
2. You should avoid all distracting forces like radio, transistor, T.V., etc. while studying.

3. Allocate a separate place for study. It should be free from noise.
4. You should study in a proper light. It would be best, if you study under a tube light. Otherwise, you should use at least a 60-walt bulb light. Don't use tinted light for study. If you study by table lamp it will be good for health.
5. You should keep all your study material at a fixed place in a systematic order. Otherwise, things get misplaced and when you are in need of something, you will waste your time in search of that and mentally also you feel frustrated.
6. You always should study by sitting in a chair at a table. Generally, people study sitting on a cot or lying on it. It is harmful for eyes and you cannot study attentively like this.
7. You should keep yourself active and enthusiastic.

3. Method of Study and Memorizing

1. You should be clear about the concepts
2. Study every topic in detail
3. Make proper use of library
4. You should develop the habit of logical thinking by asking how? Why? When? and What?
   - To memorise as I previously told you, you should revise material.
   - Retention of subject in mind is better during sleep. After that, you can revise it in the morning
   - You can memorise the material by 'whole or part' method. It depends on how long the material is. If it is short you can memorise it by studying in its entirety. If it is very long you can divide it into parts, then memorise one part, then the second part, but before going to the third, revise the first and the second parts fully so that they can be associated with one another.

Remember, you should not leave the work pending. Lastly, I will discuss something about your examinations.

Q. How do you prepare for your examinations?

Ans. ...

I will suggest you some points.

1. Sometimes students don't study the whole year and try to study when examinations are over their heads. It is a very wrong habit to adopt that last moment method.
2. Plan your schedule for preparation for examination.
3. You should have all work completed earlier so that you can revise

the material easily and can take proper rest in examination days.

4. You should prepare a time schedule for each subject.

Subject Day Hour

5. You should pay special attention to difficult points.
6. You should consult last 10 years' question papers so that you may able to understand what type of questions you should prepare for.
   (i) By improving your study habits you can improve the quality of your work. If you learn to study without difficulty, you will put your study time to better use.
   (ii) You will enjoy your work more. You will also discover new and surprising material of interest in your school courses.
   (iii) If you develop good study habits, you will become a more efficient student. You will finish your studies in less time, *i.e.,* you will have more time for leisure activities, sports etc.
   (iv) Your mental conflict will reduce and you will be satisfied with yourself and will gain self-confidence. You will get rid of most worries about your school work, worries about examinations, reports etc.

Black Board Summary:

1. Topic: Effective study habits and how to prepare for examinations
2. Introduction

Causes of differences in marks of different individuals:

Intelligence
Circumstances
Study habits

Obstacles in effective study habits

Interests and attitudes
Shifting attention
Physical conditions
Psychological factors
Schedule of time
Will power and confidence

Improving the study habits

A. Plan your study
B. Physical and emotional satisfaction
C. Method of study and memorising
D. Examination preparation.

Supported by posters and charts

4. Career Conference

Career Conference is a technique through which information about a number of occupations and educational choices may be provided to a large number of students at one time. To organise career conference, pre-planning is extremely necessary.

How to organise the Career Conference

- First of all the guidance worker should identify the needs of the students at various levels
- Career conference may be planned for two or three days
- The conference may be organised for the students of three or four schools located in the area
- Career conference may be followed by career exhibition.
- Topics may be chosen according to the needs of the students
- The place for organising the conference has to be decided. The experts for speaking on the chosen topics should be identified and contacted.
- The details of the topic to be covered in the talk may be provided to the experts
- Duration of each topic to be covered by the experts should be decided in advance.
- Career conference may include some career talks, motivational talks, group discussions as well as film shows to a smaller group. Activities like drama and group songs may be organised.
- To organise a career conference, help of the teachers, parents, community and experts has to be obtained
- The students should also be involved in preparation and organisation of the conference.
- The posters and charts may be obtained from various agencies for display. Some of these may be prepared with the help of the students.
- Topics should be chosen keeping the interest of the target groups
- Children of various classes may be invited according to the topic.
- Feedback from the students and other participants should be obtained.
- During the career conference, the employers, the bank personnel may also be invited so that they could interact with the students.
- Media people may also be invited to provide publicity to the activities.

There are several advantages of organising a career conference, which provides for orientation of the community at large about the guidance activity, direct contact with the community people, and students' interaction with the experts and employers.

5. Field Visits

Field trips provide a direct experience to the students. The visits may be organised to the employment exchanges so that the students may see the actual functioning of the exchange and may establish the rapport with the concerned officials. The field trips may also be organised to various educational institutions so that the students could observe the educational atmosphere of the institution. They could interact with the students studying there and get their opinion about the course. Visits to employers and industries provide a first hand experience to the students about the nature of occupations and jobs, working atmosphere, and relative strengths and weaknesses of various organisations. The students may discuss with the employees of the organisation and gain knowledge about the hazards of a particular job.

To organise the field visits, the concerned institution, organisation or industries should be contacted in advance through writing a letter and contacting on phone. Later on, time, date and duration should be fixed. The groups should comprise about 30 to 40 students. The students should be briefed about the field visit in advancc. The number of participants to be visiting the organisation should be conveyed the plan of the field visit in consultation with the organisation to be visited. The Manager of the organisation may be requested to deliver a lecture about the general activities of the organisation. Some experts may interact and address the queries of the students and after that the visits to the work site may be organised.

The field visits provide a very good learning experience for students to see and observe the kind of experience they may not have through talks or discussions outside.

After the visit the students may be asked to prepare a note on the field trip and their experience. A discussion session may be held after the visit to review the outcomes of the visit.

6. Guidance Through Co-curricular Activities

It is a fact that direct advice may not have much impact as the indirect advice can have. It is also important who is telling whom and at which place? For example, the campaign for 'No Smoking' may not be effective if the parents advise the children that smoking is not good for health, but a good campaign in a television programme utilising some actor or actress whom the children like, providing this message will have impact. Children would like to listen. If the same is in their community setting through songs, drama and film shows, street plays, *nukkad natak*, puppetry, etc. they have a lasting impact. Guidance counsellor should encourage that kind of activities in the school. Hobby clubs may be established, students may be asked to choose a topic and prepare some activity related to that topic to be displayed. Sometimes, the counsellor himself may give the topic. Through these activities messages may be communicated. Such activities are more influential in case of tackling personal problems or motivating the students for studies or developing the desired behaviours.

These activities, on the one hand, transmit the message, and on the other, develop creativity in the children. Their communication skill also improves. Participation of a large number of students can be had in such activities. Flower shows, science fairs, building models may develop their hobbies, which they can learn to be creative and utilise their skills as well as leisure time in an appropriate manner.

7. Film Shows

It is not possible to take large number of students for the field visits. There is another method to provide direct experience of the work sites. This can be the organisation of film shows. When a class talk is given the education of the students gets diverted and they misuse all the information provided during the talk. If the same information is provided through film shows the interest of the students remains intact; the guidance counsellor should be able to choose the film which is most appropriate to the pupils' needs and is also attractive. The time of the film show and the target group should be identified in advance, proper sitting arrangement should be made and equipments may be kept ready to show the film. After the film show, students should be asked to give their opinion and prepare a note on the film show.

8. Use of Mass Media

Group guidance programmes may use another effective technique, which is mass media. It includes the use of press, magazines, radio, TV, computers. A career information magazine may be brought out in the schools itself or otherwise the already existing magazines may be used for the articles on educational, vocational information. The panel discussion, the phone-in programmes, the quiz programmes, vacancy information etc. may be given through radio and TV.

Essential Planning

- Preparing Annual Plan
  - Consultation with AIR/TV, Newspapers
  - Subjects to be covered and the audience targeted
  - Availability of resources

- Collection of Information
  - Collection of information required
  - Labour market information
  - Other information like facing interviews, facilities available according to topic chosen
- Selection of Medium
  - Radio or TV or Newspapers/Journals/Internet/Computer Data Base.
  - Talk or Panel Discussion/Play.
- Working out Details
  - Material to be covered/Time to be taken/Speaker or Panel Members/Style of Presentation/etc.
- Rehearsal
  - Presentation
  - Time taken
  - Impact

Release of Programme

Why Mass Media

- Communication through media has a greater impact due to glamour attached to it.
- Information may be given to a larger number of people in lesser time & lesser cost.
- V.G. Programme may be publicised.
- Information may reach to diverse groups simultaneously.

Limitations

- Immediate feedback is not available
- Due to paucity of space/time details of information may be left out
- Information may not reach to the needy as many people do not read newspaper or have a TV/PC.

Some Agencies Related to Mass Media Communications:

- All India Radio
- Doordarshan
- Press Information Bureau
- Film Division
- Directorate of Advertising & Visual Publicity
- Publication Division
- Song & Drama Division
- Directorate of Field Publicity

- Photo Division
- Registrars of Newspapers of India
- Indian Institute of Mass Communications
- Film & Television Institute of India
- Children's Film Society
- National Film Development Corporation
- Directorate of Evaluation
- Research & Reference Division

(For details – Contact Ministry of Information & Broadcasting)

- State Govts. and UTs have their own departments/Directorates of information.

Fig. 6.4: Planning Vocational Guidance Programmes through Mass Media

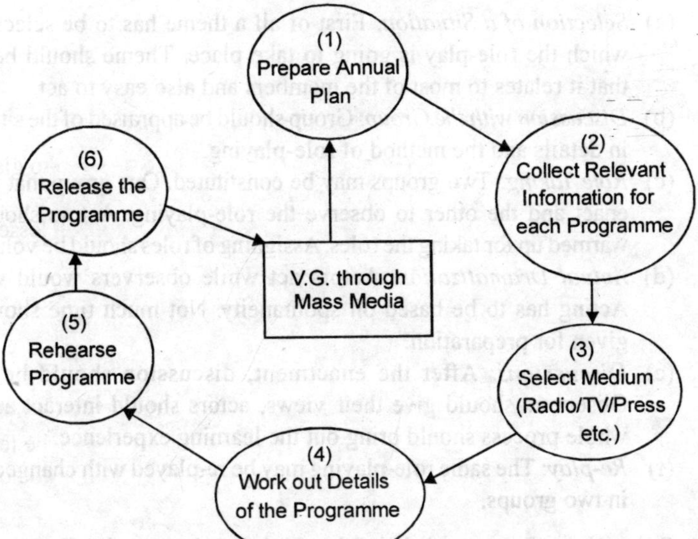

Computers are becoming very popular among the students. A database on information may be developed and disseminated through computers.

9. Role Play

Moreno gave the concept of Role-playing. According to him, it involves the "staging of a situation in which selected members of the group are "the actors" and the other members are "the spectators". Participation in role playing technique permits the individual to express his inner needs and reactions to pressures. Through Catharsis (release of tension), better insight into his repressed self is achieved. It is assumed further that constructive forces come into play, and that, by permitting them to direct the individuals-believe acting, he realizes more complete and realistic understanding of himself." Super Role-playing is voluntary, unrehearsed and spontaneous. It can be of two types.

1. Socio-drama
2. Psycho-drama

Both types are almost similar so far as their procedure and basic concepts are concerned. The basic difference between the two is the subject matter. While socio-drama takes up the topics related to social issues, under psycho-drama themes are of personal nature.

The Procedure:

(a) *Selection of a Situation:* First of all a theme has to be selected on which the role-play is going to take place. Theme should be such that it relates to most of the members and also easy to act.
(b) *Discussion with the Group*: Group should be appraised of the situation in details and the method of role-playing.
(c) *Role Taking:* Two groups may be constituted. One group that would enact and the other to observe the role-playing. Actors should be warmed up for taking the roles. Assigning of roles should be voluntary.
(d) *Actual Dramatization*: Actors act while observers would watch. Acting has to be based on spontaneity. Not much time should be given for preparation.
(e) *Discussions:* After the enactment, discussion should be held. Observers should give their views, actors should interact and the whole process should bring out the learning experience.
(f) *Re-play*: The same role-playing may be re-played with changed roles in two groups.

Role-playing is extremely helpful and is becoming popular. Enacting over a problem provides insight. Warmth, problem solving, problem analysis and exploration of resources take place in the process. Internal feelings are expressed freely and in many such situations, catharsis takes place. Once the tension is released, person starts thinking in positive direction. Shy persons are able to overcome their shyness and cultural barriers get removed.

For using this technique, communication skills are required. Problem should be understood properly.

7

Individual Guidance (Counselling)

Individual Guidance is also termed as **counselling** which has been defined as "face to face relationship in which growth takes place.' The underlying idea behind the counselling is that it is one to one interaction between an individual facing certain problems which he cannot cope up with by himself and a professional counsellor is needed who is ready to help the individual to come out of his problems. The individual guidance is focused upon the problems and needs of the client. According to the Committee on Definition of American Psychological Association counselling means "to help individuals towards overcoming obstacles to their personal growth, wherever these may be encountered and towards achieving optimum development of their personal resources." The definition shows that through counselling the behaviours of the client are expected to be modified in order to maximize personal development. The goal of counselling is self-understanding, self acceptance and finally to achieve self-realisation.

Smith (1955) has defined counselling as "essentially a process in which the counsellor assists the counselee to make interpretations of facts relating to a choice, plan or adjustment which he needs to make." Williamson & Foley (1949) said that "Counselling has been defined as a face-to-face situation in which, by reason of training, skill or confidence vested in him by the other, one person helps the second person to face, perceive, clarify, solve and resolve adjustment problems."

The above definitions describe that the counsellor knows better than the client and he has to counsel the client, *i.e.,* it is more counsellor-centered.

Contrarily, the theorists who believe that client has to be helped in understanding himself to make his own choices, propagate for client-centered approach. Wrenn (1951) following this approach of counselling stated that "counselling is a personal and dynamic relationship between two people who approach a mutually defined problem with mutual consideration for each other to the end that the younger, or less mature, or more troubled of the two is aided to a self-determined resolution of his problem". The definition does not indicate the dominant role of the counsellor.

Blackham (1977) said that "Counselling is a unique helping relationship in which the client is provided the opportunity to learn, feel, think, experience and change in ways that he or she thinks is desirable." Here the dominance of the client may be observed.

Tolbert's definition (1972) about counselling is commonly used. According to him, counselling is a "personal, face to face relationship between two people, in which the counsellor, by means of the relationship and his special competencies, provides a learning situation in which the counselee, a normal sort of person, is helped to know himself and his present and possible future situations so that he can make use of characteristics and potentialities in a way that is both satisfying to himself and beneficial to society, and further, can learn how to solve future problems and meet future needs."

Myers says "Counselling implies a relationship between two individuals in which one give a certain kind of assistance to the other."

Arbuckle (1905) defining the concept said "Counselling is helping a person to come to see who he really is, what he has and does not have; what he can do easily, what he can do with difficulty and what he probably cannot do at all…(It) is a close sharing of a human relationship with one who has for him a high regard; one who can offer him unconditional acceptance, but one who has no guarantees, no answers."

Any definition can be followed but basically counselling is a professional relationship between the counsellor and the client which helps in mutual growth and understanding. The focus is on client's problems.

Objectives

The objectives of the individual guidance (counselling) are to make the person

(a) To understand once own problems clearly
(b) To realise what he is able to do and what he should do that means to accept his abilities and weaknesses
(c) Develop insight and understanding in relation to self and environment, opportunities open to improve in respect to his potentials and goals he has chosen.
(d) Decide a course of action by making his own decisions.

Features of Counselling

- Counselling is a professional service, which is imparted by a professional counsellor who is properly trained to handle various kinds of situations.

- Problems and needs of the individuals are important.
- Counselling helps the client make his own decisions during the process of counselling. The counsellor is not supposed to make decisions for the client. Counsellor may provide various types of information so that the client could get insight to take a decision
- It is more focused on one to one relationship even when the participants are involved with group counselling programmes. They are generally some or the other time approach for individual counselling because it is personal and more confidential
- The individual counselling is more about personal problems.

Approaches to Counselling

Counselling methods may vary according to the needs of the individual. Basically it is a voluntary process from the side of the individual, which provides a structured learning situation. Here some of the approaches to counselling are discussed.

Directive Counselling

In this type of approach counsellor plays an important role. A major goal is to replace the emotional behaviour of the individual with deliberate rationale behaviour. Although he avoids dictatorial advice. This approach is also known as counsellor-centred. Under this process the counsellor plans the counselling process, his work is to analyse the problem, identify the triggers, identify the exact nature of problem and provide various options. Williamson was a great profounder of this kind of approach as he stated that this approach is good to address the problems relating to educational and vocational adjustment. This type of counselling is a concept, where educational and vocational guidance relate to the personality dynamics and interpersonal relationship. This type of counselling is more useful where the individual wants information and advice for choice of a career. This approach does not focus its attention on personality development as such.

Steps of Directive Counselling

Williamson has given six steps of directive counselling:

1. Analysis: It includes collection of information about the individual which can be collected through structured interviews, psychological case history methods, interaction with family members, friends, etc.
2. Synthesis: After collection of lot of data the information is organised

in the logical manner to analyse the individual in terms of his qualifications, assets, potentials, liabilities, adjustment, cultural background, habits, etc.

3. Diagnosis: The diagnosis consists of the interpretation of the data in relation to the nature of problem, the causes of problems.
4. *Prognosis*: Under this step a prediction is made about the future development of the problem
5. Counselling: The counselling here is to bring about adjustment and re-adjustment to the individual in relation to his problem. Attitudes and interests of the individual are considered during the counselling. It emphasises the individual to develop life cycle where an effort in the positive direction could lead to success and the success in turn could lead to further efforts and motivation.
6. Follow up: The sixth step in directive counselling is follow up which is extremely important. An individual may be able to solve immediate problem through counselling but new problems may occur or the original problem may re-occur. Follow up with the client is extremely necessary. The role of counsellor is important as he has to make the individual understand and accept his strength and also his weaknesses and faults.

This technique is considered as a most economic approach and also important for student counselling because it is less time consuming and students who lack experience are easily influenced by the counsellor's experience and specialised knowledge. The students feel that the counsellor is superior in knowledge and therefore a professional relationship takes place. The relationship is the base of this kind of approach. A submissive and highly emotionalised counselling of student can cultivate self-confidence in the individual. A relationship is based on dignity to help the student to reach his goal.

Example of Directive Counselling and Reporting

Identification Data:

Name of the Client	-	Ajay Kumar
Father's Name	-	Shri A.P. Saxena (Not alive)
Gardian's Occupation	-	Assit Editor General Office
Class & Section	-	IX B
Name of the School	-	Boys Higher Sec. School
Date of birth	-	6-1-63

Statement of the Problem:

Client has some vocational problem. He wants to go to I.I.T. and he wants information about it.

Family Background:

The client is living with his uncle. His father is dead. His family is living with some other relation. He has two brothers and three sisters. One brother is elder to him studying in IX class; others are younger to him.

His uncle has two sons and one daughter. All are elder to the client. His elder son is Engineer at Faridabad and younger is also serving as an Assistant. Uncle's daughter is studying in B.A. Final. Client is quite happy with the uncle's family.

Father: His father was a store keeper. He was suffering from cancer. He was a smoker. He sent the client to his brother's house before his death. Client has no domestic problem.

Physical Health of the Client: Client is very active and smart. He is very talkative and quick responder. Physically he is very normal. He takes part in school's activities.

Educational Information: He is a good student of the class. Since his childhood he is getting good marks and obtaining a position in the class. He likes his studies. He likes the science subjects. He has some difficulty with History but he is not at all worried about it. He wants to improve his studies. He takes a great interest in his studies. He wants to study further.

Interests & Hobbies:

He takes interest in playing Cricket and Hockey. He also has interest in reading some good books from which he can improve his knowledge. He takes interest in learning new things.

Test Reports:

Group Tests:

1. According to Standard Progressive Matrices the client's IQ is 27 – Stanine V & he comes under average category.
2. In the Verbal Ability Test he has a score of 27 which comes under VII Stanine & above average category.
3. In the Mechanical aptitude test the client's weighted score is 0 and he is low in this ability and have I Stanine. It shows that the client's mechanical aptitude is low.
4. According to interest record client has VII Stanine in Social area. In clerical and outdoor he is average.

Individual Test Report: According to Bhatia Battery Client has an IQ of 97 which comes under the category of average. He has a Pd. of 105 which is known as average performance.

Teacher's Opinion: Teacher's opinion is very good for the client. Everybody loves him. He is known as a good and active student of the school. As the teacher states – "He is naughty but lovely." He is very a small looking boy and lovely. He is intelligent also. He gives all school work in time, so everybody likes him.

Achievement Test Report:

Subjects	Total	Maximum Marks
English	65	100
Hindi	58	100
Math	96	100
S. Studies	67	100
Science	70	100
Craft	62	100
Physical Education	55	100

Counselling Interviews

Ist Interview: It was very easy to establish rapport with Ajay. He voluntarily came to discuss his problem. After some general talk such as "How are you going on with your studies?" "What are your hobbies?" "How are you preparing for your exams?"

Then when counsellor asked his future plans he was looking very enthusiastic and he answered.

Ajay – Actually I want to be an Engineer because I am keenly interested in this field. I want to join I.I.T. Can you help me in this field? Can you provide me some information about I.I.T. and other alternatives?

Couns. – It is good that you are thinking about your future. I will try to give you some information regarding I.I.T. But why do you want to go to this field?

Ajay – I have a high interest in science. My uncle's son is an Engineer. So my uncle says to me that I should be an Engineer. And secondly, when my father died he told me, "It is my desire, you try to be an Engineer". I have regard for my father and I am motivated and, I want to go to this field.

Couns. – So, how many marks you are getting in Science?

Ajay – I am getting 70 per cent But I know I should get more. I should study more. I used to study from 7.30 to 11 in the night and in the morning also I study but I am getting low marks in science.

Couns. – So, what can you do for it?

Ajay – Now I will give more time to science subjects. I am trying to get some good magazines concerned with science. I can solve some of my problems with my brother.

Couns. – So, it is all right. You are thinking seriously about your studies and you know how should you improve your studies. So, come next time I will give you information about I.I.T.

IInd Interview: Next Thursday the client came

Ajay – Today can I know something about I.I.T. What type of courses are available there & how can I get admission there?

Couns. – Yh. There are following Engg. courses. These are in

1. Chemical Engg.
2. Civil Engg.
3. Electrical Engg.
4. Mechanical Engg.
5. Textile Engg.
6. Computers

You can take admission in any one of these. They provide B. Tech. degree. Course is of five years. You can get admission through Joint Entrance Examination. Qualification should be a pass in the +2 examination of a Central or State Board of Secondary Education or Pre-University or Pre-Degree examination, Indian School Certificates or any equivalent examination is necessary. At this stage the counsellor provided the prospectus of courses and other material relating to IIT courses and entrance examination

Ajay – What are the physical standards needed?

Couns. – No special physical standard is needed but as Engg. Profession demands good physique and stamina, the candidate should not suffer from any organic defect and should be physically fit to bear the strain of the course and later of the professional life.

Ajay – When the would examination be?

Couns. – Examination medium is English and Admission notices are published as advertisement in the national dailies some time in December, January every year.

Ajay – From where I can get the form?

Couns. – From the I.I.T's.

Ajay – What about the expenditure?

Couns. – Counsellor gave the information about expenditure.

Ajay – What about the scholarships?

Couns. – Yh. Scholarships are given on to merit basis after entrance examination. Loans are also available for education

Ajay – What else I can do if I am not able to get admission in I.IT.'s

Couns. – You can go to Engg. Colleges such as Rurkee, Ranchi, Kanpur etc. In some colleges the selection is on merit basis and in some colleges there is an entrance examination. You can apply for that after +2 stage. Other than Engg. courses there are options for pure sciences. You can do B.Sc. then M.Sc. in any specialised field from any university and then you can do some job such as research work in various research laboratories/institutes or you can be a science teacher. There are good future prospects in it. After M.Sc. you can do Ph.D. and chances of going abroad are very good. Anything else if you want to ask me?

Ajay – No that is all right. I will try my best to do it; thank you very much. If I am in need of some other information from where I can get?

Coun. – First you choose from the options and make up your mind, detailed information for each option is available with me. You can refer to the career literature which is available in the centre

Ajay – Thank you very much.

Coun. –Thank you and you are most welcome any time you like

Counsellors' Comments and Suggestions

As the client was in need of some information regarding his vocation, counsellor provided that to the best of his knowledge. Client wanted to select a direction and the counsellor helped him in choosing that. Counsellor gave some alternatives in the same line so that client may be able to select a vocation according to his choice and can choose a career if he is not able to go to IIT.

During counselling, the counsellor tried to explore the reason for his choice of vocation. Why is he motivated towards this job? Is his selection worthy and genuine?

Follow up: Follow up was not needed in this case immediately because this time client was in IX class. The problem was connected with his vocational career and just then he was studying.

2. Non-directive Counselling

While Directive Counselling involves a counsellor-centred approach, Non-Directive Counselling is client-centred counselling. Rogers was the pioneer of this kind of technique. It is assumed in this approach that the individual is capable of making decisions, once his emotions and tensions are released. He can think in a positive direction and can help himself to come out of his problems. The counsellor's role is of that of a listener and facilitator.

Psychological tests are not essential in this kind of technique. Rogers was of the view that people are self-directed. They need only a congenial atmosphere where they can explore themselves. Counsellor does not provide analytical input to the client, he only empathises with the client and responds only to his feelings and emotions. This type of counselling is more useful in the case of personal and emotional problems.

By providing this theoretical base Rogers explained how the change takes place in the client. He said that the individual has personal anxiety or is in distress. The Counsellor relates himself with the problems of the client and pays positive regard to him. An empathetic relationship takes place where counsellor keeps himself in the place of the client and plays the role of a 'facilitator' or 'reflector'. In this approach it is assumed that each individual is basically good and has capability to develop his insight.

Steps in Client Centered Counselling

Rogers gave the following steps in the process of Non-directive counselling.

1. The individual comes for help. He has taken a tentative step.
2. The helping situation is usually defined. He is made aware at once that the counsellor does not have the answers; the client is merely helped to work out his own answers. The counselling time is his, if he wants it.
3. The counsellor encourages free expression of feelings in regard to the problem. He tries to keep from blocking (and even encourages) the flow of hostility and anxiety, the feelings of concern and of guilt, and the indecisions that come out freely if we have succeeded in making the client feel that the hour is his to use as he wishes. The counsellor does not attempt to persuade the client that he is wrong or that he is right. He accepts him as he is. He merely tries to encourage free expression.
4. The counsellor accepts, recognises, and clarifies those negative feelings. The counsellor must respond to the feelings of the client, not to the intellectual context of what the person is saying, not to the rightness or wrongness of the position or belief taken by the client. He tries to verbalise it and clarify it without undue sympathy.
5. When the individual's negative feelings have been quite fully expressed, they are followed by the faint and tentative expressions of the positive impulses that make for growth. This is one of the most certain and predictable aspects of the whole process.
6. The counsellor accepts and recognises the positive feelings which are expressed in the same manner in which he has accepted and recognised

in the same manner in which he has accepted and recognised the negative feeling. They are not accepted with approval or blame.

7. This results in an understanding of and insight into the self and an acceptance of the self. This provides a basis on which the individual can go ahead to new levels of integration.
8. A clarification of possible decisions, possible courses of action.
9. The initiation by the individual of minute, but highly significant, positive actions. The client is not urged; he still is merely accepted and encouraged.
10. A development of further insight, a more complete and accurate understanding. This is a further element of growth.
11. Increasingly integrated positive action.
12. A feeling of increased independence, of decreasing need for help. (The relationship must terminate.)

Counselling and Psychotherapy

Sometimes the concepts of counselling and psychotherapy are misunderstood as one. But these two concepts are different. While counselling deals with normal people, psychotherapy deals with abnormal people. Another difference is that counselling relates to conscious mind, while psychotherapy relates to unconscious mind. Counselling is said to be focused on cognitive and rational behaviour whereas psychotherapy relates more to emotions and feelings. (Bordin)

Differences have also been observed in the ultimate aim of both. The aim of counselling is to help a person, the aim of psychotherapy is to change the personality of a person (Tyler 1961). Buchheimer and Balogh (1961) tried to differentiate the two concepts stating that counselling refers to individual's present and immediate awareness while therapy refers more to past experiences and symbolism.

On the other hand, Byrne (1963) sees the two concepts as having many similarities, except that the difference is in "degree to which psychotherapists uncover and work with hidden psychological dynamics because the individual seeking help reports a long-standing dissatisfaction with life, accompanied by long-standing ineffective or unwanted behaviours."

Example of Non-directive Counselling

Identification Data:

Name of the Client Mahinder

Father's Name	-	Shri Guru Vachan
Father's Occupation	-	Lift Operator
Client's Class & Section	-	IX
Name of the School	-	Govt. Co-Educational School
Date of birth	-	20-9-60
Age	-	16 years 6 months

Statement of the Problem:

1. He is weak in English & Maths – Educational problem.
2. Adjustment problem – The client is not able to adjust with the teachers.

Family Background: Client has two brothers, one is elder to him. This elder brother is a writer. He used to write poems and stories. Client has one younger brother who is studying in VIII class in the same school. He has no real sister. There is a cousin sister who stayed with client's family. His father was a lift operator and just now, as he stated in his last interview, he has retired and is doing agricultural work. Client's mother is a housewife. Because his father has retired client wants to support his family by joining some night school so that he may be able to do some job. His mother and brothers are going with the father and he himself stayed with his sister because he thinks he will get some good job over here. His sister is working in some office.

Physical Health of the Client: Physically the client is quite normal. He takes active part in school's activities. He was the monitor of his class as it was observed that he is good at administration.

Educational Information: Client is interested in his studies. Since his childhood he likes photography and now at this stage when he is in class IX he has taken photography as a subject. He likes this subject very much. As he stated he was normal with his studies. While at school every teacher used to like him. Since his childhood he is weak in Maths and English. He was weak in Maths so he doesn't like it. Whenever he is not able to solve any problem he skips it. He doesn't try further. He says, 'when I am not able to solve the previous question how can I be successful in this'. He doesn't pay any extra attention to Maths. He is weak in English also but even then he likes it. He takes much interest in other subjects such as Hindi.

Interest & Hobbies: Client takes interest in music. He plays on instruments such as Tabla or Drum. He has learnt this from his father. He father is a musician and he usually goes to some musical sittings. Client also wants to learn some specific instrument in music and he wants to develop his hobby of music.

Sports: He likes cricket very much. Whenever he gets time he plays cricket with some of his good friends. Client also feels pleasure in seeing new places.

Test Reports: Group Tests:

1. Standard Progressive Matrices: According to this group test, client has an average IQ.
2. In the verbal ability test client's score is 33. He comes under VIII Stanine and he is above average in this category.
3. According to the Interest Record he is getting VII Stanine in artistic field. He is above average in this interest area. In some fields such as clerical and out-door fields he is average.

Individual Testing: According to C.*I.E.* Individual scale of Intelligence client's IQ is 83.33 and he is slightly below average according to the IQ's categories.

Bhatia Battery Individual Test Report:

The client has an IQ of 86 and his PQ is 96. According to this report client's IQ comes under slightly below average and according to PQ he is average person.

Achievement Test Report:

	Subjects	Evaluation I	II	III	Total
1.	English	09	04	10	23
2.	Hindi	20	15	13	48
3.	Maths	20	02	16	38
4.	Social Studies	20	14	12	46
5.	Science	11	13	16	40
6.	Craft	25	21	12	48
7.	Physical Education	08	11	A	19

Teacher's Opinion: Teacher's opinion about the client is not very good. They regard him as an aggressive boy. Principal and other teachers referred his case for his adjustment problem. The client voluntarily came for his educational problems.

Teachers don't complain anything about his studies. They only stated – "He is very disobedient and doesn't listen to anybody."

General Opinion: As it was observed that client was very open, there was no difficulty in establishing rapport with the client. During the tests, he was taking interest in the activity.

Counselling Interviews

Ist Interview: The first interview was in reality an initial interview. As stated earlier, it was very easy to establish rapport with the client. He was feeling friendly with the counsellor. A good relationship was established during the test administration. Therefore, it was very easy to talk with the client in first interview. After some general talk such as, "What are your hobbies"? "How did you like the tests which have been administered to you?" and some other questions about his family, the client was feeling relaxed and then he stated his problem. The client so opened up with the counsellor that he himself stated his adjustment problem also. But in this initial interview counsellor didn't talk anything about his adjustment problem. He overlooked the client's statement and tried to lay emphasis mainly upon the educational problem.

Mahinder stated – "I am weak in Maths and English. Main problem is with Maths. I can't understand anything in this subject.

Counsellor asked him to come next time so that he may discuss his problem.

2nd Interview: Couns. – How many marks are you getting in maths?

Mahinder – Only 38 out of 100.

Couns. – What are the things you are not able to understand in maths?

Mahinder – You see, I can't understand anything. I am weak in maths from the very beginning.

Couns. – Why are you weak in maths from very beginning? Can you think of any reason? Were you not paying much attention or any thing else?

Mahinder – Yes. This was the reason. Now I pay more attention. In the beginning I was not paying any attention. Wherever I could not solve any question I skipped it because I got puzzled. In the beginning, I always used to get 0 marks but now I get some marks.

Couns. – So you are understanding what should you do?

Mahinder – Yes.. I am ..... but ......

Couns. – How much time do you give to your studies?

Mahinder – Not much, only 2 hours in the night from 9 to 11.

Couns. – You study two hours in the night. How do you plan it? For how much time do you study maths?

Mahinder – I study maths for one-hour daily, half an hour English and rest half an hour Science. Other subjects I feel very easy and I study other subjects very little.

Couns. – Do you study in the morning?

Mahinder – No, I don't, because I wake up in the morning at 9.

Couns. – What you can do for it?

Mahinder – Now I have taken an alarm piece and I try to wake up early in the morning.

Couns. – What are the courses in the maths?

Mahinder – Algebra, Geometry and Trigonometry I can't understand a word of them.

Couns. – What is the thing? Do you think teacher is not good or you don't concentrate?

Mahinder – No, teacher is quite nice but actually I don't pay much attention because I have no interest

Couns. – But you know, you have to study all subjects upto 10th standard and Maths is a very scoring subject.

Mahinder – That is right but what can I do? Can you tell me?

Couns. – Yes. You come next time. I will think over your problem, you should also think and then we will try to find a solution for your problem.

3rd Interview: Next Thursday the client came. After some general talk we started–

Mahinder – Yes, can you tell me something to solve my problem?

Couns. – You see, as you have stated previously, it seems that you have no interest in Mathematics because you are not able to understand it.

Mahinder – ..... Yes, that's right.

Couns. – And you were not paying any attention in the beginning, therefore you are not able to understand it.

Mahinder – Yes. When I don't know about previous things, how can I understand further?

Couns. – You can tell your problem to the teacher.

Mahinder – Till now I never went to him, but if you say so, I will go.

Couns. – No, you should not go just because I am saying so you. You should think about it yourself, whether to go or not. Is there any other person in your house who can teach you?

Mahinder – No, there is non but I will go to my teacher personally.

Couns. – And, what is your problem in English

Mahinder – I can't understand grammar. My teacher says you have to study new grammar. I don't know even what parts of speech are. I don't know the difference between a noun and pronoun.

Couns. – What about other students?

Mahinder – Nobody understands.

Couns. – You haven't studied it in class VIII?

Mahinder – No, there was no grammar in VIII class. When we ask the teacher, he says 'you are so foolish that you don't know even these things'.

Couns. – You can study in groups in the class.

Mahinder – There is too much noise in the class. There is no study room and they don't allow us to sit in the library. They think we are cutting our classes.

Couns. – You can study in any class where there is no lecture going on.

Mahinder – Then other boys disturb us. They laugh at us.

Couns. – So it means you are afraid of them.

Mahinder – Yes

Couns. – Why?

Mahinder – Because, if friends insult me I feel bad.

Couns. – Do you think it insulting, if you are studying.

Mahinder – ....No .... that is not the thing. But when they want me and I am studying, then they say 'Oh you have to top'—or something like that.

Couns. – But you can also tell them that you have to study. If they say, 'you leave studies' will you leave?

Mahinder – No, I will not. How it can be?

Couns. – So, you can tell them that at this time you have to study or at this time you can complain to your teachers.

Mahinder – They don't do anything.

Couns. – Then, what do you think, what can be done? It is a problem but studies are more important. Are they not?

Mahinder – That's right. Now, I have to make my time table. Now I won't talk with any body. There is only one friend of mine. I usually to study with him. We solve our problems with the help of each another.

Couns. – Yes. You can do like this. Everybody can't understand everything and you can solve your problems with the help of each other. Tell me one thing what do you want to be in future?

Mahinder – There are some family problems with me. I have to join some night school. To support my family I want to take up some job. I am having photography in my work experience; I want to have my own shop.

Couns. – How has your interest in photography developed?

Mahinder – Since my childhood I have interest in photography. Some relations had cameras with them. I wanted to know about it. When I asked something about photography, they told, "you are a child, when you grow up, you will be able to understand it". Now when I came in IX class I took photography as a subject.

Couns. – Do you have any friend or somebody or relation with whom you want to open your shop?

Mahinder – Yes, a friend of mine is interested in photography but he doesn't know about it. I am teaching him and when we have decided that we will contribute fifty-fifty we will open a shop.

Couns. – Do you want to open your shop after completing your studies or, as you have stated, you will join some night school, and start your work right from now.

Mahinder – Yes, I will do some other job, because we don't have so much money. I will save some money and then I will do my own work.

Couns. – It is very good that you think in this way and want to do your work on your own. If you are not able to open your own shop, you can do some other job in photography. For example, you can be a photographer in any company, or advertising agencies or in some newspaper.

Mahinder – That's all right.

Couns. – Any thing else you want to say?

Mahinder – No. Now I don't have anything to say.

Couns. – So, I think now you will study well. You are a good student.

Mahinder – Yes, I will try my best. Now I can solve my problems. Thank you very much.

4th Interview:

Couns. – Last time we were discussing about the problem of difficulties in your studies. Once you told me about your adjustment problem. Will you discuss it today?

Mahinder – Yes, of course I will.

Couns. – Then tell me what the matter is.

Mahinder – You see, teachers used to harass me. Once the entire class was making noise. So the teacher punished the whole class and even those who were not at fault were punished. Then there was my brother. He asked some teacher how to make me remember things. The teacher told him to cut my hairs. I felt very bad. It is a kind of comment on my *Dharm*. This was in class VIII. In class IX there was a boy. He commented "Hello Sardarji. Is it twelve o'clock?" I felt very bad and I slapped him. He went to the teacher. The teacher abused me and beat me. The boy is the same fellow who was talking against the teacher last year.

Couns. – From the very beginning you had bad relations with the teachers.

Mahinder – No. not so. When I was in class V, some incident took place. Some teacher told something nasty to my brother. These things I cannot tolerate. One day I went to a palmist. He told me, "you could never tolerate injustice. You are very aggressive type. You will be just like Gandhiji, who could never tolerate injustice and started non-cooperative movement. You will also do like that."

Couns. – Have you read anything about Gandhiji?

Mahinder – Yes, I have. There was a book on Gandhiji, I have read that.

Couns. – Do you think he was very aggressive?

Mahinder – No, he was not. He was very calm and quiet. He was a very simple man. Whatever step he took he took it peacefully.

Couns. – Yes, you are right. He never tried to win any injustice through anger. Is it not so?

Mahinder – Yes.

Couns. – He told that if anybody is angry, you can win him by love and not with anger. Now, take your fight with that boy. Actually it may not be any comment. He is just like your friend. Friends can say anything. You see, when you like Gandhiji and you want to be like him, you study more about him then you can understand the real facts about him.

Mahinder – Yes, I will study more.

Couns. – You were a monitor of your class. I have seen that you were doing a good job in the class. You can enforce discipline in the class. But, do you feel you can control the people only with aggression?

Mahinder – They don't understand the things otherwise. I can't do anything else.

Couns. – No, you can. Why not? You see, if your parents always tell you, "you have to do like this, otherwise we will punish you," would you like it? Would you do the work by such type of threats or when they ask you to do the work with affection?

Mahinder – Yes, I will not do by force.

Couns. – Then.

Mahinder – But when I was in class V there was a teacher of mine. He told me to beat the students if they are not controllable. So I became hostile.

Couns. – But hostile ones can be ..... Is it not?

Mahinder – Yes. It is but it cannot be in one moment. It will go gradually.

Couns. – Will you try not to be hostile?

Mahinder – Yes, I will. You see, every teacher used to like my brothers. They always tell me "you are so bad but your brothers are very simple". I also feel that I am not a good boy and my brothers are so good.

Couns. – You don't want to be like your brothers?

Mahinder – I want, but now it is not possible because now teachers could not forgive me.

Couns. – Do you feel if someone has done something wrong he can never be a good man.

Mahinder – Some people think like that.

Couns. – No, it is not. Suppose somebody has done some mistake, will you not forgive him if in future he realises his mistake?

Mahinder – Yes, I will.

Couns. – Have you heard about Valmiki?

Mahinder – No I haven't. You tell me.

Couns. – Yes, I will. He was a dacoit. One day some saints came to him. Valmiki asked them to give him whatever things they had. The saints said that they would give, but asked "you are committing sins to support your family. When you will be punished by god, will the members of your family help you or not?" Valmiki replied I don't know. They should support me. Valmiki went to his home and asked the members of his family. They told that they would not help him when God punished him. Since that very day Valmiki got reformed and became a very good man. So, don't you think a bad man too can be good some day?

Mahinder – You are right. Actually I am a weak person, so I was thinking like this. I was feeling that teachers would not change their opinion.

Couns. – Now you understand you can be a good man through your behaviour. It is good that you should not tolerate injustice, but you should not be aggressive. You think yourself which is better?

Mahinder – Now I will try my best to change myself. I will study some good books.

Follow up – The time was not much but in the limited time, counsellor observed client takes interest in his studies. He has left the monitorship because of his studies. He is friendly to his classmates. He respects his teachers. His classmates also gave positive comments.

Counsellor's Comments and Suggestions: If counsellor was able to get more time he could do much better. Problem was much lengthy, it needed time. As counsellor knew about the adjustment problem of the client he observed that client couldn't listen anything against about his '*Dharm*'. Counsellor gave the example of Valmiki because counsellor observed that he could be changed only through such an example. For the study problems of the client counsellor tried to open up the client and asked for suggestions as to what he could do to tackle the problem.

The Process of Counselling

It cannot be expected that a person would just come for counselling, would state his problem, that the counsellor would give a solution and the person would be happy that his problem is resolved. Counselling is a time consuming process where trust building between the two is extremely essential. There are no readymade solutions. A long process is involved in the problem solving.

Brammer (1973) has pointed out four stages of the counselling process. These are: entry, clarification, planning and termination. Similarly, Blackham has identified the stages as problem identification and relationship establishment stage; exploration and analysis stage; and termination stage. Although the stages relating to identification and analysis of the problem as well as planning a solution are the most important where the actual work takes place, but the initial stage of rapport building and the last stage, *i.e.*, termination stage are extremely crucial and difficult. It is the responsibility of the counsellor to prepare an atmosphere where the client could feel relaxed and accepted. The client has to have faith in the counsellor to confide himself. This trust building takes time. It develops gradually in a friendly harmonious relationship. Non-verbal communication like shaking hands, smiles, eye contacts etc. play an important role. The counsellor should understand the importance of such clues.

Similarly, the termination stage is difficult because during the whole counselling process, even though the relationship between the client and counsellor is said to be professional, it is, in fact, extremely sensitive. Many a time; the client develops special affection for the counsellor, totally depends upon him and looks forward to continued relationship. At this stage the counsellor needs to be tactful. Gradually he should withdraw from the relationship of dependability. The counsellor should, however, welcome in case the client really needs some help.

Table 7.1: Comparative Analysis of Directive and Non-Directive Counselling

Directive	*Non Directive*
1. Economical	• Time Consuming
2. Emphasis is on the problem	• Emphasis on individual
3. Emphasis on the intellectual aspect	• Emphasis on emotional aspect
4. Methodology is direct and persuasive	• Methodology is indirect
5. Solves immediate problems	• Deals with self analysis and new problems of adjustment may be taken care of
6. Uses psychological assessment data	• May not use psychological assessment
7. Counselor plays active role	• Counselor plays passive role
8. Direct counseling sometimes may be done by supporting staff	• A highly professional, competent and trained person with understanding of relationship skills is required
9. Help is offered by counselor to take decisions	• Client takes his own decisions
10. It is more information giving, rapport formation is not that significant	• It is to develop self-insight and more towards solving the personal problems-rapport formation is essential.

3. Eclectic Counselling

This is the middle path between Direct and Non-direct approaches where both approaches are adopted simultaneously. There may be cases and situations where one approach exclusively may not help to reach the desired results. Hence a middle path, in which both the approaches can be combined under this technique as and when needed. Here the counsellor accepts that an individual can choose his goals but motivation on the part of the counsellor is essential so that the client may solve the problems. Counsellor takes an initiative in providing information and suggestions wherever he feels that these are necessary for the client to take the decisions. In cases where school environment or work environment is responsible for individual's problems, the counsellor, under this approach, tries to amend the environment with the help of other members of the school. Under this approach it is also believed that the present behaviour is influenced by past and, therefore, information about the client is collected from various sources. The counsellor also takes into account the support services available in the client's environment like family, community, friends' circle, and other agencies that can help the client in solving his problems and reaching the goal. In this eclectic counselling approach finding the solution to the problem is joint responsibility of the counsellor and the client.

4. Cognitive Therapies

Under the cognitive therapies, Rational-Emotive therapy by Albert Eliss (1950) and Cognitive Restructuring Therapy by Aaron Becks are the two important ones to mention. These are based on the concept that problems occur in people because of the distortions in the cognitive or the thought process.

While explaining the Rational-emotive therapy, Eliss considered that whenever the person has irrational thought, emotional problems emerge. The person starts feeling anger, anxiety, depression etc. People sometimes make illogical interpretations of the events, they compare themselves with others and develop self-defeating attitudes. This therapy helps in changing such thoughts and beliefs into rationality by challenging the irrational thoughts through arguments and rational interpretation of the situation.

Restructuring therapy also tries to change the client's negative self-images through restructuring their thoughts, but in this case the situation is not analysed in a more rational manner but the client is told of certain experiences that could disapprove the client's negative self-image. For example, if the client comes with an image 'He is no good and cannot do anything'; the counsellor has to talk with him about those activities where the client excelled earlier.

5. Behavioural Counselling

Behavioural counselling is based on social learning theory, which relate to process of changing the behaviours and how the learning takes place. The outer symptoms of behaviour are most important. It is believed that a person is not behaving properly because his learning is faulty. Re-learning has to take place and mal-adaptive learning has to be unlearned. These therapies concentrate on a person's present behaviour.

Various techniques are used to change the undesirable behaviour known as classical conditioning and operant conditioning.

The following two techniques are used in classical conditioning :

(a) Desensitisation

Joseph Walpe developed this technique in 1950. Desensitisation for a problem situation is conducted systematically under this technique. People are trained to relax in the situations that create anxiety. The process involves identifying the triggers that induce anxiety and their intensity. In the second step, the person is asked to relax physically and mentally. When a person is totally relaxed, he is asked to think about the triggers according to their intensity till he feels anxious. When the person is trained to be relaxed in such situations, which he imagines as anxiety situations, he is asked to face the real situation. This technique is effective in dealing with anxiety and phobias.

(b) Aversive Conditioning

In this technique, the person is asked to feel discomfort with the behaviour he wants to change. For example, if a person wants to leave his habit of smoking, he is asked to feel that his mouth has a bad taste, he is not enjoying, and he is feeling physically uncomfortable while smoking. In this technique, some drugs are administered after which the person would develop such discomfort when he would smoke or drink. This technique is used generally to deal with the problems of smoking and alcoholism.

Operant Conditioning

These therapies are also known as behaviour modifications methods through providing positive reinforcements to encourage desired behaviour and to remove some existing stimuli to punish the undesirable behaviour. In other words, reinforces are used manipulatively to change the behaviour. The techniques used under this therapy are positive reinforcement, extinction, and punishment. In the positive reinforcement technique some rewards are given for encouraging the desirable behaviours. When a child is rewarded for his desirable behaviour for example, by giving a toy and by giving the food he likes, he may get encouragement for his behaviour and would continue to act in the same manner. In extinction technique, when a child's behaviour is not liked, the reinforce to encourage that behaviour is eliminated. In cases where children cry for getting attention and parents immediately attend to the child when he cries, he develops crying as a behaviour. If such situations have to be dealt with, the parents are advised to heed to the child before crying and not to encourage crying by responding to it.

In punishment technique the child is punished for his undesirable behaviour. Modeling is also a technique for behaviour change. Successful stories of people and identification of children with their ideals is common for behaviour modifications. This also involves role-playing, in which people try to act in hypothetical situations. Once they are confident in such situations, they will be comfortable when placed in real life activities.

6. Group Therapy

In dealing with emotional problems of people, the concept of group therapy is a recent phenomenon. Problems such as alcoholism, smoking, introversive ness, etc. may be dealt collectively. The groups may be the families, the couples or the people having similar problems. For example, in marriage counselling, the therapists call both the husband and the wife. Group therapy provides a therapeutic effect. It also encourages the group relationships and feeling of togetherness and support. Interaction with the group develops interpersonal skills. Suggestions come from various members and there is an opportunity to see how others are coping with the problems. For example, in case of alcoholism the people who want to get rid of this habit may come together, where they can discuss their problems, or a person who earlier had this problem and has been successful in coming out of it, may interact with the group and discuss the strategies to change the habit. These behaviour therapies have been criticised to be over simplistic and ignoring the individual's growth and development process.

Specific Skills Required in Counselling

One to one counselling is a specialised activity, which requires besides training, some special skills in the counsellor.

1. *Ethics*: The ethical attitudes of the counsellor matter most, as client is providing extremely personal information to the counsellor, in other words, the client is confiding in the counsellor, and the counsellor should have

professional attitude and also some basic ethics that personal information should not be revealed to others and would not be used other than professional. The counsellor should also have respect and regards for the client for 'what he is'. The client's feelings should also be respected.: Counselling requires unconditional warmth towards the client. In a counselling process, counsellor should always be welcoming with a smiling face; he should not say "say it fast, I have to do some other work." He should not even give the non-verbal clues like seeing the watch many times. Client may feel that his is not wanted.

2. *Sensitivity and Empathy*: The counsellor should be sensitive towards the client's needs and problems. He should not pass remarks 'what you are wearing is not a proper dress' or 'I was told you are a mischievous boy'. Empathy is the competence of the counsellor to experience the client's experience. Rogers (1990) defined empathy as 'perceiving the internal frame of reference of another person'. Egan (1990) defined the concept of empathy as 'entering the private perceptual world of the client and being sensitive to his/her feelings, whether good or bad.' For example if the client comes to the counsellor for confessing some act he is guilty of now, counsellor should not go into the value judgement about the act, expressing his feelings. He should not say, "What did you do? You should have not done it" but try to listen to the client patiently and help him to come out of his feeling of guilt. Such situations can be handled by giving some examples, indicating that these things can and do happen. Self-disclosure also helps in dealing such situations.

3. *Communication and Listening*: Communicating through listening is most important in counselling. The counsellor should possess that intellectual competence to react verbally as well as non-verbally wherever required. Most of the problems of the clients are resolved only when the counsellor is a good listener and a good communicator. The expressions, the tone, the pitch, the body language, eye contact are equally or even more important than words. If a client comes and counsellor says 'Hello, I am happy to see you' but the expressions of the counsellor do not reflect that happiness, the communication would not be effective. A small touch is better than thousand words to the crying.

4. *Giving Leads*: In communicating with the client, the counsellor makes use of statements called 'leads'. Such leads may be classified into the following categories of techniques.

(a) Restatement : The counsellor attempts to convey his understanding of what the client communicated by repeating or rewording the client's statement.

(b) Questioning : The counsellor seeks additional information from the client.

(c) Reflection of feeling : The counsellor expresses understanding of the client's point of view and communicates that understanding.

(d) Reassurance : The counsellor's statement serves as a reward or reinforcing agent. This technique is often used to support the client's exploration of ideas and feelings or test different behaviour.

(e) Interpretation : The counsellor tries to explain the meaning of what the client stated.

Example: The counsellor met the student for the first time. The student said: "The teacher asked me to see you, I do not know why. She says I should learn to stay awake in the class. I feel sleepy because I walk five kilometers to reach the school. Moreover her lessons bore everyone."

In response, the counsellor may say one of the following:

(a) "You were bored and felt sleepy in the class and the teacher asked you to leave the class".

– Restatement

(b) "Why do you get bored in that teacher's class?"

– Questioning

(c) "So, you felt bad when she asked you to go"

– Reflection of feeling = Understanding

(d) "Do not worry! It should be possible to find a solution soon"

– Reassurance = Supporting

(e) "Do you think that you are making the teacher responsible for what happened?"

– Interpretation

Importance of Interview in Counselling

Interview plays an important role in counselling, be it directive, non-directive or eclectic. The process of interview changes according to the type of counselling. While in directive counselling, the counsellor can directly ask questions to get information from the client and can ask about his needs, in non-directive counselling, the role of the counsellor is to encourage the client to speak about himself. The counsellor has to be supportive and empathetic in his approach. Direct questions should be avoided. Silence and non-verbal clues are to be interpreted adequately. In general, according to Humphreys a counsellor has to perform five basic functions in an interview,. These are:

1. *Rapport Formation*: To establish harmonious and congenial relationship with the client.
2. *To Secure Information*: Counsellor may seek information from the client during interview or can have the information from other sources like Cumulative Record Card, Anecdotal Records, School Records.
3. *To Impart Information:* During the interviews counsellor can impart the information to the client as per his need.
4. *To Motivate:* Motivation here is not forcing the client to do something but to help the counselee to understand and develop his motivational forces inside.
5. *To Help*: Under this function counsellor helps the counselee to make adjustments and have long-term planning.

For conducting an interview, counsellor should:

1. *Prepare*: Such as collection of information about the client from various sources; note down the gaps, fix up the appointment, see the physical settings, keep himself prepared to face the client.
2. *Create a Pleasant Atmosphere*: Counsellor should be able to create such a pleasant atmosphere that the client is ready to trust the counsellor and open up his feelings.
3. *Be a Good Listener*: The counsellor should have patience in dealing with the client. He should be a good listener and should not interrupt the client to cut his speech. He should not comment like 'I know this, go further'.
4. *Be Unbiased*: While interacting with teachers, or peers or parents about an individual, the counsellor should not form any opinion. He should meet with the client without any pre-conceived ideas.
5. *Be Accepting*: The counsellor should not pronounce value judgement. He should receive the client with open heart. He should accept him as 'what he is' and not as 'what he should be'.
6. *Be Aware of his Limitations*: The counsellor himself may not deal with all cases. He should take the help of others wherever required or he should be willing to refer the client to the appropriate agency wherever needed.
7. *Be Able to Maintain the Privacy*: Total privacy should be maintained during the interview process. The counsellor should ensure that others are not waiting in the queue. Counsellor should keep himself free from other activities.

8. *End the Interview on a Positive Note*: At the end of the interview session, counsellor should be positive. He should not be depressed or gloomy or leave the client in depressing mood.
9. *Interpret with Full Understanding*: Counsellor should be able to make interpretation from the discussions with counselling properly and with adequate understanding.
10. *Recording of Procedures*: Wherever client agrees, the interview may be recorded so that information and clues given by the client are not forgotten.

How to Conduct Interview in Counselling

1. *Rapport Formation*:
   - Have the interview where privacy can be maintained.
   - Welcome the client, with smile or a handshake or with pleasant greetings.
   - Make him/her sit comfortably and relax
   - So far as possible use only first name of the client. With this the client will get a feeling of intimacy.
   - Start with informal conversation like – How are you doing today, or how was your day today, or how you did in the class today, etc.
   - Use the native language of the client as far as possible.
   - Avoid interruptions created by other visitors, phone calls.
   - Listen attentively and slow empathy towards the problem of the client.
   - Patience is required in establishing rapport. Sometimes no words are required, only small gestures of affection like smile, welcoming attitude may help while with some clients, it may take a long time. In a case where student came with saying 'I want to commit suicide' the reply from the counsellor's we will talk it over, first let us have a cup of tea together; was enough to form the rapport.
   - Sincerity, non-judgmental attitude and friendly behaviour is essential.
2. *Client's Problem*:
   - In counselling, it is important to know how the client perceives his problems. Questions like 'you want to share something with me', or 'what would you like to talk with me?' may be the initial questions that may encourage the client to start talking.
   - When the client narrates his problem, listen. With small words Oh! or O.K. or with some non-verbal gestures show that you are concerned with the problem of the client.

- When the client stops speaking questions like 'what your parents feel about this problem; or whether you have discussed it with any of your friends and relatives' may be asked to know how the client see others' advice.
- Thought Providing Clues:

During counselling interview, the counsellor may raise certain questions and issues that may start thought provoking process in the client other than how he perceives himself or his problem. For example, with a totally negative self-image, the counsellor may ask the client what strengths he thinks he has or what good things happened in his life or count small achievements of the day or the week, etc.

- *Self-Understanding and Self-Realisation*: It is said that sharing the problem provides a kind of catharsis (release of tension) and client starts understanding the self in a positive manner. Factual data on the clients performance or the environment should be provided to the client so that he could start realising and accepting him self like 'you got good marks in Science', or 'you did extremely well in the annual function of the school.'
- *Information Providing*: Wherever necessary counsellor should provide the information to the client to facilitate his decision making, *e.g.,* where the client is confused in making a choice of career, or has no choice.
- *Motivation*: During the interview, motivate the client when he puts forth some idea towards the process of decision making in solving his problem like 'yes that's a good idea' or 'yes it would work out'
- *Self-insight or Change in behaviour*: When the client is able to get self-insight into the problem and says 'yes it can be done like this' or I will do this, counsellor should help the client in executing the idea with follow up.

Interview with the client may not be complete in one sitting. The whole process takes three or four interviews.

Guidance and Counselling—The Distinction

Sometimes the two words Guidance and Counselling are used synonymously, although both are not the same. Guidance is a broader concept whereas counselling is only one technique of providing guidance. Counselling is one to one interaction while guidance can be both individual as well as in groups. Guidance includes various other services such as display of material using Audio Visuals, etc. while counselling uses interview techniques only.

8

Career Information

Because of the vast changes in and expansion of the world of education and world of work, the decision making process has become difficult and complex. Wrong decision in the choice of the educational stream and/or career may cost anyone a lot of money, time, energy and happiness. To make right decisions at the right time is the need of the day, which can be made only if supported by a proper information management system. Career information is the foundation of the career guidance programme. Hoppock has rightly pointed out that "choice always involves knowledge, one cannot choose what one does not know… the wise choice of an occupation requires accurate information about what occupations are available, what they require and what they offer." If a question is put to a small boy or girl of 3rd or 4th standard as to what he/she would like to be, his/her answer probably would be—a milkman, or a teacher or a gardener and so on. The reason is that they know only about these simple occupations they come across in everyday life. As they grow up, their choices change not because of growing but because they receive more and more information about the world of work. There is today an enormous variety of educational streams, skill development avenues and occupations, each requiring its own preparation and each having its own opportunities. The scene is getting increasingly complex day by day with innumerable number of specialisations in each field. Thus, it would almost be impossible to organise a guidance programme unless there is a strong information system.

Specific Need for the Information

(a) There are gaps in the information available and information required. Moreover, career information is not a one-time activity. As the educational and occupational scene changes, more information would be required. Therefore, a continuous collection of information is necessary

(b) One of the major services of a guidance programme is 'Pupil Information Service' where collection of information becomes a pre-requisite.

(c) To organise group guidance activities and also the individual guidance information is required. For example, if a guidance worker wants to organise career exhibition cum career conference, information is required to prepare posters and charts, career films etc.

Objectives of Career Information

Some of the basic objectives of collecting career information for a guidance programme are as follows:

- To help students in understanding, comparing and analysing various occupations and assessing their own potentials.
- To assist students in choosing a right field of education on the basis of the information
- To help in developing appropriate attitudes towards various kinds of occupations
- To provide a clear picture of various fields of occupations in terms of the actual working conditions, life style associated with each occupation, working hours, etc.
- To familiarise students about the various problems they may face in choosing an educational stream or a career.
- To analyse and provide information about the future trends and prospects of various careers.
- To provide information about the demands of various jobs and supply of people for the same and if there are any surplus or shortage categories of occupations.
- To give information about the financial aspects of pursuing a career.
- To assist the students in developing tentative career plans.
- To keep a watch on labour market changes and provide information to schools for modifications in course content as well as to students to amend their career plans, if necessary.

Sources of Information

There can be two types of sources of information. One can be the direct or primary source, *i.e.,* discussions with the employers, industries and collection of primary data, and, another the secondary source, *i.e.,* the published material. The information from secondary sources is available from:

1. *Career Publications*: A number of agencies – governmental as well as private are producing career literature. Some of these agencies are Central Institute for Research and Training in Employment Services (CIRTES), Employment Exchanges, State Directorates of Employment, National Council

for Educational Research and Training, University Bureaus and private organisations like – YMCA, YWCA, Publishers, Newspapers, etc. Recently, many of the career publications of CIRTES have been placed on the official website of Ministry of Labour and can be accessed by anyone.

2. *Other Publications*: Other publications for career information include various magazines and journals such as Economic and Political Weekly, Yojana, magazines, Employment News, etc.

3. *Reports of Ministries and Other Departments*: Institute of Applied Manpower Research brings out a Manpower Profile which provides the overall statistics about labour market. Technical Manpower Bulletin of the Council of Scientific and Industrial Research, Reports from Ministry of Education, Ministry of Employment, UPSC, handbooks from Association of Indian Universities, Ministry of Health, Five Year Plan documents of reports of Planning Commissions, National Sample Survey Organisation and Directorate General of Employment & Training (DGE&T) provide information about various aspects of education & employment such as trades and courses in ITIs, polytechnics, apprenticeship training, competitive exams, statistics about education and employment, higher level courses and intake etc. The DGE&T also brings out a Bulletin on Job Opportunities.

4. *Prospectus of Institutes:* The prospectus of professional and technical institutions contain detailed information about courses available in the respective institutions, eligibility, seats, duration and prospects of the course, financial liabilities etc.

5. *Surveys:* Surveys conducted from time to time by various organisations provide a lot of information about employment market trends, prospects, shortage and surplus of vacancies, unfilled vacancies etc. Some of these surveys are Occupational Pattern surveys, Employment Exchange statistics, reports of the Employment Market Information (EMI) programme operated by DGE&T, Census, Industries Surveys and Census of Central Government Employees.

6. *Advertisements*: Various Vacancy and educational advertisements appearing in newspapers and their special job issues (like ASCENT of Times of India), internet, etc. provide a wealth of career information.

Primary Sources

1. *Interviews with People*: One way to collect the information directly from the source can be interviewing the experts in the field. For example, to collect information about self-employment opportunities, or loan facilities or on how to start self-employment ventures, interviews can be had with bank officials,

personnel of District Industries Centres, persons who are already in the self-employment, or associations of small entrepreneurs.

2. *Mailing Questionnaires*: Another method of collecting the information from primary sources is to structure a questionnaire and mail it to the concerned department, industry or persons. For example, to collect the information about textile industry, a questionnaire has to be prepared on the items like, job-positions, nature of duties, hours of work, pay scales, perks, terms & conditions, annual vacancies at various levels, future prospects, skills required, method of recruitment, working conditions, health hazards in that industry. The questionnaire may then be mailed to the Personnel Managers of some of the textile industry units.

3. *Industry Visits*: This is yet another way to collect the information. It provides first hand information about a field of occupation. One can visit some industry units and see for himself the job openings, the working atmosphere etc.

4. *Trade Unions and Employers' organisations*: Information can also be collected from the persons associated with trade unions and organisations of employers. In India apex employers' organisations such as Federation of Indian Chambers of Commerce and Industry (FICCI), Local chambers of commerce, Confederation of Indian Industries (CII) and trade unions such as Indian National Trade Union Congress (INDUC), Bharatya Mazdoor Sangh (BMS), All India Trade Union Congress (AITUC), can provide information about future trends of employment. The local industries associations and plant level trade unions can provide first hand information on specific occupations and industries.

How to Evaluate the Information

After collection of information, the following criteria should be followed to check the authenticity of the information. All the collected information may not be relevant. Some may be obsolete. Some may not be required. It is, therefore, necessary to sift and check the information collected from various sources to avoid duplication.

1. *When Published*: Year of publication of the information is important. Very old information may not be useful on most of the aspects, as eligibility conditions for a particular job change from time to time. On the other hand, analysing the trends in a particular occupation overtime using time series data may be useful.

2. *Who Published or Provided*: It has to be checked as to what is the source of the information. For example, the authentic person to provide data about ITI trades in a particular ITI may be the principal or a teacher of that

particular ITI. If the material is in published form, the relevant question is who the author is. Is he providing his opinion or the facts? These aspects should be looked into.

3. *Where from the Information has been Brought:* This refers to the source. Was it a primary source or the secondary source? If it is from a secondary source the question to look into is whether the published material provides authentic information, and if the source is primary, whether the person who collected the information from primary source could understand and note down the details properly or the person has provided the information without bias.

4. *Why:* Information has to be evaluated on the basis of the purpose of collection. Information should be sorted out on the basis of the purpose and irrelevant information should be scrapped.

5. *How:* The method of collection and dissemination of information is extremely important so that it is properly collated, checked and understood. To evaluate the authenticity of information, more than one method may be used. If the information has been collected through mailing the questionnaires, some interviews may be had with the experts to check the correctness, or it may be verified through a comparison with published material.

What Information should be Collected by a Guidance Worker?

1. *Educational Purposes*: Courses of various levels, directory of training institutions, eligibility and entry reauirements, how to prepare, duration of courses, fees, content of the course, future prospects, scholarships, training opportunities at various levels, linkages with further education/training/employment, suitability of individuals to particular courses, hostel and other facilities, placement programmers, preparation for entrance examinations, institutions that assist for appearing in entrance examinations. *Narris et al* (1960) has summarised the educational information as "valid and usable data about all types of present ad probable future educational or training opportunities and requirements including curricular and co-curricular offerings, requirements for entrance and conditions and problems of student life."

2. *Vocational Purposes*: Nature of work, duties, service conditions, method of recruitment, pay packet, personal qualities required, promotional avenues, employment trends of various occupations, employing organisations, working environment, hours of working, perks and hazards, physical requirements, eligibility conditions, preparation for competitive examinations and sources of assistance, apprenticeship training, on-the-job training, preparation of CVs, assistance for appearing in interviews in terms of discussions with experts in the field who may like to help, employers' list, placement agencies, placement

facilities, employers' requirements. Narris *et al.* (1960) defined occupational information as "valid and usable data about positions, jobs and occupations, including duties, requirements for entrance, conditions of work, rewards offered, advancement patterns, existing and predicted supply and demand of workers and sources for further information."

3. *Personal Guidance Purposes:* Information about the environment where the person is living, family background and culture, assisting agencies where the individual could be referred to for health problems, occupational experience through field visits, personal information about the person's needs, attitudes, potentials, experience, weaknesses, strengths are also required. The importance of personal information has got special focus in recent years in the field of occupational information as the personal information has to be collated with educational and occupational information. Without facilitating the personal matching with courses and jobs, help in vocational planning may turn out to be a useless affair. Norris *et al* define social information and its uses as "valid and usable data about the opportunities and influences of the human and physical environment which bear on personal and inter-personal relations. It is that information about human beings which will help a student to understand himself better and to improve his relations with others."

4. *For Setting up Self-employment Ventures*: List of agencies involved in promotion of self-employment, market demand surveys for launching of self-employment ventures, availability of raw material, project profile preparation, samples of project profiles, credit and loan facilities and eligibility conditions, raw material sources, marketing outlets, personal qualities needed to start and continue with the ventures, experience in the field.

Classification of Information

Once the information has been collected, it is essential to store the collected information in such a way that what is required in a particular case could be easily accessed as per individual's needs. There can be a number of ways to file the collected information.

1. Alphabetical order
2. By interests
3. Geographical locations
4. By industry/occupation
5. By levels of education
6. Separate folders for specific information such as part-time employment, correspondence courses, lists of various web sites,

facilities for special categories, information for women candidates, self-employment opportunities.

7. Computerised data base
8. Dr. Mehta's method of classification:

1. *Alphabetical Order*: In this method, information about various educational/technical courses and occupations may be arranged in alphabetical order. Separate files may be opened for each alphabet. If for some alphabets, occupations or information is bulky, more than one file may be opened. For example for teaching occupation, file may be opened under the alphabet 'T' and then separate files may be for school teacher, college teachers, technical teachers, teachers for professional courses as T-1, T-2, T-3 and so on.

2. *By Interest*: Files may be opened according to the vocational interests. Super's classification of interest may be used for this purposed:

(a) Scientific
(b) Social Welfare
(c) Literary
(d) Material technical
(e) Business detail
(f) Business contact
(g) Artistic
(h) Musical

If some occupations do not fall under this classification, separate files with name of the interest area can be opened.

3. *Geographical Locations*: Information may also be classified according to geographical locations. The geographical area may be divided in several ways. One can be – plains, hilly areas and coastal areas related occupations. Other method could be to divide the information as East, West, North, South, North-East or Statewise classification.

4. *By Levels of Education*: Separate files may be kept about courses available or about training options or job openings according to educational levels especially after VIII standard, after X or after XII standard and so on. At XII level these can be further divided according to occupational streams such as for science students, for commerce students and for arts students.

5. *By Industry/Occupation*: National Classification of Occupation (NCO) provides a detailed method to classify the information on the basis of occupations. In this method a specific code number is assigned to each occupation in a systematic manner.

The National Classification of Occupations (1968) which was in use till now, has been revised in 2004 due to the emergence of new occupations and the need for taking into account the skill levels of occupations. The career information can be classified according to the system given under the revised NCO. In this revised NCO, all the identified occupations (2484 in number) are broadly divided into 10 Occupational Groups, and each Group into Families of occupations. A single digit code is assigned to each Division, two digit code to a Sub-Division, three digit code to each Group and a four digit code to each Family. Within each occupational family the individual occupations are assigned two digits each. There are 10 occupational Divisions, 11 Sub-divisions Groups and 462 occupational Families. For classification of career information, classification upto three digit code level may be followed or depending upon the volume of information, two digit code may be followed.

The 10 divisions given by NCO are

Codes

1. Legislators, Senior Officials and Managers
2. Professionals
3. Technicians and Associate Professionals
4. Clerks
5. Service Workers and Shop & Market Sales Workers
6. Skilled Agricultural and Fishery Workers
7. Craft and Related Trade Workers
8. Plant and Machine Operators and Assemblers
9. Elementary Occupations
10. Workers Not Classified by Occupations

Table 8.1: Divisons, Sub-divisions, Groups and Families

DIVISION:	1	LEGISLATORS, SENIOR OFFICIALS AND MANAGERS
Sub-Divisions	11	Legislators and Senior Officials
Group	111	Legislators
Family	1111	Elected Officials
	1112	Elected Officials, State Government
	1113	Elected Officials, Local Bodies
	1119	Elected Officials, n.e.c.
Group	112	Administrative and Executive Officials
Family	1121	Administrative and Executive Officials, Union Government
	1122	Administrative and Executive Officials, State Government
	1123	Administrative and Executive Officials, Quasi Government

	1124	Administrative and Executive Officials, Local Bodies
	1125	Administrative and Executive Officials, Government and Local Bodies, n.e.c.
Group	113	Traditional Chiefs and Heads of Villages
Family	1131	Traditional Chiefs and Heads of Villages
Group	114	Senior Officials of Special-Interest Organisations
Family	1141	Senior Officials of Political Party Organisations
	1142	Senior Officials of Employers, Workers and Other Economic Interest Organisations
	1143	Senior Officials of Humanitarian and Other Special Interest Organisations
Sub-Division	***12***	***Corporate Managers***
Group	121	Directors and Chief Executives
Family	1211	Working Proprietors and Directors, Electricity, Gas, Water Supply
	1212	Directors, Financial Institutions
	1213	Working Proprietors and Directors, Mining, Construction
	1214	Working Proprietors and Directors, Manufacturing, Wholesale & Retail Trade
	1215	Working Proprietors and Directors and Related Executives in Transport and Communication
	1216	Working Proprietors and Directors, Storage and Warehousing
	1217	Working Proprietors and Directors, Lodging and Catering Services
	1218	Working Proprietors and Directors, Recreation and Entertainment
	1219	Working Proprietors and Directors, Other Services, n.e.c.
Group	121	Production and Operations Department Managers
Family	1221	Production and Operations Department Managers in Agriculture, Hunting, Forestry & Fishing
	1222	Production and Operations Department Managers in Manufacturing
	1223	Production and Operations Department Managers in Construction
	1224	Production and Operations Department Managers in Wholesale and Retail Trade
	1225	Production and Operations Department Managers in Restaurants and Hotels
	1226	Production and Operations Department Managers in Transport, Storage and Communication
	1227	Production and Operations Department Managers in Business Services
	1228	Production and Operations Department Managers in Personal Care, Cleaning and Related Services
	1229	Production and Operations Department Managers, n.e.c.

Group	123	Other Department Managers
Family	1231	Finance and Administration Department Managers
	1232	Personnel and Industrial Relations Managers
	1233	Sales and Marketing Managers
	1234	Advertising and Public Relations Department Managers
	1235	Supply and Distribution Department Managers
	1236	Manager, Computing Services
	1237	Manager, Research and Development
	1238	Other Department Managers, n.e.c.
Sub-Division	***13***	***General Managers***
Group	130	General Managers
Family	1301	General Managers, Forestry and Fishing
	1302	General Managers in Manufacturing
	1303	General Managers in Construction
	1304	General Managers in Wholesale and Retail Trade
	1305	General Managers of Restaurants & Hotels
	1306	General Managers in Transport, Storage and Communications
	1307	General Managers of Business Services
	1308	General Managers in Personal Care, Cleaning and Related Services
	1309	General Managers, n.e.c.
DIVISION:	**2**	**PROFESSIONALS**
Sub-Divisions	***21***	***Physical, Mathematical and Engineering Science Professionals***
Group	211	Physicists, Chemists and Related Professionals
Family	2111	Physicists and Astronomers
	2112	Meteorologists
	2113	Chemists
	2114	Geologists and Geophysicists
	2119	Physical Scientists, n.e.c.
Group	212	Mathematicians, Statisticians and Related Professionals
Family	2121	Mathematicians and Related Professionals
	2122	Statisticians
	2129	Mathematicians, Statisticians and Related Professionals, n.e.c.
Group	213	Computing Professionals
Family	2131	Computer Systems Designers and Analysts
	2132	Computer Programmers
	2139	Computer Professionals, n.e.c.
Group	214	Architects, Engineers and Related Professionals
Family	2141	Architects, Town and Traffic Planners
	2142	Civil Engineers
	2143	Electrical Engineers
	2144	Electronics and Telecommunication Engineers

	2145	Mechanical Engineers
	2146	Chemical Engineers
	2147	Mining Engineers, Metallurgists and Related Professionals
	2148	Cartographers and Surveyors
	2149	Architects, Engineers and Related Professionals, n.e.c.
Sub-Division	***22***	***Life Science and Health Professionals***
Group	221	Life Science Professionals
Family	2211	Biologists, Botanists, Zoologists and Related Professionals
	2212	Pharmacologists, Pathologists and Related Professionals
	2213	Agronomists and Related Professionals
	2214	Life Science Professionals, n.e.c.
Group	222	Health Professionals (except Nursing)
Family	2221	Physicians and Surgeons, Allopathic
	2222	Physicians and Surgeons, Ayurvedic
	2223	Physicians and Surgeons, Homeopathic
	2224	Physicians and Surgeons, Unani
	2225	Dental Specialists
	2226	Veterinarians
	2227	Health Professionals (except Nursing), n.e.c.
Group	223	Nursing Professionals
	2230	Nursing Professionals
Sub-Division	***23***	***Teaching Professionals***
Group	231	College, University and Higher Education Teaching Professionals
Family	2310	College, University and Higher Education Teaching Professionals
Group	232	Secondary Education Teaching Professional
Family	2320	Senior Secondary and Secondary School Teaching Professionals
Group	233	Other Teaching Professionals
Family	2331	Education Methods Specialists
	2332	School Inspectors
	2339	Teaching Professionals, n.e.c.
Sub-Division	***24***	***Other Professionals***
Group	241	Business Professionals
Family	2411	Accountants
	2412	Personnel and Careers Professionals
	2419	Business Professionals, n.e.c.
Group	242	Legal Professionals
Family	2431	Archivists and Curators
	2432	Librarians and Related Information Professionals
Group	244	Social Science and Related Professionals

Family	2441	Economists
	2442	Sociologists, Anthropologists and Related Professionals
	2443	Philosophers, Historians and Political Scientists
	2444	Philologists, Translators and Interpreters
	2445	Psychologists
	2446	Social Work Professionals
Group	245	Writers and Creative or Performing Artists
Family	2451	Authors, Journalists and Other Writers
	2452	Sculptors, Painters and Related Artists
	2453	Composers, Musicians and Singers
	2454	Choreographers and Dancers
	2455	Film, Stage and Related Actors and Directors
Group	246	Religious Professionals
Family	2461	Ordained Religious Workers
	2462	Non-Ordained Religious Workers
DIVISION:	**3**	**TECHNICIANS AND ASSOCIATE PROFESSIONALS**
Sub-Division	***31***	***Physical and Engineering Science Associate Professionals***
Group	311	Physical and Engineering Science Technicians
Family	3111	Chemical and Physical Science Technicians
	3112	Civil Engineering Technicians
	3113	Electrical Engineering Technicians
	3114	Electronics and Telecommunications Engineering Technicians
	3115	Mechanical Engineering Technicians
	3116	Chemical Engineering Technicians
	3117	Mining and Metallurgical Technicians
	3118	Draughtpersons
	3119	Physical and Engineering Science Technicians, n.e.c.
Group	312	Computer Associate Professionals
Family	3121	Computer Assistant
	3122	Computer Equipment Operators
	3123	Industrial Robot Controllers
Group	313	Optical and Electronic Equipment Operators
Family	3131	Photographers and Image and Sound Recording Equipment Operators
	3132	Broadcasting and Telecommunication Equipment Operators
	3133	Medical Equipment Operators
	3139	Other Optical and Electronic Equipment Operators, n.e.c.
Group	314	Ship and Aircraft Controllers and Technicians
Family	3141	Ship's Engineers
	3142	Ship's Deck Officers and Pilots
	3143	Aircraft Pilots and Related Associate Professionals
	3144	Air Traffic Controller

	3145	Air Traffic Safety Technicians
Group	315	Safety and Quality Inspectors
Family	3151	Fire Inspectors
	3152	Safety, Health and Quality Inspectors
Sub-Division	***32***	***Life Science and Health Associate Professionals***
Group	321	Life Science Technicians and Related Health Associate Professionals
Family	3211	Life Science Technicians
	3212	Agronomy and Forestry Technicians
	3213	Farming and Forestry Advisers
	3214	Environment Science and Protection Technicians
Group	322	Modern Health Associate Professionals (Except Nursing)
Family	3221	Medical Assistants
	3222	Sanitarians
	3223	Dieticians and Nutritionists
	3224	Optometrists and Opticians
	3225	Dental Assistants
	3226	Physiotherapists and Related Associate Professionals
	3227	Veterinary Assistants
	3228	Pharmaceutical Assistants
	3229	Modern Health Associate Professionals (except Nursing) n.e.c.
Group	323	Nursing and Midwifery Associate Professionals
Family	3231	Nursing Associate Professionals
	3232	Midwifery Associate Professionals
Group	324	Traditional Medicine Practitioners and Faith Healers
Family	3241	Traditional Medicine Practitioners
	3242	Faith Healers
Sub-Division	***33***	***Teaching Associate Professionals***
Group	331	Middle & Primary Education Teaching Associate Professionals
Family	3311	Middle School Teaching Associate Professionals
	3312	Primary School Education Teaching Associate Professionals
Group	332	Pre-Primary Education Teaching Associate Professionals
Family	3320	Pre-Primary Education Teaching Associate Professionals
Group	333	Special Education Teaching Associate Professionals
Family	3330	Special Education Teaching Associate Professionals
Group	334	Other Teaching Associate Professionals
Family	3340	Other Teaching Associate Professionals
Sub-Division	***34***	***Other Associate Professionals***

Group	341	Finance and Sales Associate Professionals
Family	3411	Securities and Finance Dealers and Brokers
	3412	Insurance Representatives
	3413	Estate Agents
	3414	Travel Consultants & Organisers
	3415	Technical and Commercial Sales Representatives
	3416	Buyers
	3417	Appraisers, Valuers and Auctioneers
	3418	Finance and Sales Associate Professionals, n.e.c.
Group	342	Business Services Agents and Trade Brokers
Family	3421	Trade Brokers
	3422	Clearing and Forwarding Agents
	3423	Employment Agents and Labour Contractors
	3429	Business Services Agents and Trade Brokers, n.e.c.
Group	343	Administrative Associate Professionals
Family	3431	Administrative Secretaries and Related Associate Professionals
	3432	Legal and Related Business Associate Professionals
	3433	Statistical, Mathematical and Related Associated Professionals
	3439	Administrative Associate Professionals, n.e.c.
Group	344	Customs, Tax and Related Government Associate Professionals
Family	3441	Customs and Border Inspectors
	3442	Govt. Tax and Excise Officials
	3443	Government Social Benefits Officials
	3444	Government Licensing Officials
	3449	Customs, Tax and Related Govt. Associate Professionals, n.e.c.
Group	345	Police Inspectors and Detectives
Family	3450	Police Inspectors and Detectives
Group	346	Social Work Associate Professionals
Family	3460	Social Work Associate Professionals
Group	347	Artistic, Entertainment and Sports Associate Professionals
Family	3471	Decorators and Commercial Designers
	3472	Radio, Television and Other Announcers
	3473	Street, Night-club and Related Musicians, Singers and Dancers
	3474	Clowns, Magicians, Acrobats and Related Associate Professionals
	3475	Athletes, Sports, Persons and Related Associate Professionals
Group	348	Religious Associate Professionals
Family	3480	Religious Associate Professionals
DIVISION:	**4**	**CLERKS**

Sub-Division	***41***	***Office Clerks***
Group	411	Secretaries and Key Board-Operating Clerks
Family	4111	Stenographers and Typists
	4112	Word Processor and Related Operators
	4113	Data Entry Operators
	4114	Calculating Machine Operators
	4115	Secretaries
Group	412	Numerical Clerks
Family	4121	Accounting and Book Keeping Clerks
	4122	Statistical and Finance Clerks
Group	413	Material Recording and Transport Clerks
Family	4131	Stock Clerks
	4132	Production Clerks
	4133	Transport Clerks
Group	414	Library, Mail and Related Clerks
Family	4141	Library and Filing Clerks
	4142	Mail Carriers and Sorting Clerks
	4143	Coding, Proof-Reading and Related Clerks
	4144	Scribes and Related Clerks
Group	419	Other Office Clerks
Family	4190	Other Office Clerks
Sub-Division	***42***	***Customer Services Clerks***
Group	421	Cashiers and Ticket Clerks
Family	4211	Cashiers and Ticket Clerks
	4212	Tellers and Other Counter Clerks
	4213	Book Makers
	4214	Pawnbrokers and Money Lenders
	4215	Debt Collectors and Related Workers
Group	422	Client Information Clerks
Family	4221	Receptionists and Information Clerks
	4222	Telephone Switch Board Operators
DIVISION:	**5**	**SERVICE WORKERS AND SHOP & MARKET SALES WORKERS**
Sub-Division	***51***	***Personal and Protective Service Workers***
Group	511	Travel Attendants, Guides and Related Workers
Family	5111	Flight Attendants & Travel Stewards
	5112	Transport Conductors
	5113	Travel Guides and Ground Hosts
Group	512	Housing Keeping and Restaurant Service Workers
Family	5121	Housing Keeping and Restaurant Services Workers
	5122	Cooks
	5123	Waiters and Bartenders
Group	513	Personal Care and Related Workers
Family	5131	Child Care Workers

	5132	Institution Based Personal Care Workers
	5133	Home Based Personal Care Workers
	5139	Personal Care and Related Workers, n.e.c.
Group	514	Other Personal Services Workers
Family	5141	Hair Dressers, Barbers, Beauticians and Related Workers
	5142	Companions and Valets
	5143	Undertakers and Embalmers
	5149	Personal Services Workers, n.e.c.
Group	515	Astrologers, Fortune-Tellers and Related Workers
Family	5151	Astrologers and Related Workers
	5152	Fortune-Tellers, Palmists and Related Workers
Group	516	Protective Services Workers
Family	5161	Fire Fighters
	5162	Police Officers
	5163	Prison Guards
	5169	Protective Services Workers, n.e.c.
Sub-Division	***52***	***Models, Salesperson and Demonstrators***
Group	521	Fashion and Mother Models
Family	5210	Fashion and Mother Models
Group	522	Shop Salesperson and Demonstrators
Family	5220	Shop Salesperson and Demonstrators
Group	523	Stall and Market Salespersons
Family	5230	Stall and Market Salespersons
DIVISION:	**6**	**SKILLED AGRICULTURAL AND FISHERY WORKERS**
Sub-Division	***61***	***Market Oriented Skilled Agricultural and Fishery Workers***
Group	611	Market Gardeners & Crop Growers
Family	6111	Field Crop and Vegetable Growers
	6112	Tree and Shrub Crop Growers
	6113	Gardeners, Horticultural and Nursery Growers
	6114	Mixed Crop Growers
Group	612	Market-Oriented Animal Producers and Related Workers
Family	6121	Dairy and Livestock Producers
	6122	Poultry Producers
	6123	Apiarists and Sericulturists
	6124	Mixed Animal Producers
	6129	Market-Oriented Animal Producers and Related Workers, n.e.c.
Group	613	Market-Oriented Crop and Animal Producers
Family	6130	Market-Oriented Crop and Animal Producers
Group	614	Forestry and Related Workers
Family	6141	Forestry Workers and Loggers

	6142	Charcoal Burners and Related Workers
Group	615	Fishery Workers, Hunters and Trappers
Family	6151	Aquatic Life Cultivation Workers
	6152	Inland and Coastal Water Fishery Workers
	6153	Deep Sea Fishery Workers
	6154	Hunters and Trappers
	6159	Fishermen, Hunters, Trappers and Related Workers, n.e.c.
Sub-Division	***62***	***Subsistence Agricultural and Fishery Workers***
Group	620	Subsistence Agricultural and Fishery Workers
Family	6200	Subsistence Agricultural and Fishery Workers
DIVISION:	**7**	**CRAFT AND RELATED TRADES WORKERS**
Sub-Division	71	Extraction and Building Trades Workers
Group	711	Miners, Shot-Fires, Stone Cutters and Carvers
Family	7111	Mines and Quarry Workers
	7112	Short Firers and Blasters
	7113	Stone Splitters, Cutters and Carvers
	7119	Miners, Quarry Workers, Shot Firers and Blasters, Stone Splitters, Cutters and Carvers, n.e.c.
Group	712	Building Frame and Related Trades Workers
Family	7121	Builders, Traditional Materials
	7122	Bricklayer and Stone Masons
	7123	Concrete Placers, Concrete Finishers and Related Workers
	7124	Carpenters and Joiners
	7129	Building, Frame and Related Trades Workers, n.e.c.
Group	713	Building Finishers and Related Trades Workers
Family	7131	Roofers
	7132	Floor Layers and Tile Setters
	7133	Plasterers
	7134	Insulation Workers
	7135	Glaziers
	7136	Plumbers and Pipe Fitters
	7137	Building and Related Electricians
	7138	Supervisors in Building Finishing and Related Trade Workers
Group	714	Painters, Building Structure Cleaners and Related Trades Workers
Family	7141	Painters and Related Workers
	7142	Varnishers and Related Painters
	7143	Building Structure Cleaners
	7148	Supervisors and Foremen and Related Trades Workers in Painting, Building, Structure Cleaning
Sub-Division	***72***	***Metal, Machinery and Related Trades Workers***

Group	721	Metal Moulders, Welders, Sheet Metal Workers, Structural Metal Preparers and Related Trades Workers
Family	7211	Metal Moulders and Core Makers
	7212	Welders and Flame Cutters
	7213	Sheet Metal Workers
	7214	Structural Metal Preparers and Erectors
	7215	Riggers and Cable Splicers
	7216	Underwater Workers
	7217	Supervisors, Foremen and Related Workers in Metal Moulding, Welding, Sheet Metal Work, Structural Metal Preparation and Related Trades
Group	722	Blacksmiths, Toolmakers and Related Trades Workers
Family	7221	Blacksmiths, Hammersmiths and Forging Press Workers
	7222	Tool Makers and Related Workers
	7223	Machine Tool Setters and Setter Operators
	7224	Metal Wheel Grinders, Polishers and Tool Sharpeners
	7228	Supervisors, Foremen and Related Workers in Blacksmithy, Tookmaking & Related Trades
	7229	Blacksmiths, Tool Makers and Related Workers, n.e.c.
Group	723	Machinery Mechanics and Fitters
Family	7231	Motor Vehicle Mechanics and Fitters
	7232	Aircraft Engine Mechanics and Fitters
	7233	Agricultural or Industrial Machinery Mechanics and Fitters
	7238	Supervisors, Foremen and Related Workers in Machinery Repair and Fitting
Group	724	Electrical and Electronic Equipment Mechanics and Fitters
Family	7241	Electrical Mechanics and Fitters
	7242	Electronic Fitters
	7243	Electronic Mechanics and Servicers
	7244	Telegraph and Telephone Installers and Servicers
	7245	Electrical Line Installers, Repairers and Cable Joiners
	7248	Supervisors and Foremen, Electrical and Electronic Equipment Mechanics and Fitters
	7249	Electrical and Electronic Equipment Mechanics and Fitters and Related Workers, n.e.c.
Sub-Division	***73***	***Precision, Handicraft, Printing and Related Trades Workers***
Group	731	Precision Workers in Metal and Related Materials
Family	7311	Precision Instrument Makers and Repairers
	7312	Musical Instrument Makers and Tuners
	7318	Supervisors, Foremen and Related Workers in Precision Work in Metal and Related Materials
Group	732	Potters, Glass Makers and Related Trades Workers

Family	7321	Abrasive Wheel Formers, Potters and Related Workers
	7322	Glass Makers, Cutters, Grinders and Finishers
	7323	Glass Engravers and Etchers
	7324	Glass, Ceramics and Related Decorative Painters
	7329	Glass Makers, Potters and Related Workers, n.e.c.
Group	733	Handicraft Workers in Wood, Textile, Leather and Related Materials
Family	7331	Handicraft Workers in Wood and Related Materials
	7332	Handicraft Workers in Textiles, Leather and Related Materials
Group	734	Printing and Related Trades Workers
Family	7341	Compositors, Type Setters and Related Workers
	7342	Stereotypers and Type Setters and Related Workers
	7343	Printing Engravers and Etchers
	7344	Photographic and Related Workers
	7345	Book Binders and Related Workers
	7346	Silk Screen, Block and Textile Printers
	7348	Supervisors and Foremen in Printing and Related Trades
Sub-Division	***74***	***Other Craft and Related Trades Workers***
Group	741	Food Processing and Related Trades Workers
Family	7411	Butchers, Fishmongers and Related Food Preparers
	7412	Bakers, Pastry-Cooks and Confectionery Makers
	7413	Dairy Products Makers
	7414	Fruits, Vegetables and Related Preservers
	7415	Food and Beverage Tasters and Graders
	7416	Tobacco Prepares and Tobacco Products Makers
	7418	Supervisors and Foremen in Food Processing and Related Trades
Group	742	Wood Treaters, Cabinet Makers and Related Trades Workers
Family	7421	Wood Treaters
	7422	Cabinet Makers and Related Workers
	7423	Wood Working Machine Setters and Setter Operators
	7424	Basketry Weavers, Brush Makers and Related Workers
Group	743	Textile, Garment and Related Trades Workers
Family	7431	Fibre Preparers
	7432	Weavers, Knitters and Related Workers
	7433	Tailors, Dress Makers and Hatters
	7434	Furriers and Related Workers
	7435	Textile, Leather and Related Pattern Makers and Cutters
	7436	Sewers, Embroiderers and Related Workers
	7437	Upholsterers and Related Workers
Group	744	Pelt, Leather and Shoe Making Trades Workers
Family	7441	Pelt Dressers, Taners and Fell Mongers

	7442	Shoe Makers and Related Workers
DIVISION:	**8**	**PLANT AND MACHINE OPERATORS AND ASSEMBERS**
Sub-Division	***81***	***Stationery Plant and Related Operators***
Group	811	Mining and Mineral Processing Plant Operators
Family	8111	Mining Plant Operators
	8112	Mineral Ore and Stone Processing Plant Operators
	8113	Well Drillers and Borers and Related Workers
	8118	Supervisors and Foremen, Mining and Mineral Processing Plant Operation Activities
Group	812	Metal Processing Plant Operators
Family	8121	Ore and Metal Furnace Operators
	8122	Metal Melters, Casters and Rolling Mill Operators
	8123	Metal Heat Treating Plant Operators
	8124	Metal Drawers and Extruders
	8128	Supervisors and Foremen in Metal Processing Plant Operation
Group	813	Glass, Ceramics and Related Plant Operators
Family	8131	Glass and Ceramics Kiln and Related Machine Operators
	8138	Supervisors and Foremen, Glass, Ceramics and Related Plant Workers
	8139	Glass, Ceramics and Related Plant Operators, n.e.c.
Group	814	Wood Processing and Paper Making Plant Operators
Family	8141	Wood Processing Plant Operators
	8142	Paper Pulp Plant Operators
	8143	Paper Making Plant Operators
	8148	Supervisors and Foremen, Wood Processing and Paper Making Plant Operators
Group	815	Chemical Processing Plant Operators
Family	8151	Crushing, Grinding and Chemical Mixing Machinery Operators
	8152	Chemical Heat Treating Plant Operators
	8153	Chemical Filtering and Separating Equipment Operators
	8154	Chemical Still and Reactor Operators (Except Petroleum and Natural Gas)
	8155	Petroleum and Natural Gas Refining Plant Operators
	8158	Supervisors and Foremen, Chemical Processing Plant Operators and Related Workers
	8159	Chemical Processing Plant Operators, n.e.c.
Group	816	Power Production and Related Plant Operators
Family	8161	Power Production Plant Operators
	8162	Steam-Engine and Boiler Operators
	8163	Incinerator, Water Treatment and Related Plant Operators
	8168	Supervisors and Foremen, Power Production and Related Plant Operators
	8169	Incinerator, Water Treatment and Related Plant

		Operators, n.e.c.
Group	817	Automated Assembly Line and Industrial Robot Operators
Family	8171	Automated Assembly Line Operators
	8172	Industrial Robot Operators
Sub-Division	***82***	***Machine Operators and Assemblers***
Group	821	Metal and Mineral Products Machine Operators
Family	8211	Machine Tool Operators
	8212	Cement and Other Mineral Products Machine Operators
	8218	Supervisors and Foremen, Metal and Mineral Products Machine Operators
Group	822	Chemical Products Machine Operators
Family	8221	Pharmaceutical and Toiletry Products Machine Operators
	8222	Ammunition and Explosive Products Machine Operators
	8223	Metal Finishing, Plating and Coating Machine Operators
	8224	Photographic Products Machine Operators
	8229	Chemical Products Machine Operators, n.e.c.
Group	823	Rubber and Plastic Products Machine Operators
Family	8231	Rubber Products Machine Operator
	8232	Plastic Products Machine Operator
	8238	Supervisors and Foremen, Rubber and Plastic Products Machine Operators
Group	824	Wood Products Machine Operators
Family	8241	Wood Products Machine Operators
	8248	Supervisors and Foremen, Wood Products Machine Operators
Group	825	Printing, Binding and Paper Products Machine Operators
Family	8251	Printing Machine Operators
	8252	Book Binding Machine Operators
	8253	Paper Products Machine Operators
	8258	Supervisors and Foremen, Printing, Binding and Paper Products Machine Operators
Group	826	Textile, Fur and Leather Products Machine Operators
Family	8261	Fibre Preparing, Spinning and Winding Machine Operators
	8262	Weaving and Knitting Machine Operators
	8263	Sewing Machine Operators
	8264	Bleaching, Dyeing and Cleaning Machine Operators
	8265	Fur and Leather Preparing Machine Operators
	8266	Shoe Making and Related Machine Operators
	8268	Supervisors and Foremen, Spinning, Weaving,

		Knitting, Dyeing and Related Processes
	8269	Textile, Fur and Leather Products Machine Operators, n.e.c.
Group	827	Food and Related Products Machine Operators
Family	8271	Meat and Fish Processing Machine Operators
	8272	Dairy Products Machine Operators
	8273	Grain and Spice Milling Machine Operators
	8274	Baked Goods, Cereal and Chocolate Products Machine Operators
	8275	Fruit, Vegetable and Nut Processing Machine Operators
	8276	Sugar Production Machine Operators
	8277	Tea, Coffee and Cocoa Processing Machine Operators
	8278	Brewers, Wine and Other Beverage Machine Operators
	8279	Tobacco Production Machine Operators
Group	828	Assemblers
Family	8281	Mechanical Machinery Assemblers
	8282	Electrical Equipment Assemblers
	8283	Electronic Equipment Assemblers
	8284	Metal, Rubber and Plastic Products Assemblers
	8285	Wood and Related Products Assemblers
	8286	Paper Board, Textile and Related Products Assemblers
Group	829	Other Machine Operators and Assemblers
Family	8290	Other Machine Operators and Assemblers
Sub-Division	***83***	***Drivers and Mobile Plant Operators***
Group	831	Locomotive Engine Drivers and Related Workers
Family	8311	Locomotive Engine Drivers
	8312	Railway Brakers, Signallers and Shunters
Group	832	Motor Vehicle Drivers
Family	8321	Motor Vehicle Drivers
	8322	Car, Taxi and Van Drivers
	8323	Bus and Tram Drivers
	8324	Heavy Truck and Lorry Drivers
Group	833	Agricultural and Other Mobile Plant Operators
Family	8331	Motorised Farm and Forestry Plant Operators
	8332	Earth Moving and Related Plant Operators
	8333	Crane, Hoist and Related Plant Operators
	8334	Lift Truck Operators
Group	834	Ships' Deck Crews and Related Workers
Family	8341	Ships' Deck Crews and Related Workers
DIVISION:	9	ELEMENTARY OCCUPATIONS
Sub-Division	***91***	***Sales and Service Elementary Occupations***
Group	911	Street Vendors and Related Workers
Family	9111	Street Food Vendors

	9112	Street Vendors, Non-Food Products
	9113	Door to Door and Telephone Sales Persons
Group	912	Shoe Cleaning and Other Street Services Elementary Occupations
Family	9120	Shoe Cleaning and Other Street Services Elementary Occupations
Group	913	Domestic and Related Helpers, Cleaners and Launderers
Family	9131	Domestic Helpers and Cleaners
	9132	Helpers and Cleaners in Offices, Hotels and Other Establishments
	9133	Hand Launderers and Pressers
Group	914	Building Caretakers, Window and Related Cleaners
Family	9141	Building Caretakers
	9142	Vehicle, Window and Related Cleaners
Group	915	Messengers, Porters, Door Keepers and Related Workers
Family	9151	Messengers, Package and Luggage Porters and Deliverers
	9152	Door Keepers, Watchpersons and Related Workers
	9153	Vending Machine Money Collectors, Meter Readers and Related Workers
Group	916	Garbage Collectors and Related Labourers
Family	9161	Garbage Collectors
	9162	Sweepers and Related Labourers
Sub-Division	***92***	***Agricultural, Fishery and Related Labourers***
Group	920	Agricultural, Fishery and Related Labourers
Family	9201	Farm Hands and Labourers
	9202	Forestry Labourers
	9203	Fishery, Hunting and Tapping Labourers
Sub-Division	***93***	***Labourers in Mining, Construction, Manufacturing and Transport***
Group	931	Mining and Construction Labourers
Family	9311	Mining and Quarrying Labourers
	9312	Construction and Maintenance Labourers, Dam and Similar Construction
	9313	Building Construction Labourers
Group	932	Manufacturing Labourers
Family	9321	Assembling Labourers
	9322	Hand Packers and Other Manufacturing Labourers
Group	933	Transport Labourers and Freight Handlers
Family	9331	Hand Pedal Vehicle Drivers
	9332	Drivers of Animal-Drawn Vehicle and Machinery
	9333	Freight Handlers

DIVISION:	**X**	**WORKERS NOT CLASSIFIED BY OCCUPATIONS**
Sub-Division	***X0***	***New Workers Seeking Employment***
Group	X00	New Workers Seeking Employment
Family	X001	Workers Without Occupations, Matriculates and above
	X002	Workers Without Occupations, Literates
	X003	Workers Without Occupations, n.e.c.
Sub-Division	***X1***	***Workers Reporting Occupations Unidentifiable or Inadequately Described***
Group	X10	Workers Reporting Occupations Unidentifiable or Inadequately Described
Family	X100	Workers Reporting Occupations Unidentifiable or Unclassifiable
Sub-Division	***X9***	***Workers Not Reporting Any Occupations***
Group	X99	Workers Not Reporting Any Occupations
Family	X999	Workers Not Reporting Any Occupations

6. Dr. H.P. Mehta, one of the pioneers of guidance services in India provided a three dimensional plan for classification of the career information:

(a) *Educational and Occupational Groups*: The codes can be given as follows:

00. General Education, such as general arts and science courses in college.
01. Architecture, Engineering and Crafts
    (Architects, Engineers, Craftsmen and Production Process workers of all types)
02. Physical Sciences
    (Physicists, Chemists, Geologists, Meteorologists and other physical scientists)
03. Biological Sciences
    (Biologists, Zoologists, Veterinarians, Agronomists, Silviculturists)
04. Medicine
    (Physicians and Surgeons of all types, and Dentists)
05. Nursing, Pharmacy, etc.
    (Nurses, Pharmacists, Vaccinators, Physiotherapists, Opticians, Sanitary Technicians, Health Visitors, etc.)
06. Teaching and Counselling
    (Teachers of all types and guidance personnel)
07. Law
    (Judges, Legal Practitioners, Legal Advisers, etc.)
08. Accountancy and Auditing

(Accountants, Auditors, etc.)

09. Statistics and Actuarial Science
(Statisticians, Actuaries, etc.)
10. Psychology
(Psychologists)
11. Social Work and Labour Welfare
(Social Workers, Labour Officers, etc.)
12. Economics and Political Science
(Economists and Political Scientists)
13. Sociology and Anthropology.
(Sociologists and Anthropologists)
14. History and Archaeology
(Historians, Archaeologists, Musicologists, etc.)
15. Journalism
(Authors, Editors, Journalists, Interpreters, Translators, etc.)
16. Arts
(Painters, Decorators, Commercial Artists, Sculptors, Modelers)
17. Acting, Dancing and Music
(Actors, Dancers, Musicians, etc.)
18. Administrative and Executive Work in Government offices and private firms
(Administrative, Executive and Managerial Workers, etc.)
19. Book-keeping, Typing and Stenography
(Clerks, Typists, Stenographers, Office Machine Operators, Book-keepers, Cashiers, Store-keepers, etc.)
20. Army (Army Officers and other ranks, excluding technical)
21. Navy (Naval officers and other ranks, excluding technical)
22. Air Force (Air Force Officers and other ranks, excluding technical)
23. Selling (Salesmen, Insurance Agents, etc.)
24. Farming and Fishing (Fishery Workers, Farmers, etc.)
25. Forestry (Forest Officers, Forest Rangers, etc.)
26. Merchant Marine (Deck Officers, Ship Pilots, etc.)
27. Aviation
(Aircraft Pilots & Navigators, Air Hostesses & Stewards, etc.)
28. Railways (Railways Drivers, Firemen, Conductors, Guards, Stationmasters, etc.)
29. Road Transport (Drivers of buses, tram cards, taxis, automobiles, etc.)
30. Telecommunication (Telephone Operators, Telegraphers, Signalers, etc.)
31. Police and Fire Fighting (Police Officers, Constables, Firemen, etc.)
32. Catering and Domestic Service (Caterers, Cooks, Maids, etc.)
33. Personal Service (Barbers, Hair Dressers, Beauticians, Launderers, etc.)
34. Sports and Recreation (Athletes, Sportsmen, Magicians, etc.)
35. Photography and Cinematography
(Photographers, Movie Camera Operators, etc.)

(b) *Levels of education/Training or Occupation*: Degree, Diploma and

Certificate courses may be classified as X, Y, Z.

(c) *Curriculum Stream*: Codes according to curriculum stream have been given as follows:

H– Humanities
S – Science
T – Technical
C – Commerce
A – Agriculture
F – Fine Arts
D – Domestic Science

In case the information for science students has to be classified in respect of the courses at degree level the code would be S-01-X. The first part of the code refers to the curriculum, the second to educational – occupational group and the third to level.

No one method of classification is perfect. The information is vast and keeps on changing. It is better to combine more than one method to make it 'easy to use'.

Preparation/Dissemination of Information

As discussed earlier, information is in various forms and is of various types. It may be in printed form, in the form of reports, booklets etc. that can be filed and students may make use of these by themselves. But on the other hand, lot of information may be in loose form, *i.e.,* collected through discussions, field visits, observations, etc. Moreover, similar information may be available in more than one form. It would then be necessary to collate all information and present it so that it becomes usable, attractive and less time consuming. To explore the world of work, students may need less information about more jobs or they may require detailed information about one course or job. There can be various ways to prepare the information in usable forms, which are discussed in the following paragraphs. These are only indicative. However, innovation has no boundaries:

1. *Reference Cards*: A number of reference cards may be prepared to provide information about various courses available or jobs available.

For Example: Cards may be prepared for 'Options after +2', or 'Careers Through Competitive Examinations'. Information in Reference Cards has to be short and comprehensive. For detailed information, reference may be given in the respective reference cards. See the following examples:

Competitive Exams. Organised by UPSC				
Types of Exams.	Eligibility	Advertisement	Remarks or Other Information	Detailed Reference

Institute of Hotel Management			
Courses	Eligibility	Openings	Reference

Reference Cards may be prepared in the form of series also, *i.e.,* 4-5 cards in the series on one topic for example:

Topic: What to do after Matric?

Card (a) Educational Options
(b) Vocational Options
(c) Part-time Jobs
(d) Technical Course

2. *Scrap Book*: Cuttings from Newspapers may be pasted on plane sheets and scrap-books may be prepared for various courses and jobs separately.

3. *Photo Albums*: For exploration of world of work and having a feel of real working conditions, photo albums may be prepared. This is specially useful for small children. Various types of photographs may also change the habits of learning in children. Being attractive, students may automatically be oriented for guidance services.

4. *Posters/Charts/Models*: Career Exhibitions: Details of these are discussed in the Chapter of group guidance techniques

5. *Display of Material on Bulletin Boards*: In every school Bulletin Boards are available. One or two such boards may be used specifically for guidance services. Vacancy notifications for courses or technical training or jobs may be displayed on these boards from time to time. One such Board may also display about the objectives and importance of guidance services.

6. *Use of Assembly*: As has been said earlier guidance is meant for all. Information of common interests may be announced during the school assemblies. That can also be a good platform for orientation about guidance as Principal, teachers and students are all present in the school assembly. Brief motivational talks may also be given during this time. Announcements may be made for any new courses advertised.

7. *Film shows, dramas, songs, nNukkad natak, mime shows* etc. may be other ways of disseminating information.

8. *Use of Computers*: Computer is a modern media which is very popular amongst students. Almost all the schools make use of computers. If the information is available on computers, students can themselves explore it. Information displayed through computers should be systematic and to the point.

9. *Mass Media*: Mass media can be used to disseminate information to the large masses.

10. *Small Booklets*: Small booklets containing information on specific subjects may be prepared and distributed. These can be useful for the students even after leaving the school and also can be shared with others

11. In developed countries like USA, *hot line services* for getting information are available. Telephone lines are available and people can call to get the information. Such possibilities may be explored in India also.

Type of Career Literature Available

1. *National Classification of Occupations*: Directorate General of Employment and Training, Ministry of Labour and Employment, have brought this out. This provides information about nature of work and concept of each occupation identified. This has been revised in 2004.

2. *Folders*: A series of folders published known as 'Guide to Careers' are published by Central Institute for Research and Training in Employment Services (CIRTES) under Ministry of Labour. The organisation is located in Pusa Institute, New Delhi. Each of these contain 5 to 8 pages and provide information about a particular job.

3. *World of Work Series*: CIRTES also brings out career information through a set of publications known as Career Information series. This series is in booklet form and provides detailed information about various types of jobs available under one group of occupations such as Careers in Fashion Technology, Careers in Agriculture etc. Information booklets are also available for a particular category of students and or at various levels of education such as Careers for Women, Careers for SC/STs or Careers after Matric, Careers for Science Graduates. This literature gets revised and updated from time to time and is available at nominal rates. CIRTES has recently placed a lot of career information on the official web-site of the Ministry of Labour

4. *Handbook on Training Facilities*: This handbook brought out by DGET, provides State-wise information on institutional and in plant training facilities. Detailed information is available on number of seats, duration of courses, admission requirements, hostel facilities.

5. *Bulletin on Job Opportunities*: This publication is a quarterly issue of DGET, which gives information about job vacancy trends. Vacancies analysed in this publication relate to the educational level of graduation.

6. *Posters and Charts*: Posters and charts are published under 'Choice of Careers' series. These are printed by CIRTES. Various other agencies like Employment Exchanges, NCERT, departments of State Governments also produce posters and charts to be displayed for consumers. The Ministry of Defence brings out posters on careers in Armed Forces

7. *Prospectus*: Every institution and professional college brings out its prospectus containing details about the courses being offered and other details related with the course. Copies of these can be had by contacting these institution.

8. *Handbook of Examination*: Union Public Service Commission and State Public Service Commissions publish Handbooks on Examination, which provide details of examinations conducted through these organisations.

9. *Articles*: Almost all the reputed newspapers bring out weekly special supplements on educational facilities and on careers. Current information is available in these supplements. Employment News provides information about vacancies available at various places. Detailed articles are also available in these newspapers relating to particular field of occupation. This is a good source to update the information.

10. *Career Magazines*: A number of Career Magazines are available in the market. To name a few, Competition Success Review, Competition Master, Competition Times etc.... These magazines not only provide details on how to prepare for competitive examinations but also tell about courses and careers available for various levels of students.

11. *Job Monographs*: Job Monographs containing detailed information about particular jobs are being prepared by various organisations. Some of such monographs are available in NCERT.

12. *Other Literature*: The Universities, the State Bureaux of Education, private organisations, NGOs are bringing out career literature in various forms which can be had from respective universities and state level organisations. Career books brought out by individuals and publishers are available in the market. A search in the market may be helpful in identifying career literature, which is authentic and relevant.

9

Testing and Non-testing Techniques of Guidance

Testing Techniques (Psychological Tests)

Sometimes psychologists or counsellors are considered as predictors or astrologers or magicians by common man. A gentleman 'X' was travelling by train and chatting with co-passengers. During the conversation they could get to know that 'X' was a psychologist. All of a sudden many people crowded around 'X' and started asking questions like 'Tell me about my personality'; 'See my face and tell my strengths'; 'What can I do in future', etc. It took some time for 'X' to convince the people around him that no simple answers can be given to these questions. Counsellors are neither astrologers nor magicians. They only make a study of the individual, his environment and his situation and help him to reach a conclusion or decision. In this process, they may conduct appropriate scientific investigations.

Psychological tests are instruments in the hands of the counsellor that are helpful in the assessment of an individual's skills – abilities, aptitudes, personality traits, attitudes, interests and achievements. They constitute a scientific method of individual's appraisal. A psychological test has been defined as "an objective and standardised measure of a sample of behaviour" (Anastasy, 1968). Cronback (1970) has defined a test as "a test is a systematic procedure for observing a person's behaviour and describing it with the aid of a numerical scale or category system". The definitions show that while it may be extremely difficult to tell about a person's skills or behaviours using only non-testing techniques psychological tests make it possible to arrive at quantitative indicators of his strengths, weakness, behaviour patterns, etc. Moreover, the results of these tests enable comparisons between individuals and the same individual in different situations.

Objectives of Using Psychological Tests in a Guidance Programme

While non-testing techniques of guidance are subjective, the testing techniques are objective and unbiased. The objectives of using psychological tests as tools for guidance are:

(i) To get factual data about the student to understand him better
(ii) To find out the tentative reaction of an individual in a given situation
(iii) To identify personality characteristics and difficulties of an individual
(iv) To use the tests results as a tool to provide educational, vocational and personal guidance
(v) To use them as a tool for improving educational performance

Classification of Tests

Classification of tests has been done using various criteria. For example, *on the criterion of the process of administrability*—these have been classified as individual tests and group tests. Individual tests are those which are administered to the individual. Group tests are administered to a group of people at a time. *On technical basis*—these have been classified as paper-pencil tests or performance tests. Performance tests are language free and free from cultural bias while paper-pencil tests require reading and language ability. *According to the purpose*—these tests can be classified as survey tests where the purpose is collect the information about the individual on various variables or diagnostic tests meant for diagnosing the specific problem of the individual.

Characteristics of a Good Test

A scientifically prepared test should have the following characteristics:

1. *Objectivity*: Objectivity of a test denotes unbiasedness in administration, scoring and interpretation of the test. The test should be such that the Guidance workers' attitudes or ideals do not get reflected in the administration, interpretation and scoring of the test. The scores on the tests should be the same even when examined by more than one examiner. Higher this objectivity, higher is the probability of the test being good. Objectivity of a test is also measured in terms of item difficulty. Item difficulty in a test should be based on empirical findings. For example, if a large number of individuals are able to solve a particular item in a test, it implies that the item is easy, and the items which are solved by only a few people are termed as difficult. This shows that construction of a test should be based on experimental measurement of difficulty level.

2. *Reliability*: The reliability of a test denotes consistency of the results. In other words, if a test is administered repeatedly to an individual the test

results should be more or less similar. For example, if on an intelligence test an individual's score is above average and the test is repeated, the scores should not be below average or average.

Anastasi has defined reliability as: "Test reliability is the consistency of scores obtained by the same persons, when retested with the identical test or with an equivalent form of test."

For use of any test for guidance purposes only those tests should be used whose reliability has been tested and is high. The formulation of the test should also explain the method by which reliability of the test has been checked.

The reliability of a test can be measured through various techniques:

(a) *Test-retest reliability*: Test-retest reliability is the technique where the test is repeated on the same individual or individuals a second time. The extent to which the scores are equal indicates the extent of reliability. It should be kept in mind that the conditions during the administration of the test during the second administration should remain the same as during the first administration and the time gap between the two administrations should not be too large. This interval may vary from one month to six months. Tests, which have a probability of improved performance due to familiarity, should not be tested through this method.

(b) *Alternate form reliability*: It is also known as parallel form reliability. In this technique, two parallel tests are constructed and administered one-by-one on the same set of individuals. The correlation in the scores obtained on these two parallel forms refers to the reliability coefficient. This overcomes the problems in the technique of test-retest method to a certain extent. But in using the parallel form, it should be ensured that the two tests are truly parallel. The level of difficulty, the content, the procedure of administration, the time limit, the format, the illustrations all should have equivalence, which is very difficult in practice. Thus, many tests available do not have an equivalent form.

(c) *Split half reliability*: In this technique, one test is divided into two equivalent halves. This can be divided choosing the odd even number, or first half and second half. The division of a test depends on how the items in the test have been arranged. In this procedure the test is administered only once and two scores are obtained by splitting the test in two forms. The reliability coefficient is then measured by the correlation coefficient between the scores of the two half tests.

3. *Validity*: Anastasy has defined 'validity' as "what the test measures and how well it does so. It tells us what can be inferred from test scores." For

example, if people are to be recruited for defence services, the validity of the test depends on whether the test can predict who is suitable for this particular occupation. Validity of a test is measured on the basis of some criteria. If the correlation of the constructed test is high with the criteria, the test is known to have high validity. An aptitude test for pilots can be validated choosing criteria of achievement in flight training. Validity is based on the relationship between the performance and other variables such as behaviour characteristics. Validity of a test has several aspects to it.

(a) *Content validity*: Content validation refers to the extent to which a person has learnt a specific skill. For example, to repair a car, it is necessary to ascertain whether a person knows the details of repairing the car. The content of the test for this purpose should be such that it can measure the ability of a person in repairing the car. The content to measure specific skill or skills should be properly defined and should include the objectives, factual knowledge, application of this knowledge in practical situations, interpretation of data etc..

(b) *Face validity*: 'Content validity' is sometimes misinterpreted as 'face validity' while the two terms are different. 'Face validity' is the relevance of the test to a particular target group or the situation. In other words, the test should be acceptable to the target group. They should feel that the test is not superficial or childish. Test items should be relevant to the cultural ethos of the type of group it is meant for, e.g., the test, which has to be used for recruitment of science teachers, should ask questions relating to science and those eliciting the scientific mind of the examinees. If questions relating to literature are included in this test they would not have any relevance and the test would lose its 'face validity'. It is commonly advised that a test constructed for a particular culture should be adapted before it is chosen for use in another cultural setting.

(c) *Concurrent validity*: Concurrent validity of a test requires that the test scores should be consistent with other test of assessment.. For example, if a test of intelligence is correlated with the other available test of intelligence of similar nature, it is known as measuring the concurrent validity.

(d) *Predictive validity*: Predictive validity of a test is measured when the test has to predict the performance for future.

Standardisation of a Test

Whenever the term psychological testing is used, the question of 'standardisation' arises. It is said that while choosing a test to be administered, it should be ensured that it is a standardised test. What is the meaning of standardisation? It is "uniformity of procedure in administering and scoring the test".

For ensuring the uniformity of procedure of administration, detailed instructions for administration of the test should be made available. It includes time duration, sample items, verbal instructions, the material required, conditions, if any. Standardisation implies that all the individuals being tested should receive exactly the same information, directions, examples, time limit.

Norms

For maintaining the uniformity of scoring, the second aspect of standardisation, proper 'norms' should be established. A 'norm' is the average performance with which the individual's performance could be compared. For example, if, on an average, children of 12 years are able to complete 30 items out of 50 on an abstract reasoning test, then the norm for a 12 year's old child would be 30 and the scores obtained by an individual are compared with this norm. The actual scores obtained by individuals are known as raw scores. For establishing such norms of test scores, a test is administered to a large number of persons of a specified age group, educational level, according to the fixed time limit and controlling other variables. The scores are averaged to prepare norms.

Evaluation of a Test Score

Once the norms for a test are available, and a person is administered the test and scored, the question arises as to how the score is to be evaluated. The obvious way to measure the individual's score against a norm is to take the deviation of the score from the norm. For example, if the norm is 'm' and the individual score is X, the deviation is X – m. How to evaluate the magnitude of this deviation? Usually, in distributions based on large number of individuals, the statistical measure called the 'standard deviation' (denoted by 's') can be used to divide the population into sections containing fixed percentage of scores. For example, about 68 per cent of the scores would lie within one standard deviation's distance from the mean (34 per cent on each side). About 96 per cent of the scores would lie within two standard deviation' distance from the mean (48 per cent on each side) and over 99 per cent with three standard deviations' distance.

Fig. 9.1: Distribution of Scores

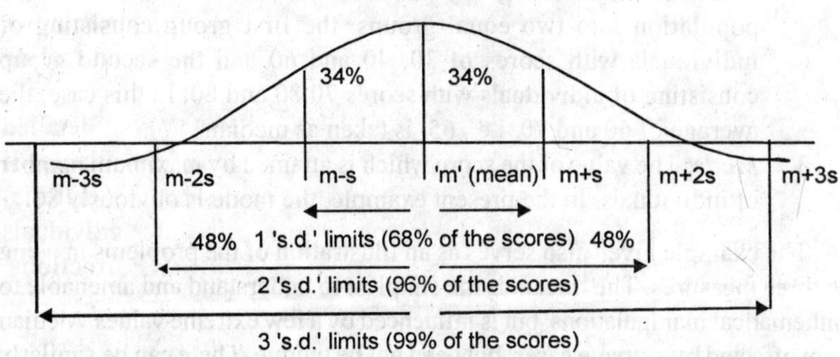

In view of this, an individual score is evaluated not merely as its deviation from the norm, but as the ratio of the deviation to the standard deviation, as this ratio enables us to evaluate how the deviation observed in the case of the individual compares with the standard deviation and whether the observed deviation can be expected with a high level of probability. This ratio, called the 'Z' score, is $Z = \frac{X - m}{s}$.

Thus, from the raw scores obtained by the individuals 'Z' scores are derived. 'Z' scores are amenable to further statistical analysis and interpretation. Statistical tables are available, with the help of which it may be inferred if, for example, an observed 'Z' score can lead to the conclusion that there is no 'significant' deviation from the norm, or whether it is 'significantly' different from the norm.

Statistical Concepts

In evaluating psychological tests, one has to deal with the scores of several (at times thousands) of individuals. These raw scores by themselves do not lead us to any worthwhile conclusion. Questions like "Is there any value around which the scores center, and which can be taken as a representative value of the population's score?" or "Are the individual scores closely packed or are dispersed over a wide range?" arise. The first question is answered by computing what are called 'measures of central tendency'. These measures are:

1. *Mean*: The arithmetic average of all scores. For example, if there are 6 individuals with scores of 60, 30, 70, 80, 40 & 80, the average is (60+30+70+80+40+80)/6 = 60.
2. *Median*: The value of the score, which divides all individuals into two equal groups. Sometimes, there may be more than one such value

In the above example, any value between 60 and 70 divides the population into two equal groups, the first group consisting of individuals with scores of 30, 40 and 60 and the second group consisting of individuals with scores 70,80 and 80. In this case, the average of 60 and 70, i.e., 65, is taken as median.

3. *Mode*: The value of the score which is attained by maximum number of individuals. In the present example, the mode is obviously 80.

The example given also serves as an illustration of the problems in using the three measures. The 'mean' is the simplest to understand and amenable to mathematical manipulations, but is influenced by a few extreme values. Median is not affected by extreme cases, but need not be unique. There can be similarly more than one mode. Both median and mode are relatively difficult to handle statistically.

The second question raised above is answered by what are called 'measures of dispersion'. Some measures of dispersion used in the context of testing are standard deviation, range and percentiles.

1. Standard deviation is computed by the formula

$$s = \sqrt{\frac{1}{n}\sum_{1}^{n}(x_i - m)^2}$$

where X_i is the individual score of the 'i'th individual, m is the average score of all individuals and 'n' is the total number of individuals. The formula derives standard deviation as the square root of the average of the squares of deviations of the individual scores from the mean.

2. Range of a distribution of scores is the difference between the maximum and minimum of the scores. In the example given above, the minimum score is 30 and the maximum is 80. The range is therefore 50. It may be noted that the Range is dependent only on the minimum and maximum scores and does not take account of the other scores.

3. Percentiles are the levels of scores, which divide the population into fixed, equal percentage groups. For example, 'quartiles' divide the population into four equal groups and 'deciles' divide into ten equal groups. There will be four quartiles Q1,Q2, Q3,Q4 and one-fourth of the scores would be less than Q1, one-fourth between Q2 and Q3, one-fourth between Q3 and Q4 and the remaining one-fourth above Q4. Similarly, in the case of deciles, D1,D2,....D10, one tenth of the individuals have scores less than D1, one-tenth between D1 and D2, and so on, and one tenth above D10.

Uses of Psychological Tests

1. Tests are useful in measuring the individual differences.
2. They can indicate the behaviours of an individual in various circumstances, enabling identification of problems in adjustments.
3. They can identify children with special talents and also the slow learners.
4. On the basis of the psychological tests students may be provided education and vocational guidance, after assessing their suitability to various technical and professional courses.
5. The tests are helpful to the employers to hire employees according to the needs of specific jobs. For example, these tests are used in recruitment in the Defence Services.
6. Similarly tests are helpful to professional educational institutions in their admissions, *e.g.*, in Management courses.
7. The result of the tests may be helpful for the parents in understanding their children better and making a future plan along with their children.
8. The tests results are useful for teachers in understanding the children and preparing remedial plans wherever required. With such an understanding teachers may be able to deal with the child in a better way.
9. Tests provide a foundation for self-understanding, which helps an individual in taking decisions. The emotionally disturbed persons may also be identified through tests for individual counselling.
10. Tests provide data for conducting researches on a number of issues such as developmental process and problems therein, group variations, cultural variations, etc.

Fig. 9.2: Psychological Tests and Guidance

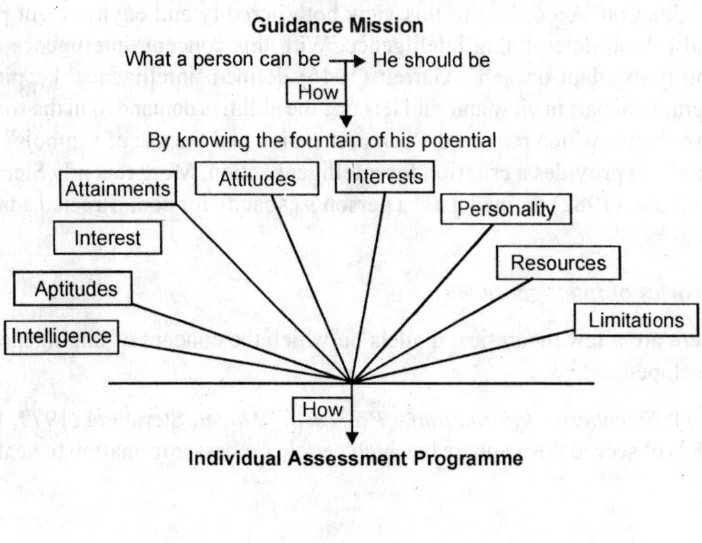

Types of Tests

Intelligence and Aptitude

These two terms are sometimes used interchangeably, but there are differences in these two terms. While intelligence is the general ability related to one's potential for learning, aptitudes measure specific ability, such as for clerical, mechanical or artistic work. Intelligence was considered to be an innate characteristic that could not be changed while aptitude could be developed and nurtured.

Intelligence Tests

It is common to hear people say 'she is brilliant', or 'he is very intelligent' or 'he is so dull that he cannot understand anything'. What does it mean? What is intelligence?

Various psychologists on the basis of their researches have defined the term. Terman (1921) defined it as the 'ability to think abstractly'. Wechsler (1944), who also developed tests to measure intelligence said that "intelligence is the ability to act purposefully, to think rationally, and to deal effectively with the environment". There are different points of view from which the term may be defined. One view emphasises the role of heredity (organic view) in the individual's attempts to adapt himself to environment. Another view focuses its attention on environment (social view) that influences person's adaptation to environment, and the third view (behaviouristic view), which stresses the importance of the capacities of the individual to adapt himself to the situation. According to this view both heredity and environment play a vital role in determining intelligence. With this concept, intelligence is the 'ability to adapt oneself'. Garrett (1946) defined 'intelligence' keeping its operational part in view and said it is "... the abilities demanded in the solution of problems which require the comprehension and the use of symbols". This definition provides a criterion for intelligent action. More recently Sternberg and Salter (1982) defined it as "a person's capacity for goal-directed adaptive behaviour".

Theories of Intelligence

There are a few theoretical models on which the concept of intelligence has developed.

1. *Sternberg's Information – Processing Model*: Sternberg (1979, 1981, 1982) observed the manners in which people process information to deal with

various situations. He listed six steps in the process – Encoding, Inferring, Mapping, Application, Justification and Response. During his research, he found that intelligent people analyse a problem more thoroughly at the initial stage (encoding). He saw that intelligence and speed were not necessarily inter-correlated.

In this model people can be motivated to devise their own problem solving technique. In this approach, information about facts is important.

2. *Spearman's Two factor Model*: This model is based on the structure of intelligence. On the basis of his experiments, Spearman stated that intelligence is made up of two factors. One is 'g' factor, *i.e.*, general factor and another 's' factor – a collection of specific abilities. He was of the view that every body is endowed with some general intelligence, which is reflected in all his behaviours. Specific factors help in doing some specific activities.

3. *Thurston's Primary Mental Abilities Model*: Contrary to Spearman, Thurston's research and factor analysis didn't find any general factor. He argued that intelligence consists of seven primary abilities. These are verbal comprehension, numerical ability, spatial ability, perceptual speed, word fluency, memory and inductive reasoning. According to him each ability is independent and can be measured independently. To see the overall intelligence of a person, there is a need to measure all seven primary abilities.

4. *Guilford's Structure of Intellect Model*: Guilford conducted researches during the period 1967 to 1982 and based his model of intelligence on factor analysis. According to him, there is no general mental ability but intelligence consists of 150 separate abilities. He believed that each task involves three major intellectual functions.

(a) Operations – how we think
(b) Content – what we think about
(c) Products – applying particular operation to a particular content

Each of the above major functions has numerous sub-functions. Guilford identified 150 such sub-functions

Measurement of Intelligence

(a) In 1905, Simon and Binet devised an intelligence test, which was revised in 1908 and again in 1911. Terman further revised this later in 1916. This revision is known as Stanford-Binet test. The test has been devised to be used at various age levels with varying levels of difficulty. In this revised form, the concept of IQ (Intelligence Quotient) was introduced for the first time. The basic idea behind the scale is that intelligence can be measured through behaviours. The Stanford-Binet test assumes that intellectual ability improves with age. Thus, a child's composite score on the test was his mental level. A 5-year-old child who scores the same on this test as an 8 year-old child scores, is said to have a mental age of 8 years.

Intelligence Quotient: – On the basis of the Binet's work, Stanford gave a formula to calculate mental age corresponding to chronological age (actual age of a person). Stanford used the ratio of a person's mental age (MA) to his chronological age (CA) to measure the intelligence level and designated it as Intelligence Quotient (IQ). To avoid the problems of fractions, the ratio is multiplied by 100. Thus, IQ = MA/CA x 100. In the above example, the I.Q. of the child is 8/5 x 100 = 160

To Recapitualte: *Mental age* can be defined as a measure of mental ability defined in terms of the average capabilities of individual at each age. It means his mental ability as distinct from age in years

Chronological Age – Actual age: IQ – Index of intelligence defined as a person's mental age divided by his chronological age multiplied by 100.

(b) *The Wechsler Intelligence Scale*: Wechsler Scale is in three forms, one designed for adults, one for school-age children and one for pre-school children. Wechsler scale has verbal and non-verbal sub-tests. It is possible in this test to have separate scores for the verbal test and non-verbal test and also a composite score.

Both the Binet scale and Wechsler Scale are individual tests and can be administered to one person at a time. There are other tests that can be administered to groups also. Group tests are economical as well as less time consuming. Initially, two tests called Army Alpha test and Army Beta test were developed as group tests. These tests were developed, as their names suggest, to be used for soldiers.

As said earlier, administration of individual test is very time consuming. Verbal tests have cultural bias. Tests have, therefore, been designed, which can be administered to groups and are also free from cultural bias. Some such tests are:

(a) *Raven's Progressive Matrices (RPM)*: This test was designed to measure the 'general' factor of intelligence propounded by Spearman. The test contains abstract design items in the form of matrices. From each of these matrices, a part is missing. Alternatives for this missing part have been provided and the client is asked to choose the correct missing part from the given alternatives. The administration and scoring of the test is simple.

The test is available in three forms. Coloured Progressive Matrices (CPM) is for young children, Standard Progressive Matrices (SPM) is for school children and Advanced Progressive Matrices (APM) is for above average adolescents and adults.

Example of the Test

A1

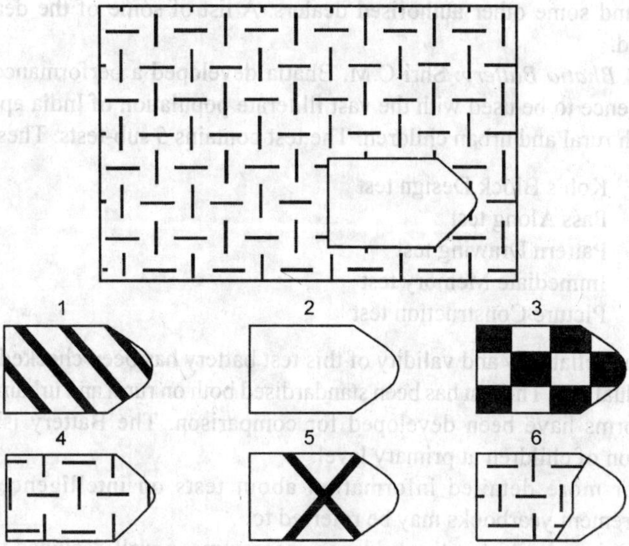

A2

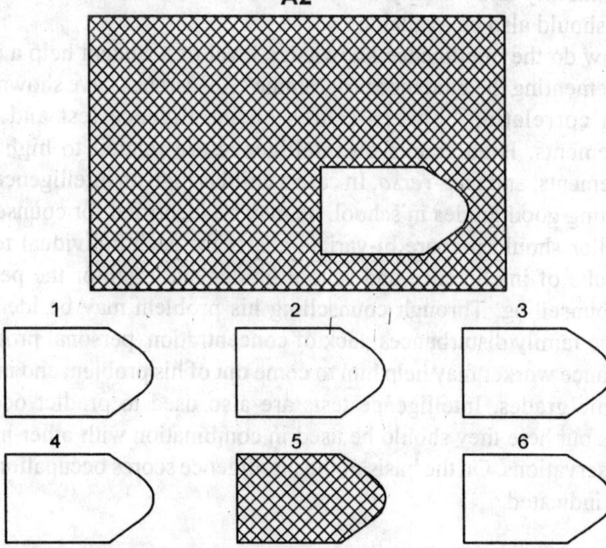

Source: Prepared by J.C. Raven, M.sc. Printd in Great Britain at the University Press, Cambridge, published by K.G. Lewis and Co. Ltd., London.

This test is being used widely in Indian schools. Indian norms have also been developed. The test can be purchased from Mansayan, located in New Delhi and some other authorised dealers. A list of some of the dealerss is annexed.

(b) *Bhatia Battery*: Shri C.M. Bhatia developed a performance test of intelligence to be used with the vast illiterate population of India applicable for both rural and urban children. The test contains 5 sub-tests. These are:

1. Koh's Block Design test
2. Pass Along test
3. Pattern Drawing test
4. Immediate Memory test
5. Picture Construction test

The reliability and validity of this test battery has been checked. It is an individual test. The test has been standardised both on rural and urban children and norms have been developed for comparison. The Battery is used in selection of children at primary level.

For more detailed information about tests on intelligence mental measurement yearbooks may be referred to.

To choose a test in the guidance programme, a well-designed test, with high reliability and validity should be taken. Local norms to compare the results should also be available.

How do the intelligence/knowledge level of a student help a counsellor in implementing the guidance programme? Researches have shown that there is high correlation between scores on intelligence test and academic achievements. High scores on intelligence are related to high academic achievements, and *vice-versa*. In case a child is high on intelligence score but not getting good grades in school, he may be identified for counselling. The counsellor should prepare bi-variate charts for each individual to compare the results of intelligence and school grades and monitor the performance after counselling. Through counselling his problem may be identified – it could be family disturbances, lack of concentration, personal problems, etc. A guidance worker may help him to come out of his problem and improve the academic grades. Intelligence tests are also used to predict occupational success but here they should be used in combination with other information and observations. On the basis of the intelligence scores occupational choices can be indicated.

Aptitude Tests

Aptitudes are generally known as latent and undeveloped abilities which can be developed through their proper identification and training. In Warren's dictionary aptitude has been defined as "a condition or set of characteristics regarded as symptomatic of an individual's ability to acquire with training some (usually specific) knowledge, skill, or set of responses such as the ability to speak a language, to produce music etc." The definition shows that aptitude is a present indication of skill that is capable of future development.

Taking this definition into account Bingham (1937) defined 'aptitude' as "a condition symptomatic of a person's relative fitness, of which one essential aspect is his readiness to acquire proficiency – his potential ability – and another is his readiness to develop an interest in that ability". Super in 1949 stated that "an aptitude is not necessarily an entity, but rather a constellation of entities; the set of characteristics which enables one person to learn something may even be different from that which enables another person to learn the same thing". Thus Super indicates the unitary character of aptitudes. Hann and MacLeanc (1955) gave a more comprehensive definition of 'aptitude' as "latent potentialities, undeveloped capacities to acquire abilities and skills and to demonstrate achievements".

Thus, aptitudes are latent potentials, which can be developed. With the development of such potential one can acquire and excel in related activity. For example, if a child has potential for music, with training in music he can be a singer, a composer or a music teacher. A child may be found dancing on listening to various musical tunes, or a small child may be able to solve mathematical sums very fast and comfortably. It can be said in the former case that the child has musical aptitude and in the latter case an aptitude for mathematics. If given an opportunity and training both these children may excel in their respective fields.

Basic Characteristics of Aptitudes

(a) Aptitudes are relatively stable for a long time. If a child has aptitude for music, it is relatively consistent throughout his adulthood.
(b) Relative differences in traits can be identified, and measured with accuracy.
(c) Individuals can excel and develop their aptitudes if provided training and an environment to develop themselves. It may be observed that some children who have good aptitudes for art, painting or music, if not encouraged by teachers or parents, loose their aptitudes in the long run.

Objectives of Using Aptitude Tests

(a) To identify individual's potential, of which he is not aware. Thus, these tests help in self-discovery
(b) To develop the special identified potentials.
(c) To help in educational and vocational choice on the basis of specific potentials identified.
(d) To predict academic and vocational success.
(e) To enable grouping of individuals for educational purposes according to their aptitudes.

How to measure aptitudes: A number of tests are available to measure relative strength of aptitudes in an individual that are used by counsellors. The aptitude areas identified are:

1. Verbal Aptitude: whether an individual is able to understand the meaning of words and their related ideas, ability to present ideas through language, comprehend and understand the information or not.
2. Numerical Aptitude: Numerical aptitude relates to the ability to understand and calculate the arithmetic problems with speed and accuracy.
3. Verbal Reasoning: It is the ability to identify the concepts in a text and their inter linkages. It is not the language proficiency but ability to reason, think, read and take out the substance of a written or verbal communication.
4. Clerical Aptitude: Clerical aptitude is the ability to understand details of tabulated material and to observe accuracy in handling words and numbers.
5. Spatial Aptitude: It is the ability to observe two or three dimensional objects.
6. Form Perception: This aptitude relates to the ability to perceive details in graphic or pictorial material and observe similarities and differences in shapes.
7. Motor Coordination: The ability to coordinate eyes and hands.
8. Finger Dexterity: The ability to move fingers to place small objects in right positions with accuracy and speed.
9. Manual Dexterity: It is the coordination of hands to move skillfully so that the work could be performed in a desirable way.

Some examples of classification of aptitudes may be seen in the following tables.

Table 9.1: Classifications of Human Aptitudes and Abilities

*Aptitude or ability and description**	*Aptitude or ability and description†*	*Occupational outlets†*
Verbal – Ability to define, understand, and use words as symbols of meaning and experiences.	Verbal and linguistic – Fluency in use of one's own language and facility in learning other languages. Perception of verbal relations	Author, lawyer, professor, minister, editor, advertising copywriter, etc.
Numerical – Ability to manipulate (mentally) numbers as symbols of experience or meaning; to solve problems which involve numbers.	Mathematical – Facility with abstract symbols (and relations of cause and effect). Perception of complex number relations.	Mathematics teacher, accountant, statistician, engineer, comptroller, etc.
Spatial – Ability to think or solve problems (mentally) involving objects and the geometrical forms which represent actual objects in space.	Constructive and mechanical – Perception of spatial relations, facility in designing, calculating, working with machinery, etc.	Engineer, architect, inventor, toolmaker, printer, etc.
Memory for detail Drill – Routine memorising or learning.	Manual skills – Dexterity in using tools, skill with hands and fingers, precision in coordinating movements.	Surgeon, dentist, sculptor, artist, skilled mechanic, special skilled trades, etc.
Physical ability – Ability to coordinate large and small muscles; to manipulate objects with speed and precision.	Artistic (inc. musical) – Appreciation of form and color, facility in crafts and in imaginative interpretations	Artist, sculptor, architect, designer, composer, actor, dancer, etc.
Musical – Ability to understand musical forms and to perform on a musical instrument	Social – Sociability, cooperativeness, tact, personal pleasingness, helpfulness.	Politician, teacher, personnel or social welfare worker, salesman, etc.
Artistic – Ability to understand form, balance, color harmony, and their use in artistic creation and interpretation.	Scientific – Facility in defining, classifying, grasping principles, inductive relation of rule to example.	Research worker, physician, physicist, chemist, geologist, psychologist, etc.
Social – Ability to work with people without friction; leadership	Clerical and commercial – Accuracy and speed in handling numbers, names, systems, and details.	Bookkeeper, credit man, purchasing agent, cashier, clerk.
	Executive – Initiative, self-reliance, ambition, leadership, etc.	Director, manager, foreman, inspector, etc.
	Practical – Efficiency in practical affairs, calmness under pressure, persistence, courage.	Airplane pilot, sea captain, army officer, surgeon, etc.

* Kelly, T.L., 1929, *Interpretation of educational measurements*, Yonkers, N.Y.: World Book, pp.124-125.

† **Williamson,** *E.G.*, 1937. *Students and occupations*. New York: Holt. pp. 31-33.

Classifications of Human Aptitudes and Abilities

Aptitude or ability and description ‡	*Levels ‡*	*Occupational outlets ‡*
Academic – The ability to understand and manage ideas and symbols.	Professional, semiprofessional, and executive occupations Technical, clerical, supervisory Skilled tradesmen, low-grade clerical	Lawyers, college presidents, president of a large manufacturing concern, teachers at all levels. Minor executive, or highly technical work, railroad clerks, shop foreman, stenographers. Auto mechanic, stationary engineer, typist.
Mechanical – Includes both the ability to manipulate concrete objects – to work with tools and machinery and the materials of the physical world – and the ability to deal mentally with mechanical movements.	Professional and higher technological Skilled tradesman, high level Skilled tradesman, low level Semi-and unskilled tradesmen	Inventive mechanical genius, mechanical engineer, toolmaker. Draftsman, engraver, general automobile mechanic, bricklayer. Boiler maker, tire repairer, cobbler. Wrapper, bench assembly worker
Artistic – Refers both to the capacity to create forms of artistic merit and the capacity to recognize the comparative merits of forms already created.	Professional Commercial Crafts and mechanical	Sculptor, artist, etcher, university art teacher. Magazine illustrator, interior decorator, landscape gardener. Potter, draftsman, weaver.
Social – The ability to understand and manage people; to act wisely in human relations.	Persuasive – direct or indirect Administrative Business contact and service	Politician, life insurance salesman, minister, social service worker Executives, foreman, lawyer, physician. Sales clerk, information clerk, hotel clerk, telephone salesman.
Clerical – The ability to do rapidly and accurately detail work such as checking, measuring, classifying, computing, recording, proofreading, and similar activities.	Professional and higher technical Technical Routine	Accountant, actuary, statistician, secretary, bank teller. Bookkeeper, stenographer, calculating machine operator, railway mail clerk. File clerk, mimeograph operator, retail sales clerk, messenger.
Musical – The capacity to sense sounds, to image these sounds in reproductive and creative imagination, to be aroused by them emotionally, to be capable of sustained thinking, to give some form of musical expression	Creative, interpretive, higher professional Technical, lower professional General and mechanical	Composer, concert artist, symphony soloist, teacher in university. Arranger of music, critic, player in dance orchestra. Instrument repairman, music store clerk, factory instrument tester.

‡ Paterson, Donald G., Gerken, Clayton d'A., and Hahn, Milton E. 1953. The Minnesota Occupational Rating Scales (revised). Minneapolis: University of Minnesota Press.

A number of Tests and Test Batteries are available to measure various aptitudes. While Test is a single test, measuring a single aptitude, a test battery consists of number of tests, which can measure a number of aptitudes simultaneously. Scores of a test battery provide information about relative strengths of various aptitudes, while a single test can tell whether a person has aptitude for a particular skill or not. Some commonly used tests for measuring aptitudes are:

(a) *Differential Aptitude Test (DAT)*: DAT is a test battery, which can be administered to a group of people at a time. This is a commonly used battery, which is useful for educational and vocational guidance purposes. This battery has 8 sub-tests – Verbal Reasoning, Numerical Reasoning, Abstract Reasoning, Perceptual Speed and Accuracy, Mechanical Reasoning, Space Relations and Spelling and Language Usage. Instructions are available in the tests on how to administer them. Sample items in each sub-test are available to understand the test and practice. This test battery has been updated for computerised testing and is known as CAT.

Shri J.M. Ojha has adapted this Aptitude Test Battery for Indian Conditions also. Norms are available for Indian children.

Sample items from the Indian Adaptation of DAT are given below.

1. Abstract Reasoning

Problem

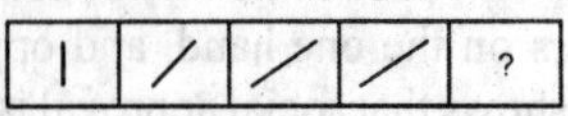

The correct answer is 'd'.

Answer alternatives

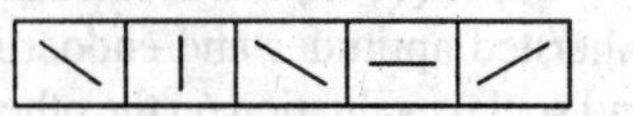

a b c d e

2. Clerical Speed & Accuracy:

Underline the same alphabet or number pairs in the answer sheet, which are underlined in question sheet.

Question sheet

AC	AE	AF	AB	AD
BA	Ba	Bb	aA	aB
7B	B7	AB	7A	A7
Aa	bA	bB	Ba	BA
BB	3B	B3	1A	33

Answer sheet

AB	AC	AD	AE	AF
aA	aB	Ba	Ba	Bb
A7	7A	B7	7B	AB
Aa	Ba	bA	BA	bB
3A	3B	33	BB	BB

Some other popular test batteries are General Aptitude Test Battery, which has 12 sub-tests. The Flanigan Aptitude Classification Tests has 19 subjects. Administration of these Tests takes 8 hours.

A number of aptitude tests suitable for Indian population covering various aptitudes are available with norms for comparability.

Scientific Aptitude Test Battery has 4 divisions relating to logic testing, arithmetic ability, scientific information and science vocabulary. Teaching Aptitude Test designed by Dr. S.D. Kapoor measures the aptitude for teaching in 10 areas – cooperative attitude, kindliness, patience, wide interest, fairness, moral character, discipline, optimism, scholarly taste and enthusiasm. Norms have been developed for the test.

Thus, a number of Test Batteries are available, which measure a number of aptitudes and tell their relative strengths. Each of these batteries consists of a series of sub-tests. It is convenient to administer and less time consuming. Comparable set of scores on various aptitudes may be considered to make a judgment. The Differential Aptitude Test Battery, commonly used to measure the aptitudes, in India includes the tests on verbal reasoning, numerical ability, abstract reasoning, space relations, mechanical reasoning, clerical speed and accuracy and language usage. The norms on Indian population are available for this test battery.

Interests Tests

People lose concentration and attention towards an activity as, according to them 'they don't have interest in it'. It is common to hear people say 'I would like to pursue my studies in literature as I am interested in that' or 'I have interest in flying, so I want to be a pilot'. What is interest? These examples show that interests are the motivating factors towards some activities or preferences for doing certain activities.

Super (1949) has defined interests as "the product of interaction between inherited aptitudes and endocrine factors on the one hand, and opportunity and social evaluation on the other". This shows that social approval is required for interest. It would vary from culture to culture.

Strong (1953) was of the view that "since interest involves reaction to specific things, they must all be learned. Accordingly, they may be modified later on by re-education".

Cronback (1949) states that "An interest may be defined a tendency to seek out an activity or object, or a tendency to choose it rather than some alternative".

Interests are thus, determined both by heredity and environment and lead to personal satisfaction. Here it may also be mentioned that the interests may not always be related to individuals' capabilities or aptitudes. One may be interested in music but may not have ability to be a musician.

Characteristics of Interests

1. Interests relate to personality shaping
2. New interests can be created through exposure
3. Preferences may be expressed towards certain occupational activities through a wide range of stimuli
4. Interest may not necessarily be associated with academic or occupational achievement
5. Peer groups, friends and family influence interests.
6. Interests need social confirmation also. Interest in smoking may not develop if the culture disapproves it.

7. Interest patterns are visible at the age of 15 and become crystallised at a later age. Some persons are not able to identify their interests, which lead them to change jobs frequently.
8. The interests that are measured through inventories show the needs and motivations of a person. These are not necessarily be reflective of success in a specific occupation. However, they can predict certain kind of job satisfaction.
9. A number of jobs are available to persons having a particular interest.
10. Interest test results should be seen in combination with the results on personality assessment and aptitudes.

How to Measure Interests

Several methods can be used to measure the interests, such as putting direct questions to the individual, observing the behaviour of the individual and by using interests tests or inventories. Using interests tests or inventories is a more scientific method and is as such more objective.

There are two most popular Interest Inventories known as Kuder Preference Records and Strong Vocational Interest Blanks. Kuder developed a number of interest inventories of which Kuder Preference Record is most commonly used. The interest items in this record are arranged in triads' alternatives from which the most preferred and the least preferred have to be chosen. The results can be used in the occupational choices relating to outdoor activities, mechanical, computational, scientific, persuasive, artistic, literacy, music, social service and clerical. Kuder Inventory is interpreted as 'relative degree of interests' in the given areas.

Strong Vocational Interest Blank was revised as Strong – Campbell Interest Inventory. This has 325 items grouped according to occupations, school subjects, activities, amusements, types of people, preference between activities and personal characteristics. Results can be obtained on a variety of scales through computers.

How a Guidance Worker can use the Interest Test Results

1. Tests may bring out hidden interest, of which a person may not be aware.
2. An individual expresses some interests during conversation. Inventories may confirm these interests, and the results can be utilised to help the student in choosing an educational/vocational stream.
3. When all the results on the psychological tests are analysed, discrepancies among aptitudes, interests, claimed interests and personality may be identified to guide the student in right direction.

4. If the interests are not on desired patterns, counselling can be done.

Achievement Tests

Achievement tests are used to measure the outcome of specific education. These are related to course curriculum. Examinations held in the school system are a kind of achievement test. Achievement can be measured using two types of tests, one the objective type and another the subjective type. The objective type achievement tests have only one correct answer. These can be either in the form of 'True', 'False' answer type, or of multiple choice answer type. Subjective kinds of achievement tests are where a student has to write 'Essay' type answers. Essay type method of measuring achievement is very subjective and scoring depends not only upon the person's understanding, but also the expectations of the person correcting the papers. Such teacher made achievement tests are not standardised.

Attempts have been made to make standardised tests also. Thorndike developed a handwriting scale. After World War II Iowa Tests of Educational Development and the Sequential Tests of Educational Progress were developed. The Iowa test contains 9 objective tests which measure the understanding of social concepts, natural sciences, correctness and appropriateness of expression, qualitative thinking, interpretation of reading materials in social studies, interpretation of reading materials in natural sciences, interpretation of literary materials, general vocabulary, and use of sources of information. This test can be given to IX to XII grade students.

The Sequential Tests of Educational Progress measures critical skills in the areas of essay writing, listening comprehension, reading comprehension, writing, science, mathematics and social studies. The tests are available for various students of various grades.

There are other tests such as Stanford Achievement Tests available in J, K, L, M and N Forms applicable for students of various grades.

A number of Achievements Tests have been developed for Indian students also. Some of these are Mathematics Attainment Test Series, Progress in English, Biology Achievement Test, Statistics achievement etc.

The achievement tests measure the present level of educational status of the student, and are helpful in guidance programme to get the achievement level of the student in different areas. The standardised test scores can supplement the judgements received from the teachers and comparison among the students can be made. On the basis of these test results students may be guided to plan their future course of action or to improve the areas where they are lacking. Tests results may also be used to make prediction for future success in various educational streams.

Personality Tests

Personality is a term, which is used in various ways. Sometimes it is referred to how a person looks, *i.e.,* the outer looks of a person; sometimes it is referred to the manner in which a person behaves. From another point of view, it is the combination of both. Various words are used to type a person such as 'he is lazy', 'he is shy and introvert', 'he is quick tempered', 'he is arrogant', etc. So, let us first define personality. Coleman (1960) defined personality as "the individual's unique pattern of traits, the pattern that distinguishes him as an individual and accounts for his unique and relatively consistent way of interacting with his environment'.

More recently, Mischel (1986) defined 'personality' as what "usually refers to the distinctive patterns of behaviour (including thoughts and emotions) that characterise each individual's adaptation to the situations of his or her life". This is the common theme of various definitions of personality and the emphasis is on individual. The function of personality test is "the measurement of emotional, motivational, interpersonal and attitudinal characteristics, as distinguished from abilities", Aiken (1993), Surger (1993) and Maddi (1989).

Theories of Personality

(a) *Trait Theories*: Trait theorists believe that personality is the sum of certain traits that each individual has in clusters. Allport said that the pattern of these traits is unique in each individual and it determines his behaviours. He said "bona fide mental structures in each personality that account for the consistency of its behaviour (1937)". This consistency in behaviours is because of the endurance of traits. If the personalities of two persons, one being outgoing and another being introvert, are compared it can be observed that the out-going person would be social, happy go lucky and would make friends easily while the introvert's behaviour would be of shyness. He would not be happy in meeting people. He would be withdrawn and would not socialise. Thus, the traits in one's personality determine his reactions to various situations.

Allport described three major traits – cardinal trait, central trait and secondary traits in personality. The special trait in the personality that makes a person totally different from others and provides uniqueness is known as cardinal trait. Allport is of the view that some extraordinary people have this trait. The cardinal trait can be seen in almost all the behaviours throughout one's life. A child who becomes the monitor of the class since **beginning tries** to lead in sports and games, instructs people at work place, can be said to have 'leading' as cardinal trait. Central trait refers to major characteristics such as honesty, dependability, cooperativeness etc. These are the general traits of a person. Finally, secondary trait relate to the behaviours in special situations. These traits are less enduring. A person is invited for an interview. He may wear a suit for this purpose but in general he may like to wear casuals. Allport's approach to study the individual is known as 'idiographic' approach. This approach emphasises the study of individuals in depth on some distinctive qualities of their personalities. Another approach, termed as 'nomothetic' approach, propagated by Cattell emphasises the study of personality as studies of groups of people and not as individual. Cattell argued that personality is made of two types of traits – the surface traits and the source traits. He identified some general traits and named them as surface traits. He researched on these surface traits and applied factor analysis and found 16 source traits that he called the care factors of personality. He listed each of these traits as pairs of polar opposites as Reserved/Outgoing, Submissive/Dominant, etc.

Trait theories have been criticised on the ground that they are silent on the issue how the personality develops.

(b) *Psycho-analytic Theory*: Freud propounded the psychoanalytic theory, which states that personalities of people develop through on-going conflict between their primary drives (sex and aggression) and social pressures, and that early childhood experience are extremely important in the development of the personality.

(i) *Structure of personality*: The structure of personality consists of Id, Ego and Supere go as detailed below :

	Structure	Consciousness level	Function
1.	Id	Unconscious	Need immediate gratification of desires
2.	Ego	Predominantly conscious	Rational and logical
3.	Super ego	Both conscious and unconscious	Idealistic and perfectionist

(ii) *Dynamics of personality*:

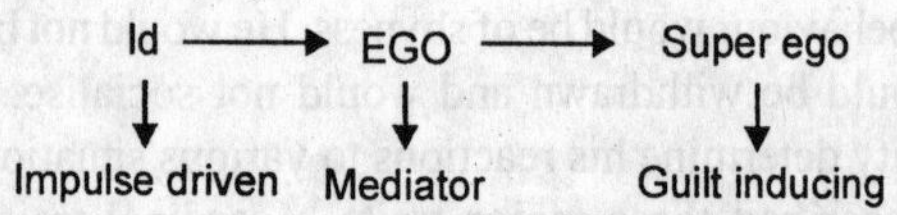

Acting as mediator, ego is pressurised with anxiety by Id and super ego. To release this anxiety, ego uses a number of defence mechanisms to save the personality from disintegration. These mechanisms are repression, rationalisation, projection, displacement, sublimation, regression and reaction formation.

(iii) *Personality development*: Freud was of the view that personality is formed during the first few years of life. He emphasised on psychosexual development, which has three stages – the oral stage – (first 12 to 18 months), the anal stage (12-18 months to 3 years) and the phallic stage (3 to 5 or 6 years). He said that during these three phases, a child goes through psychosexual development. If this psychosexual development is not proper, it may influence the adult behaviours. For example, frustration at oral stage may result in verbal hostility. Excessive gratification at this stage where a child is always given milk or a substitute may develop as dependent adult. This situation is termed as 'fixation'.

This theory has been criticised due to its overemphasis on childhood experiences. It is also not clear in stating as to how specific experiences would affect the personality in specific manner. This theory also does not take into account the importance of healthy personalities.

(c) *Behaviour Theories*: Contrary to the view that internal system shapes the personality, behavioural and social learning theories are based on the concept that environmental events build personality. Skinner, the pioneer of this approach, said that two persons may react to the same situation differently not because of their varying traits or their super egos but because they have different experiences of events in their lives. The reinforcements to certain behaviour or lack of them shape a person's personality. Social learning theorists also believe that events have a cognitive analysis dimensions. The role of thoughts, feelings, perceptions in shaping the personalities cannot be ignored. Bandura gave the concept of learning through observing others.

Behaviourist theorists were interested in modifications of behaviours and they concentrated on how the interaction between cognitive factors and environmental factors can result in modifications of behaviours.

These theories have been criticised for overemphasising the role of external factors and ignoring the human dimensions of personalities like spontaneity or creativity.

(d) *Humanistic Theories*: Humanistic theories believe that each individual is motivated to develop and tries to develop his full potential and capabilities Rogers was the pioneer of this school of thought. He said that congruence between the self-concept and experiences determining the happiness. Maslow's theory of need hierarchy says that people try to achieve highest order need, which is self-actualisation.

Humanistic theories have been criticised as being based on abstract and non-verifiable concepts.

How to Measure Personality: Personality tests are available but one drawback with such tests is that a person may manipulate the answer if he does not want to be honest. In such a situation, the real picture of the personality would not emerge.

Some commonly used tests are:

1. *Mooney problem checklist*: It consists of a series of problems and the person has to identify the problem as most important for him and the least important. This checklist is useful to identify individuals from groups for counselling.
2. *Minnesota multiphasic personality inventory (MMPI)*: In this Inventory, there are 556 statements about behaviour, thoughts, or emotional reactions, which a person rates as 'true', 'false' or 'cannot say'. Hathaway & McKinley prepared the Inventory in 1942. The statements are like 'I am a happy person'. Trained persons should use this Inventory. Generally, this is not used in school settings.
3. *Cattel's 16 personality Factors (16PF)*: As discussed earlier, Cattel's researches on personalities of people show that there are certain surface traits, which occur in clusters. His analysis led a list of 16 primary traits, which he says is the core of personality. He listed these traits in bi-polar method as Reserved/Out-going or Submissive/Dominant etc. On the basis of 16 P F Questionnaire, individual profiles may be developed. This is designed for persons of the age 16 years and above. It provides 16 scores on the trait clusters of social, boldness, dominance, vigilance, emotional stability and rule conscious.
4. *California psychological inventory (CPI)*: This Inventory was developed by Gough. Its format is similar to that of MMPI. There are 15 traits that can be identified in each individual. The Questionnaire has good predictive validity.

The Inventory has been developed to be used with normal adult population.

There are numerous scale Inventories and Tests that measure one or more traits of personality. There are adjustment scales, locus of control scales, anxiety tests, self-esteem inventories, emotional problem measurement scales, leadership traits measurement questionnaire, etc. A number of these scales are available in India, many tests for personality measurement have been adapted and developed for Indian population also, which are available with Indian dealers dealing with psychological assessment tools. Udai Pareek has compiled a number of personality measurement tools in the form of books, which may be consulted for detailed information.

Projective Techniques to Measure Personality: Projective techniques to measure personality have been developed to delve into the unconscious thoughts and feelings of a person. As explained by *Anastasy*, "It is expected that the test materials will serve as a sort of screen on which respondents 'project' their characteristic thought processes, needs, anxieties, and conflicts." The purpose of the projective technique is to measure the whole personality and not any specific trait.

Strong defined projective technique as a "method of understanding the inner world of the individual." Murrary said that "The purpose of this procedure is to stimulate literacy creativity and thereby evoke fantasies that reveal covert and unconscious complexes. The test is based on the well-recognised fact that when a person interprets an ambiguous social situation, he is apt to expose his own personality as much as the phenomenon to which he is attending."

Several methods are in use to know the personality through projective methods. Two most popular tests are Rorschach Inkblot Test and Thematic Apperception Test (TAT). The Inkblot Test was developed by Rorschach (1921). There are 10 cards in this test with inkblots in them. During the administration of this test the client is shown the cards, one by one, and is asked to tell what he sees in the card. The psychologist also records duration of response, remarks, emotional expressions and other non-verbal clues. A system to analyse the responses received from the client has been given in the Manual Sample of design. A sample of this test may be seen as follows:

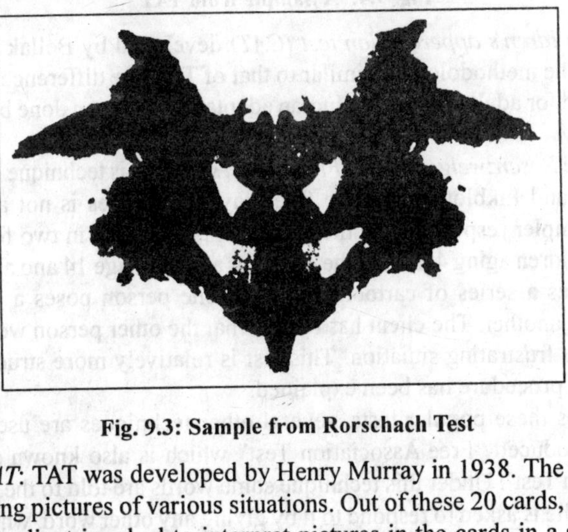

Fig. 9.3: Sample from Rorschach Test

(a) *TAT*: TAT was developed by Henry Murray in 1938. The test has 20 cards having pictures of various situations. Out of these 20 cards, one card is blank. The client is asked to interpret pictures in the cards in a story form. Here the pictures are more structured in comparison to Rorschach test. After the administration of the test, a procedure to analyse the results has been given which is based on content analysis.

This test is popularly used in clinical settings. Many adaptations of TAT have been made.

A sample from the test:

Fig. 9.4: A Sample from TAT

(b) *Children's apperception test (CAT)* developed by Bellak is used on children. The methodology is similar to that of TAT, the difference being that TAT is used for adult population. Indian adaptation has been done by Dr. Uma Chowdhary.

(c) *The Rosenzweig picture – Frustration study*: This technique is different from TAT and Inkblot tests. Here free play of fantacies is not allowed. It requires simpler response from the clients. It is available in two forms – the first for children aging 4-13 and the other for adults of age 14 and above. This test provides a series of cartoons in which one person poses a frustrating situation to another. The client has to tell what the other person would say in reply to the frustrating situation. This test is relatively more structured and the scoring procedure has been explained.

Besides these popular tests, several other techniques are used. Galton (1879) introduced "Free Association Test" which is also known as 'Word-Association Test'. Under this technique some words are told to the client one by one and he is asked to respond to it by giving any other word, which comes to his mind after listening to this word. This technique is being used to study the thought processes. It is also used for clinical purposes. Sometimes clients are asked to use the word in sentences and the way they use the words may be analysed to assess their personality characteristics. This technique is a verbal projective technique, which requires language skills. For example, if the word said is 'snake', the client can answer by saying 'poison', 'pretty', 'scares', etc., or for sentence completion, if the word is 'accident', the client may use it as – 'I saw an accident, victim died', 'Accidents on road are very common', 'I met with him accidentally'. When given a series of words either for making the sentences or for responding by another word, the full picture of the personality emerges – the complexes, the positive-negative thinking, the anxiety, etc.

Another verbal technique is 'sentence completion test'. In this test, half a sentence is already there and client is supposed to complete the sentence. There can be several possible answers to complete the sentence. For example, the sentence may be "My brother...". To complete the sentence, one may say 'is lively', 'is cruel', 'is not good', 'beats me', 'loves my sister more than me'. The type of sentence the client uses is expected to reveal his internal feelings and thoughts.

Both word Association Tests and Sentence Completion tests have been standardised.

Drawing and Painting

Drawing and painting technique is known as performance technique of projective method. This activity provides a platform for self-expression. This technique is generally used with children. Machover (1949) test of Draw-a-Person Test is very popular. In this test the child is asked to make a picture of a person on a paper. After completion of the picture if the picture is of a female, the child is asked to draw a picture of a male. After he completes the drawings, the child may be asked certain questions about the pictures he has made. The procedure for analysis has been detailed in the test, which is qualitative.

The other tests of this kind are House-Tree-Person technique where the child has to draw pictures of a house, a tree and a person, and Kinetic Family Drawing, where the child has to draw the picture of the family along with himself doing something. Emotional problems, internal conflicts, family adjustment indicators may be worked out through these tests.

Play Techniques

The toy tests where dolls, puppets, and other playing material used are also a kind of projective technique. The play material should be such that with it the person can associate himself. Psychologists have standarised such play material. Playing with toys tells about the child's feelings about his fears, attitudes towards siblings, family, and the problems he is facing. Which toy the child opts for and what he does with it is to be observed in this test. His non-verbal clues are also observed while he plays with the objects.

All the projective techniques provide generally qualitative data. Only a person with psychology background and well trained in using these techniques and interpreting the results should use it. Personal bias may affect the scoring and interpretation.

These techniques are useful as it is easy to form a rapport with the client. Information about the children can be derived easily with these techniques, which may be difficult with paper-pencil tests. Moreover, the clients would not be able to manipulate the responses under this technique as they can in self-reporting methods.

How to Use Personality Tests in Guidance

1. The tests can help in identifying the students who have adjustment problems.
2. They can help the students in assessing their suitability to various occupations. For example, a student with shy and introvert personality would not be suitable for jobs that require dealing with the public.
3. Personality tests may help the individuals in knowing their weaknesses. They can overcome some of these through special efforts.
4. Students may know their strengths and utilise them in proper channels.
5. Tests can help the students in identifying the reasons for their poor academic performance, as this may be related to their emotional handicaps.
6. Choice of educational stream may be made according to the personality characteristics.
7. Leisure time activities may be chosen suiting to the personality.
8. Ultimately, personality tests help a person in self-understanding, self-acceptance and self-realisation.

Administration of Tests

(a) *Who should administer*: A properly trained person with psychology background only, should administer the tests.

(b) *How the tests should be administered*: The counsellor should make the necessary preparations before the administration of tests. He should orient the students about the testing programme. He should decide which tests are to be given and at what level of difficulty, and whether it would be an individual testing programme or a group testing. The purpose of the assessment should properly be explained to the clients. The material such as booklets, answer sheets, pencils etc. should be kept ready and counted. The counsellor should be well versed with the instructions and examples to be explained that are given in the test.

(c) *General conditions to administer the test*: The counsellor should ensure a congenial environment where students could feel easy in taking the test programme. The place should be free from noise. It should have proper arrangement for ventilation, lighting, etc. Seating arrangement should be adequate for each student. To stop interruptions during the testing programme, a board 'Don't disturb', may be placed outside the room where the testing is on.

The students should be in proper mental and physical frame. If they have any pressures, *e.g.*, if they have to appear for some subject test soon after the psychological testing, it would affect their performance on these tests. Similarly, they will not do well in the test if they are sick.

To reduce the anxiety among students, the counsellor should form good rapport with them before administering the test.

(d) *Considerations for selection of test:*

- Purpose and target group
- What information is required
- Duration of test
- Test's reliability, validity and availability of norms
- Cost of test
- Scoring is easy or difficult
- Availability of information for interpretation. Objectivity in interpretation.

(e) *How to Communicate the test results*: Communication of test results is important as well as a delicate issue. Results can be useful for students, teachers as well as for parents in decision-making. Before communication of the results the counsellor should fully understand the purpose of the psychological assessment programme and limitations of various tests. The students, teachers and parents should be made familiar with the vocabulary used to interpret the test results. When to communicate the test results should be kept in mind. Results, specially when the results are not encouraging, should not be communicated at the time when students are preparing for some annual examinations. In case students or parents do not show much interest in the results, counsellor should not insist upon communicating the results.

Tests results should be communicated in such a manner that they do not lead to the development of negative self-concept or an individual gets demotivated. While communicating the test results it should be made clear that the test results show the present status of the child and the prediction of immediate future, and that as the child grows, many aspects may change in the long run. Some sensitive children may get emotional after knowing many things about themselves after the communication of test results. Counsellor should be able to handle such emotional reactions.

The test results should be authenticated with the information received from other sources also.

The results of the child should be communicated to parents in such a manner that it facilitates understanding of the child. The results should not disappoint the parents and should not lead to their exerting undue pressure on the child to act in a directed manner.

Similarly, the results should be told to teachers to facilitate proper handling of the student or planning remedial programmes in the weak areas of achievements.

Non-Testing Techniques of Guidance

All the information about the total life of individual cannot be obtained only through psychological tests. Therefore, the guidance workers have to adopt a number of other techniques as well to gather information about the individual. Such non-testing techniques have, however, limitations as they are of qualitative nature, the results cannot be quantified. Therefore, they have an element of subjectivity in interpretation of data. Moreover, the guidance workers' mindset may also get reflected in the information collected through non-testing techniques. It is always better to use more than one technique and source to collect the information and organise the same in its totality. Information collected through various techniques may be verified from each other.

Non-testing techniques may be of the following types:

(a) Self-reporting
(b) Observational
(c) Socio-metric

(a) Self-Reporting Methods

(i) *Autobiography*: Autobiography is a personal account of individual, in which he records about himself, his frustrations, tensions, goals, aspirations, etc. It helps the counsellor because, due to the paucity of time, it may not be possible for the counsellor to give time to each and every student to collect his life history. This autobiographical record may be had through obtaining his personal diary or through structured questionnaire that the students may fill. This can be given as a class assignment or as homework. When it is given as a class assignment, there may be obstruction to spontaneity. It is always better that students write it comfortably outside the school premises. The students may be asked to write their biographies in two ways. One way is to provide basic outlines of what is to be written and the second option is to ask them to write freely whatever relevant information they can think of. For dealing with the emotional problems of the students, the second option is always better, while in educational, vocational services, the structured autobiography may be obtained.

Autobiographies may be helpful in understanding the past experiences of the individuals, their environment, their friends circle, etc. In this process, the students should be assured that their writings would be used only for professional purposes. The autobiographical information may be verified with the students through further interviews or other sources to check the reliability and validity of the information.

Sample of Guidelines for an Autobiography

Write about yourself

1. Your schooling and academic achievements
2. Your strengths and weaknesses
3. Your likes and dislikes
4. Your family and friends
5. Your interests and hobbies
6. Your goals
7. Your problems and frustrations
8. How you deal with your problems
9. Who helps you in need – support system?

The above format may be modified according to the purpose and need of the student.

How to Analyse Autobiographies – A Sample Format

1. Identify important and relevant incidents
2. Support system available with the child or lack of it
3. Expression – whether there are certain omissions. If yes deliberate or inadvertent, the depth of expression, the tone.
4. Organisation of thoughts
5. Indicative problem

6. Verifiable information
7. Observations and comments

The limitation of this technique is the difficulty of expression through writing. Moreover if a child does not want to disclose some information, he may mislead. To seek attention and sympathies from the counsellor, the student may record events that have never happened. It may also be difficult for the student to remember all the facts.

(ii) *Self-Assessment*: In this technique, the student is asked to indicate his strengths and weaknesses. He can also indicate the problems he is facing at home or in school.

It is generally observed that many people record only their plus points and do not mention their weaknesses. Some children with low self-esteem always mention about their inability in doing things.

The counsellor may look into the real problem of the child and verify the reported information from other sources.

(iii) *Essays*: Essay writing is a kind of self-reporting method, which resembles autobiographies. But while autobiographies are direct and the child has to write about his own background, essays can be on various topics. In essays, the client may reflect some of his feelings, which he otherwise does not want to disclose. The topics of the essay may be 'If I become a teacher', 'Importance of friends in life', etc. Such topics motivate a child to think also. He can imagine instead of giving only factual information as in the case of autobiography.

(b) Observation Method

Assessment of people through observing their behaviours comes very naturally to all. All of us observe others and draw conclusions about them. This is a popular technique in guidance also. Teachers and the counsellor observe the behaviour of students in natural atmosphere and reach certain conclusions. These observations may be structured, where the students may be asked to do certain activity, or unstructured where observations are made about the students in their normal daily routines.

It is important to note here that drawing conclusion through observing a person during one incident is not appropriate. It is necessary to make observations over a long time in varying situations and circumstances with varying groups. Observations thus made should be verified with information from other sources. The totality of the situation should also be kept in mind. For example, if a person is showing aggressive behaviour, the situations where he is aggressive should be analysed properly before aiming at any definite conclusion. To reach any conclusion his behaviour should be observed in more than one situation. For structured observations, a number of techniques have been developed.

(i) *Anecdotal Record*: Randall has defined Anecdotal record as "A record of some significant item of conduct, a record of an episode in the life of the student, a word picture of the student in action... a word snapshot at the moment of the incident: any narration of events in which the student takes such a part as to reveal something which may be significant about his personality".

Anecdotal record is a useful instrument where the behaviour of a student is observed during some specific incident in which the student was also a party. It is also called a word picture because the person who observes the behaviour of the student describes the incident to show the real picture of his behaviour. The teacher may provide such records to the counsellor to understand the student better. The reporting person should be very clear and free from prejudices. He should not confuse between the facts and his own feelings. The purpose of anecdotal record is to narrate the behaviour of the student during the incident. Anecdotal records are used in combination of various other techniques. Moreover, there should be a series of anecdotes at different timings. Only one incident cannot describe the behaviour of a person.

Anecdotal reports may be prepared in a given format.

A Sample Format of Anecdotal Report

1. *Name of the Student*
2. *Class*
3. *Observation made by with date*
4. *Place where observation was made*
5. *Narration of the Incident*
6. *Situational details and setting*
7. *Any triggers identified*
8. *Observations of the observer*
9. *Comments from the observer*
10. *Recommendations*

Such records about the individual should be maintained and collated for integration and guidance. This kind of behaviour observation may provide clues about the individual's relationship with peer group, with teachers, his aspirations and motivations, aggression, fears etc.

It is not possible to record anecdotes for each and every student. It has to be considered carefully as to who should be chosen and why. At primary level a teacher can identify a child who does not speak or at secondary level child can be identified who is a slow achiever. Anecdotes may be written about those children, who are difficult to understand during normal interactions.

Example

Name	:	Miss Anita Singh
Class	:	X
Observation made by		Mrs. Sushma Acharya, Games teacher
With date		on 10.9.04
Place where observation made	–	Hockey ground
Narration of the incident	–	While playing with the group, and situational details she was looking withdrawn. When she was unable to listen to the call of another girl Nina to pass the ball, the Nina commented What's wrong with you'?

On this Anita hit the other girl with her hockey stick.

Triggers identified:

(a) Anita was upset due to some reason.
(b) Comment of Nina hurt her and triggered her mental state.

Observations and Comments from the teacher:

Anita is good in sports. She is always cooperative and helping. She remains smiling while playing.

Recommendations: Guidance worker should find out the reason of such behaviour from Anita and provide help.

(ii) *The (Problem) Checklist*

Checklist method in observation is used when the purpose of the counsellor is to identify certain specific personality characteristics in a student. The list of traits is provided to the observer and he has to tick the trait, which he observes the individual to have. For example the traits may be hardworking, calm, decision maker, irritable, etc.

Example

Problems: A girl has mental ability. She is studying in IX standard. Her academic achievement is not upto mark.

Checklist:

- Concentrates in the class
- Takes notes
- Brings the books and note books to the class
- Irritable or calm
- Aggressive
- Talks with classmates during the class
- Writes something in the class
- She is hardworking
- Attentive to the lectures
- Takes interest in the subjects.

The above checklist would provide information about the listening and learning methods of the girl in the class, her characteristics whether she is hardworking and laborious. Analysis of what the real problem is can be made in the light of the fact.

(iii) *Rating Scales*

Rating scales may also be used as instruments for observation, Rating scales provide comparability of observations. These scales may be designed according to the purpose. Observations on a particular characteristic can be rated on 5 or 7 point scale.

Example

Purpose: To observe maladjustment with the peer group.

Items:	*Never*	*Rarely*	*Sometimes*	*Often*	*Always*
• Talks with the classmate sitting next to him					
• Talks with other classmates					
• Shares his things with others					
• During lunch time eats food all alone					
• During recess plays with others					

While Anecdotal records are 'observer descriptions', the Rating Scales are 'observer evaluations'. The Rating scales also provide information about the degree of the characteristics.

How to prepare Rating Scales: For preparing a Rating Scale, one should list out the characteristics that are to be rated. These could be self-confidence in the student, self-dependence, industriousness, cheerfulness, helping attitude. Each characteristic should be well defined and be understood by the Rater. Moreover, only such characteristics should be chosen that are relevant and observable in the given situation. In a school situation where teachers are supposed to rate a student's 'love for siblings' would not be an observable characteristic.

A few things should be kept in mind before making a Rating Scale.

(a) It should be free from prejudices and subjectivity. This difficulty may be overcome by choosing more than one Rater.

(b) Some observers have a tendency to rate a person at one point on all the characteristics. This is known as 'halo effect'. For example, the

Rater may rate a student as excellent on all the characteristics. This does not give the real picture about the person. In such cases, more than one student may be rated on one characteristic, then on another, and so on.

The problems of rating scales may be lessened if the Rater is also asked to support his Ratings with justifications.

(iv) Systematic Case Study

Under this method, the major activity is to collate all the information collected from various sources and techniques. This can be the information from the school record, from achievement record of the students, the psychological tests, or information collected by teachers. All these collected bits of information may be systematically reviewed and analysed and prepared in the form of the case study. Allport says that "It provides a framework within which the psychologist can place all of his observations gathered by other methods; it is his final affirmation of the individuality and uniqueness of every personality. It is completely synthetic method; the only one that is spacious enough to embrace all assembled facts. Unskillfully used, it becomes a meaningless chronology, or a confusion of fact and fiction, of guesswork and misinterpretation. Properly used, it is the most revealing method of all."

For preparing the case study, some order of reporting may be prescribed, say, introduction, scores on achievement test, school progress, teacher's observations, learning defects, family history, social background, health background, scores on psychological tests, personal problems, pupil groups observations and the interpretation.

Case studies are important records in situations where individual counselling is required. They can serve as successful cases to be referred by other students. Case study record also indicates tne gaps in information.

Example

How to prepare case study?

Problem: Child belongs to first generation learner's category and has problems in adjustment in the school.

Case Record:

Name - Amita Kumari
Class - III
Age - 14 years

1. *Family Background*: Amita's parents are illiterate and are landless labourers. She is the eldest child in the family. She has three younger sisters and one brother. The brother is the youngest of them.
2. *Economic Background of the family*: Being landless labourers, the family

lives hand to mouth. They hardly get meals a day. The family migrated from a remote village of Bihar to the town area where they work on someone else's farms or sometimes are engaged by some Transporter for loading unloading work.

3. *Social background of the family*: The family belonged to Scheduled Tribe category. The village they were living in belonged to high castes. The family was working in the village on the farm of the Head of the Panchayat. They were paid a very meager wage or sometimes no wage at all. So they moved out of the village.
4. *Educational background of the family*: The family is illiterate. No body in the family got any education through generations After migration from the remote village to a small town, they started to send their eldest child to school. Her younger sister who was 11 years' old looked after the other siblings while parents were at work.

Problem stated by the teacher: The case was referred to counsellor by the teacher stating that the girl was unable to concentrate in the class. She does not complete her home work. She forgets to bring the note book or the pencil or the text book to the school. If she is asked to prepare a model etc. she does not bring the material. Even after scolding the child, no improvement has taken place.

Interview with the Child and her problem: During the interviews with the child it was understood that the parents were sending the child to school for 'mid-day meal' scheme, as they were not able to feed all their children. She was unable to understand the study material, as there was nobody to help her at home. She used to get more tensed when scolded by the teacher in the presence of the other girls of her class. The other girls also teased her. She didn't want to continue with the school.

Interaction with Parents: In this case, interactions were had by counsellor with the parents, who told him that they were unable to meet the demands of the school to buy things for preparing charts, or raw-material for preparing models etc.

Counsellor's Observations:

- Neither the parents nor the child knew the importance of education.
- Financial problems of the child.
- Teacher was not able to understand the adjustment problems of the child and was unable to handle her with sensitivity.
- Child required remedial teaching.

Counselling and Outcome Summary: Counsellor discussed the case with the teacher and suggested as to how to be sensitive towards the child's problems. Remedial classes to help the child in doing homework etc. were arranged. Parents were counseled to understand the importance of education. Financial support for education was arranged from school's fund meant for poor children. Group activities were arranged so that the child could be friendly with other classmates.

Follow up: Follow up was done after 15 days. Teacher reported a little improvement in the child. The child also reported better adjustment with the school environment.

(c) Sociometry

The socio metric technique is used when information is required on how a person perceives himself and others in the group *i.e.* which members in the group are near to him and who are at a distance. This tells about the relationship of the person among peers; the leader in the group and the atmosphere. Whether the person is a rejected lot or he is accepted in the group.

In this technique, children are asked to name two or three of their peers, with whom they would like to work. Sometimes they are also asked to name those with whom they may not like to sit or work. This kind of technique is used where adequate group activities and interaction among people is there. Information, thus, collected provides clues on the patterns of interactions among individuals.

Moreno J.L., has defined sociometry as “the mathematical study of psychological properties of populations; the experimental technique of, and the results obtained by, application of quantitative and qualitative methods”. Sociometry is a study of feelings, which come out spontaneously through this technique.

Example: Suppose there are 7 students (A, B, C, D, E, F and G). Each of them is asked to name three others in the group with whom they prefer to work, in the order of preferences – as first preference, second preference and third preference. The following table shows how each of them indicated their preferences.

Table 9.2: Relationship Preferences

Selector/selected	*About their relationship with others*						
	A	*B*	*C*	*D*	*E*	*F*	*G*
A	-	1	2	-	-	3	-
B	-	-	2	1	-	-	3
C	2	-	-	1	3	-	-
D	3	2	-	-	-	1	-
E	1	-	-	2	-	-	3
F	-	1	-	-	3	-	2
G	1	-	3	-	2	-	-

For example, A indicated B as his first preference, C as second preference and F as third preference. Similarly, G’s first preference is A, second preference is E and the third preference is C.

The following chart indicates the first choices of each of the seven students through arrows. For example, A’s first choice is B, B’s first choice is D, D’s first choice is F. F’s first choice is B, and so on. The number of times each student is picked up by his peers as their first choice is indicative of the student’s popularity. In this example, there are 3 students A, B and D who are the first choices of two others (maximum number) and so may be considered as more popular than the other four.

Fig. 9.5: Relationship Preferences

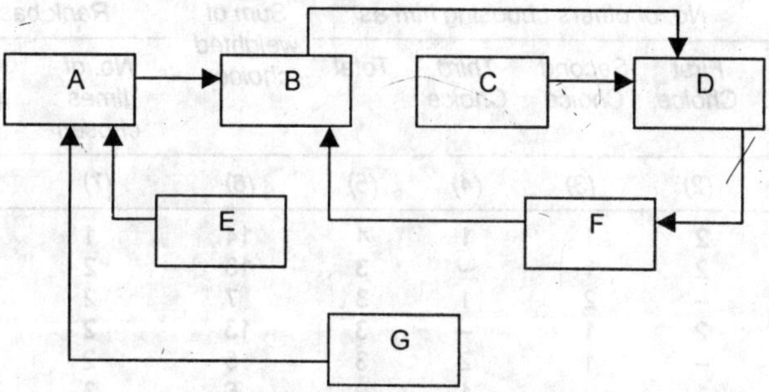

The study may be made more comprehensive by including not only the first choices but the second and the third choices as well. The following diagram depicts the complete situation — simple → arrow indicating first preference, curved arrow indicating second choice and scribble line arrow suggesting the third choice. For combining all the preferences of each individual, it would be necessary to assign some sort of weights to each preference. For example, first choice may be assigned 5, second choice may be assigned 3 and the third choice 1. To obtain a combined score for an individual, the number of times he is chosen as first, second or third preference is multiplied by the respective weight and added.

Fig. 9.6: Sociometric Presentation

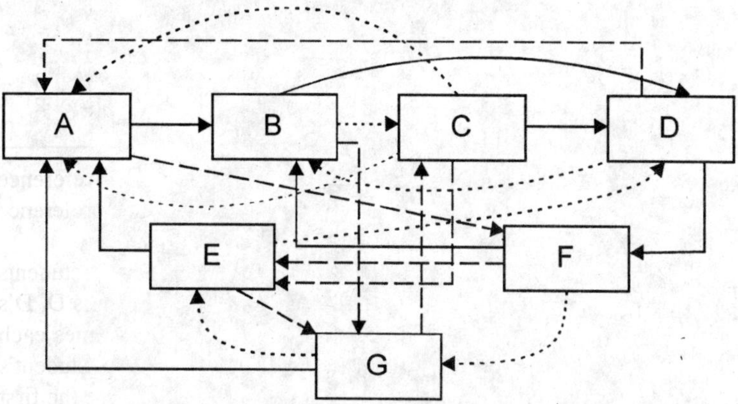

For example, A is chosen twice as first choice, and once each as second and third choice. The combined weighted sum of choices would be $2 \times 5 + 1 \times 3 + 1 \times 1 = 14$. In this manner, the following table may be generated:

Table 9.3: Choices in Sociometry

Student	No. of others choosing him as				Sum of weighted choices	Rank based on	
	First Choice	Second Choice	Third Choice	Total		No. of times chosen	Sum of weighted choices
(1)	(2)	(3)	(4)	(5)	(6)	(7)	(8)
A	2	1	1	4	14	1	1
B	2	1	–	3	13	2	2
C	–	2	1	3	7	2	4
D	2	1	–	3	13	2	2
E	–	1	2	3	5	2	6
F	1	–	1	2	6	3	5
G	–	2	2	4	8	1	3

For interpretation of the results, one could go either by the ranks on the basis of the number of times a person is chosen irrespective of the order of choice (Col. 7 of the table) or on the basis of the sum of weighted choices (Col.8 of the table). Each has its own limitation. While the rank based on simple number of times chosen ignores the orders of choice, the combined weighted sum depends on the subjectively chosen weights. However, if there is sufficient justification for the weights chosen, the latter is a more comprehensive indicator on one's popularity. In the present example, it may be observed that, whatever may be the method followed 'A' ranks above all the other six.

10

Career Education Models

The concept of 'career education' is relatively new having emerged during the past thirty years or so. It has assumed special significance in the light of the fast changing labour market scenario with some of the jobs vanishing from the labour marketand some new jobs emerging. There is also increasing demand for personnel with upgraded and multiple skills as has been discussed earlier.

Emergence of Career Education

There was the 'world of schooling' as well as the 'world of work'-perhaps at two poles far apart from each other. It was thought that these should be bridged by introducing a 'third world' to make the transition from school to work smooth and comfortable. Career education is that third world. which bridges the school system and the job market system.

Marland had been the pioneer of the concept of career education. He named it as 'educational reforms' while he was working as United States Commissioner of Education during the period 1970-1973. In America, educational reforms in terms of career education started in the form of a movement which got accelerated with the introduction of career education programmes in a large number of schools.

Similar problems were also experienced in the educational system of Britain. The period of sixties and early seventies in Great Britain had been one of mass unemployment and significant social changes. There was a lot of hue and cry about the education system. The youth of the country, faced with growing unemployment considered the education system of the country totally irrelevant. In these circumstances, Montford studied the concept of career education in America and in 1975 stressed upon the need to introduce career education in Britain also. Thus, career education came into being in Britain.

The definition of career education is given by Hoyt as follows:

"Career education offers a systematic, sequential, integrated, coordinated opportunity for the connections of education, work and career. Career education starts at an early age in the home, extends with formal and informal education throughout the life-time and occurs as a result of the collaboration of all parts of the community." (Hoyt 2001). In his words (Hoyt 1975) it is "the totality of experiences through which one learns about and prepares to engage in work as part of her or his way of living."

It is also important to note here that career education means differently to various people according to their age and perception of the surroundings. For example a young child would see it as a learning process by which he can see a variety of opportunities available from which he can choose. For adolescents career education means the work demands and what would he get with a particular kind of work in terms of salary, perks, promotion, job satisfaction life style etc. For older persons career education may be related to the learning how to be useful to others according to their experiences.

We can summarise the definition of career education as it should start from elementary school level, it should be applicable to all students and it should emphasise the relationship between education and work. In other words, education should mean preparation for work which means that every person should be taught some skill along with general education. Thus, vocational education is a part of the total career education programme. Career education includes general education, technical education and vocational education. Choice of a career means choosing a life style and value system.

Objectives of Career Education

(i) To provide skills to the persons to make them employable and rise in their careers.

(ii) To help persons in knowing about various career options available to them and make proper decision to choose careers according to their interests abilities and aptitudes.

(iii) To relate education and work so that better choice of both can be made.

(iv) To reform education by including careers information in the syllabus.

(v) To have greater involvement of employers in the educational experience of all students.

(vi) To impart career counselling starting at an early age.

(vii) To provide counselling for re-entry and re-training wherever needed.

(viii) To have flexibility in entering the skills development programme or take up work or opting for higher education as and when one wants. Exit point should enable the student to be employable.

(ix) To give notion about limitations of the world of work.

In general, objectives of career education are

- to make people familiar with the resources available in the school as well as outside which could be utilised for achieving their goals in life;
- to make people familiar with the process of career decision making by experiencing the actual working conditions.

Career education is thus expected to make education and work more satisfying and valuable and shape education as preparation for work which could equip persons for entry into the job market.

Principles of Career Education

Integration of School Education and Work

Career education makes education a process of preparation for work, both a prominent and permanent goal of all who learn. This will become more clear if we recollect a frequent classroom situation where students ask what good it would do to them to learn a particular lesson. Too often, the reply given to them, in the absence of a career education programme is that they will need this in their next class. Thus, schooling prepares them only for more or further schooling. The end result is that the student's motivation may be affected and so may be their academic achievement. When these students go out to seek employment in the world of work, they are faced with situations where employers feel that the students are no good as productive workers. Career education seeks to remedy this situation and turn this situation around by integrating school education with the requirements of the world of work.

Career Education—A Total Life Experience

Career education integrates career development with entire life experience as it spreads over from initial educational stage and continues right through adult life. It not only involves assisting children in school, become aware of world of work regarding educational/occupational opportunities available at various stages and also for adults who desire to enter the labour market or to improve the quality of their existing employment or to re-enter the job market after a spell of job-lessness or non-participation in labour force.

Integration of School and Community

Career education is provided not only in schools but in various settings like work place, home and community and sometimes in combination of settings.

For example, linkages between school and workplace can be established through field trips to industrial units, using experts from the industry as resource persons in schools, system of campus recruitments and job-fairs, industry sponsoring specialised training according to their requirements, community contact through the services of retired persons and experts in different professions to share their first-hand experiences with the children, etc.

Career Education as a Developmental Process

Career education is a developmental process wherein individual becomes aware of one's self, abilities and limitations, capacities and constraints as well as opportunities available according to his or her abilities. He can match his abilities with the opportunities available to him and make a decision.

Hands on Experience

Career education combines within itself the academic knowledge as well as the application of that knowledge in real life situations. The latter is facilitated through direct observations and hands-on experience. For example if a child wishes to become a doctor career education may provide him the relevant knowledge about diseases and treatment, and on the conditions of work of a doctor and the personality characteristics that make a good doctor—all this can be demonstrated by arranging visits to a hospital.

Integration of General and Vocational Education

Career education demands that well before the students come out of the general school system, they should acquire some or other specific vocational skill that would help them gain entry into the world of paid or self-employment. There may be a number of vocational courses that can be introduced in general education. These could be repair of house-hold items, repair of cycles, scooters, electrician work, stitching, nursery growing, etc. suitable to specific region.

Flexibility in Learning Process

Yet another important feature of career education is that it makes no distinction between students who would drop out and others who would carry on with general education at the college level. It is not uncommon for students getting into colleges and then realizing the importance of education as a means of acquiring entry level vocational skills. Career education provides flexibility in joining, rejoining educational stream, technical stream or occupational stream.

Career Decisions

Career decisions are not to be made in a hurry. Information regarding educational and occupational opportunities available for choice has to be combined with personal understanding of interests, aptitudes and values gained from exposure to real life situations. Career education provides ample opportunities to persons to take their own decision in respect of choosing a career personally satisfying. This can be arranged by calling experts from various industries and interacting with students; or students can be taken to various places where employment could be available.

Cost Effectiveness

Career education, by making people aware of themselves as well as of the world of work, minimizes mismatch between individuals and career opportunities and wastage in terms of time, talents, energies and national and personal resources. Thus, career education makes the process of career choice a cost effective affair to the individual and the nation.

Career Education – Specialised Nature

Career education either provided in school or outside the school, is a specialised work. In case the career education is provided through guidance personnel, they have to be specially trained in the work or otherwise normal subject school teachers have to be acquainted with the concepts and procedures of career education.

Career Education Models

As has been discussed earlier, Britain and America had been the pioneers so far as the implementation of career education is concerned.

Career Education in Britain

Career education in Britain is a part of the pastoral care provisions of secondary schools, which means that its provisions are implemented outside the school curriculum. In recent times, the term pastoral care has been modified as guidance, which now includes 'all the means whereby a school identifies and responds to the individual needs of the pupils, whether the means be within or drawn from outside the institution and whether the needs be psychological or physiological or material" (Daws, 1976). The major objectives of this pastoral care are to help young persons for preparing themselves for making educational choices, making their own decisions, choosing their life styles and enrich their personal lives.

The approach adopted to achieve these objectives is allocation of the regular teachers to play subsidiary role of being a house or form teacher for about 20 to 30 students. The model also involves changes in the traditional curriculum. The career guidance in Britain consists of a wide range of activities, which include educational, vocational and personal guidance embracing health education leisure education, social and moral education as well as career education. The specific implementation of this differs from school to school and year to year according to the need of the institution. The career education in Britain is provided by pastoral and subject matter teachers, designated career teachers and by career officers. Career officers are housed in Central Career Centers and visit schools as and when required to provide career services. To implement the career education in Britain, the schools Council, which is a public funded body, has developed relevant material and activities, which could be imbibed into instructional processes. Careers Research and Advisory Centre and National Institute for Careers Education and Counselling have also developed games, books and audio-visual material to facilitate career education. Schools have initiated a systematic procedure for imparting career education by following one of the five main approaches, which are as follows:

(i) Infusion of school subjects with career education concepts
(ii) Including world of work material into social study courses
(iii) Including career education information in courses designated to examine personal values
(iv) A specific course in career education
(v) An integrated studies course in personal social and careers education

In Britain, career education is treated, generally, as outside the formal education stream, is imparted by designated career officials, is equated with guidance programme which is school based, particularly at the secondary school level and starts at the age of around 14 and ends at 16.

American Model

In United States of America, there are four basic career education models developed by the U.S. Department of Education. These are:

(a) School based Model
(b) Employer-experience based Model
(c) Rural-residential based Model
(d) Home-community based Model

(a) *The school based model*: It aims at helping students to develop awareness of career options as well as awaraeness about one's own abilities and limitations. It also includes positive attitudes about work, school, and society. Students get a realistic understanding of the relationships between the world of work and education and ability to enter employment in occupation of one's choice and/or to go on for further education. The model incorporates career development ideas and information in the normal educational curriculum, with career awareness forming a part of the instruction at the elementary school level, career exploration at the junior high school level and career preparation at the senior high school level. The school-based model takes a comprehensive view of career education spanning the entire school education. For example, the Comprehensive Career Education Model (CCEM) developed by the Ohio State University begins with the kindergarten level and goes through the entire educational stream extending to the continuing and adult education.

(b) *The employer-experience-based model*: This model attempts to provide out-of-school supplementary educational programme for students in the age group 13 to 18 in a work environment that combines the positive elements of academic and vocational education. In this model education setting is shifted from the school system to an action oriented learning environment The model seeks to enhance participation of public and private employers in the educational process and thereby increases the relevance of education to the world of work. The focus is on career planning and preparation for labour market by interacting with various employers.

(c) *Rural residential based model*: This model treats family as a unit and concentrates on rural employed and unemployed families. Ultimate goal of this model is to enable low income rural residents develop their careers through specially adopted experiences. The process of career education in this model consists of experimental demonstration involving various individuals, agencies and other resources. Family is important in this model as career counselling, training home making and family development skills; job placement facilities provided under this model make family economically independent. The development of family in this way not only helps them in accelerating their own growth, but also facilitates growth of the society as a whole. Families as well as societies' resources and energies are synergised to optimise their use. You can observe that this model attempts to make a comprehensive intervention to influence all the activities of a family not only education related activities.

(d) *Home-community based model*: The fourth model attempts to make home as a learning centre, develop educational delivery systems that reach into the home and community and provide career education at home to assist individuals in developing their careers. Efforts are made through this process to provide information through mass media and distance education to the unemployed, out of school adults and adolescents about opportunities for employment and training at community level. It guides adults about new education programmes for them and establishes guidance and placement services and also assists people to develop themselves as competent workers. Unlike the other models this model does not attempt to teach skills and attitudes directly. It is only designed to inform individuals existing work and training opportunities in the community and use mass communication media for this purpose.

It is, thus, seen that in USA career education is viewed as a process of learning from kindergarten to old age and is not confined to schools alone. It draws together efforts from educational authorities, local industry and community at large to enable people to develop themselves to have a satisfying life and in turn to develop the society as a whole. The main features of the four models can be summarised in the following table:

Table 10.1: Career Education Models in America

Model	*Target group*	*Focus*	*Learning Location*	*Means of Learning*
School-based	School children	Incorporation of career development concepts and information in the school curriculum	Schools	School Curriculum and guidance
Employer-Based	Students aged 13-18	Preparation for employment and career planning	Employer-based setting	Action learning environment
Rural-Residential-Based	Underemployed and unemployed multi-problem rurai families	Total intervention to make family economically viable	Community	Experimental demonstration activity by individuals, agencies and other agencies
Home-Based	Unemployed and out of school adults	Provision of providing information on existing work and training opportunities	Home	Mass-media and distance learning

Comparison of British and American Models

A comparison of the career education models functioning in Britain and America shows that there are significant differences in the approach and organisation of career education in the two countries. This can be understood from the following table:

Table 10.2: Comparison of British and American Models of Career Education

Characteristic	*British System*	*American System*
Approach	Career education is not viewed as a solution to unemployment	Career education and planning is viewed as a means to solve unemployment problem
Setting	Primary restricted to secondary schools	Extends beyond schools at all levels to home, wok place and community at large
Applicability	Students in the age group 14-16	Life-long process
Delivery system	As a separate subject outside traditional syllabus	Infused into the traditional curriculum
Personnel	Specially trained career teachers/ officials	Normal subject teachers
Emphasis	Career awareness and exploration and decision-making. Career preparation through vocational training is left to post-secondary schools and employers	Career awareness, exploration and preparation

Limitations of the Models

- The concept of career education came into being because of mass unemployment. But career education by itself cannot be a source for providing employment or a solution to the problem of unemployment.
- The British believed that in the post-industrial society unemployment will exist and people have to find fulfillment from other life roles. Personal satisfaction may not be available to many people through work alone. In the American system of career education, self-awareness and career planning have been taken together for solving the situations relating to unemployment. But the two concepts are linked to individual development and not with job development. Individual development may indirectly be associated with providing employment but is not directly linked with it.
- In the British system of career education, vocational training and career education are inter-linked. The emphasis in their model is on the attitudes of the students towards self and world of work as well

as general education. Actual vocational or technical training is missing from their model, which could lead to getting employment. On the other hand, the vocational education, which the American model terms as career preparation, is an essential component of American career education model. But their approach to infuse career preparation into the regular traditional subject matter syllabi may not be that fruitful because of regional variations. Separate courses along with the work experience must be planned for this purpose.

- The material developed by various agencies under British model on career education does not have clear objectives and implications to modify the behaviours of students. The officials involved in career education, therefore, take career education as an add-on work assigned to them and as such do not attach much importance to this work. In the American model, on the other hand, concepts are clear but teachers have to be properly trained to implement a career education programme.

11

Guidance Services in India

Though informal guidance systems have been functioning in India since time immemorial – between elders and the children, between the Guru and Shishyas, between the people and the ruler – guidance service in its modern sense has evolved only during the twentieth century and that too to a significant measure only its second half. This evolution has proceeded in a number of directions:

- Research and training in guidance services,
- Development of psychological tests
- Development of other material to help guidance services
- Institutional arrangements for practical guidance services

It would be, however, difficult to distinguish the evolution in each of these directions as distinct, as development in one is supported by development in other.

Theoretical development and research in the field of guidance in India had its origins in the universities. Calcutta University started a psychological laboratory as early as 1915. Research and development of psychological tests commenced with the setting up of a section for research in Applied Psychology in that university in 1936. This unit's work involved adaptation of the psychological tests and procedures developed in the United States of America to Indian conditions. A Department of Psychological Services and Research was established in Patna University in 1945. The Indian Statistical Institute at Calcutta established a Psychometry unit during the early fifties and contributed to development of psychological tests. Vocational guidance activities were started in 1957 within the National Employment Service, and as a part of these, an Aptitude Testing Centre has also been set in the Directorate General of Employment & Training (DGE&T) in the Ministry of Labour to develop aptitude tests suitable for Indian conditions. Its efforts included adaptation of the General Aptitude Test Battery developed in the United States of America to suit Indian conditions and development of tests for identification of candidates for admission to Industrial Training Institutes, and individual's suitable for self-employment. The DGE&T also developed the National

Classification of Occupations in 1968 and has recently revised it in 2004. On the pattern of International Standard Classifications of Occupations developed by International Labour Organisation.

Training in vocational guidance has taken roots in India in the early fifties. As a follow up of the recommendations of the Secondary Education Commission (1952-53), a Central Bureau of Educational and Vocational Guidance was set up in 1954 under the then Ministry of Education. The Bureau now functions as a part of the Department of Psychological Foundations of the National Institute of Education under the National Council of Educational Research and Training, an autonomous organisation under the Department of Education. The Bureau, apart from conducting regular training courses in educational and vocational guidance, engages itself in production of tools for guidance work in schools, preparation of manuals in guidance and coordination of guidance activities in all States. One of the recent activities (2004-2005) of the Bureau has been the development of curriculum for a training programme in vocational guidance and counselling for international participants. The Bureau's counterparts in the States, the State Bureaus of Educational and Vocational Guidance have responsibilities for training of guidance workers as well as research to develop tools for guidance activities. These Bureaus function under the respective State Directorates of Education in some States or under State Councils of Educational Research & Training in some others, and under State Institutes of Education in others.

The Central Institute for Research and Training in Employment Service (CIRTES) under the DGE&T in Ministry of Labour started conducting training courses for Employment Exchange officers from 1964, which included training of Vocational Guidance Officers. The activity of producing occupational information, that had been carried on in DGE&T, also became the responsibility of CIRTES. In 1971, a separate Career Study Centre was set up in CIRTES, to develop and distribute career literature providing information on the educational and vocational aspects of various occupations. In a recent development, CIRTES has placed career information on over 60 occupations in the website of Ministry of Labour.

Practical guidance services in India have a long history. The Batliboi Vocational Guidance Bureau was set up in 1941, and a Parsi Panchayat Vocational Guyidance Bureau in 1947, both at Bombay. A Bureau of Psychology was established at Allahabad in 1947 by the Government of Uttar Pradesh and a Vocational Guidance Bureau was set up in 1950 in Bombay. In the post-Independence India, the institutional network for providing educational and vocational guidance services expanded rapidly through the system of school counsellors and career masters in educational institutions, on the one hand and, on the other, through the vocational guidance units set up by the National Employment Service as a part of each Employment Exchange and the University Employment Information and Guidance Bureau (UEIGB) at most universities. There are today 938 Employment Exchanges in the country, of which 360 have separate Vocational Guidance Units. Even those without such vocational Guidance Units carry on the guidance activities as a part of the normal Exchange operations. There are also 82 University Employment Information and Guidance Bureaus attached to different universities. In additional a number of government agencies (for example, the Coaching-cum-Guidance Centres for Scheduled Castes and Scheduled Tribes under DGE&T) and the Pre-examination coaching centres under the Ministry of Personnel have been set up to guide and coach the socially backward communications.

Private sector, too, has been increasingly playing an important role in providing guidance services. Most newspapers today carry regularly special features on various career and educational opportunities and a number of magazines provide material that helps candidates in preparing for competitions (*e.g.,* Competition Success Review, Careers and Competitions, etc.). A number of private coaching institutions also prepare student and career aspirants in preparing for competitive examinations and interviews.

Today, there is, thus, an elaborate institutional set up in the field of guidance services. The detailed functions of and the range of services provided by some of the major organisations in the field of vocational guidance services are described here.

Table 11.1: Guidance Programmes in India

A. National Level Programmes

S. No.	*Organisation*	*Functions*
I. Government		
1.	NCERT (Department of Psychological Foundations)	➢ Coordination of guidance activities in the country. ➢ Training guidance personnel, particularly psychologists and counselors. ➢ Production and distribution for guidance work in schools.
2.	Directorate General of Employment & Training, Ministry of Labour (DGE&T).	➢ Evolving policies and standards for vocational guidance activities through Employment Exchanges. ➢ Coordination of vocational guidance activities through employment exchanges.

(*Contd.*)

S. No.	Organisation	Functions
		➢ Development of aptitude tests ➢ Bringing out National Classification of Occupations. ➢ Coordination of Coaching-cum-Guidance.
3.	Central Institute for Research and Training in Employment Services (CIRTES), DGE&T, Ministry of Labour	➢ Research on various occupations ➢ Production on career publications in various occupations ➢ Training of employment officers, inter alia, in vocational guidance, functions of Employment Exchanges. ➢ Employment related coaching and guidance to Schedule Caste and Tribe children to fare better in competitive examination
II. Private		
1.	National Newspapers	➢ Publication of special features on career and educational opportunities
2.	Magazines (Competition Success Review, Career and Competitions; etc.)	➢ Publication of articles on careers and educational opportunities ➢ Publication
3.	Employment News	➢ Publication of articles on various aspects of the world of work and preparations for it.
4.	All India Educational and Vocational Guidance Association	➢ To coordinate educational and vocational guidance activities all over the country and to help in maintaining standards. ➢ To provide public awareness of guidance services. ➢ To bring together guidance workers from time to time for exchange of information and ideas.
B. State Level		
I. Government		
1.	State Bureau of Educational and Vocational Guidance, Directorate of Education/SCERT/State Institutes of Education	➢ Coordination of guidance services in the State. ➢ Development of guidance services in schools. ➢ Organising State level training for guidance personnel. ➢ Collection and maintenance of occupational information. ➢ Organising services in the field of guidance.
2.	State Directorates of Employment	➢ Coordination of vocational guidance programme through Employment Exchanges in the State.

(*Contd.*)

S. No.	Organisation	Functions
		➢ Development of vocational guidance programme in the State. ➢ Production, publication and distribution of occupational information and career literature. ➢ Training of vocational guidance officers and personnel in the State. ➢ Coordination of the mode of VEIGB.
II. Private		
1.	Local newspapers and magazines	➢ Publication of articles on careers and of material for preparation for careers.
2.	State Vocational Guidance Associations (Vocational Guidance Association of Bombay was established in 1952)	➢ To coordinate the efforts of various individuals and agencies in the field of guidance.
C. District Level:		
I. Government		
1.	District Educational Counsellors	➢ To coordinate school guidance activities in the district
2.	District Employment Exchanges	➢ Pre-registration guidance and talks on world of work ➢ Organising group discussions/talks. ➢ Guidance at the time of registration. ➢ Providing individual information and/or guidance ➢ Motivational programmes for promoting self-employment. ➢ Guidance services to self-employment seekers. ➢ Vocational guidance services to special groups like Scheduled Castes and Scheduled Tribes, disabled, etc. ➢ Review of cases of candidates on live register for a long time. ➢ Career talks in the Exchange premises, in schools and in mass media. ➢ Organising career conferences, exhibitions, mock interviews, etc. ➢ Organising coaching classes. ➢ Distribution of occupational information and career pamphlets. ➢ To collect and compile information on employment market, manpower shortages and surpluses.

(*Contd.*)

S. No.	*Organisation*	*Functions*
II. Private		
1.	Rotary Clubs, Associations, etc.	➢ Organise career talks and conferences
D. Institutional Level:		
1.	Universities: (University Employment Information & Guidance Bureaux)	➢ To provide career information and vocational guidance to university alumni. ➢ To organise career conferences, exhibitions, etc. ➢ To prepare alumni for campus recruitment. ➢ To conduct studies on career patterns of alumni.
2.	Schools (School Counsellors & Career Masters)	➢ To familiarise students in the various educational and occupational avenues. ➢ To organise class talks. ➢ To conduct orientation talks for students, parents, school authorities on guidance services. ➢ To provide individual/group guidance. ➢ To organise career conferences exhibitions.

12

Guidance Programme in the Schools

Various Levels of Education

A guidance programme has to be worked out keeping in mind the population of the area, the socio-cultural traditions of various groups in the society, the resources and other guidance relating activities available in the area. The guidance programme has to be divided according to the levels of education such as at elementary school, at high school, secondary school and guidance in colleges and universities. The nature of guidance services would vary in a school according to the level of education.

Information Needs

(a) At Primary Level

- About the School – physical facilities, schedule of holidays, timings, leave rules, other rules and regulations
- School activities relating to study schedule, co-curricular activities,
- Services available in the school – availability of Doctor, transport facility, etc.
- Sports and games facilities
- Learning and facilities for coping with learning problems
- Information for career exploration, development of right attitudes and giving concept of occupation, *i.e.,* career awareness
- Guidance counsellor should have the above information ready with him to be shared with parents and new comers in the school.

(b) At Middle School Level

- Educational courses and facilities
- Information about scholarships and other financial assistance
- Technical courses after middle school
- Coping with learning difficulties and adjustment problems

- Co-curricular activities and hobby clubs
- Library facilities and how to use it
- Self-assessment

(c) At Secondary and Sr. Secondary Level

- Information about future planning
- Options available for choices of courses
- Options available for technical skill development
- Options available for occupations
- Preparation for competitive examinations.
- Self-assessment and development
- Other resources in the community and how to contact them.
- How to prepare for interviews
- Contacts with employers

Guidance at Elementary School Level

It is said that at elementary school vocational guidance is not required and it may start at the secondary level but that is not a correct conception. At primary school level it is important to inculcate in the students the basic values and ethics of the work including dignity of labour, importance of systematic and planned work, need for working in groups, taking advantage of others' experiences, develop good entrepreneur skills and also provide the orientation towards various jobs.

At elementary level the emphasis of guidance would be on various activities that would help in learning. Most of the elementary schools are one-teacher classes, where the teacher has more interaction with each individual student. The classes are relatively smaller and visits of parents are frequent at this level. The developmental needs of the child are most important. Maslow's Hierarchy Theory emphasises the developmental process up to self-actualisation and both teacher and counsellor have to support this developmental process. The purpose of the guidance at elementary school is:

- To help the child to make school progress appropriate to his age
- To help the child in adjusting himself to the school environment basically this is the level where transition from home to school takes place. At this stage, the child learns to discipline himself. The new relationships other than the child-parent relationship emerge. New relationships are with other children of the class, with teachers and other members of the school

- To help the child in managing his emotions in the new environment and new relationships

Here the objectives of the guidance are more towards personality development, developing good habits in the children, helping the child in exploring his talents and creativity. At this stage, guidance can provide the students an exposure to wide variety of activities, new learning situations and meeting the developmental needs of the children. Education and guidance go hand-in-hand at this stage.

Specific Functions of Guidance at Elementary School

1. Guidance can help the children in coping with mal-adjustment and emotional disturbances.
2. The elementary school is the base where child can have the feel of guidance services available in the school.
3. Occupational elements may be introduced.
4. The children may be given the concept of occupation by giving certain examples from their daily lives like that of milkman or postman.
5. Children may also be taken on field visits where they can observe various people working.
6. Help children to explore, understand and accept the environment and self.
7. Develop their talents and creativity.
8. Help in learning to make decisions.
9. Learn to work and share in teams.

The methods of guidance at this level should be interesting so that they could catch the interest of the children. There can be a film show, organisation of games or other forms of recreation, through which children could be made to learn to cope with their adjustment and emotional problems. Emphasis should be more on group activities. The teacher's role is extremely important at this level, as the teacher has to interact with children most of the time in the school. The teacher should be trained to deal with various types of groups of children and also about the group dynamics. The teacher can also observe the behaviours of the children and keep a record, which would help the guidance worker in providing guidance services. Continued interaction between the guidance worker and teacher is necessary. Jones stated that "guidance in the elementary school, by whateve name it may be called, is the foundation of all later attempts to help individuals..."

Guidance at Middle and Secondary Level

Special problems occur during middle and secondary level of schooling, as children are in the adolescent age. At this stage, the child is neither a small child nor a grown-up. It is a very delicate stage where lot of physical and mental changes takes place. The behaviour of adolescents becomes unpredictable and uncontrollable. This is the age when parents complain about the children saying 'they do not listen', while children say 'parents do not understand'. This may be called a transitional period between childhood and adulthood. The children start dreaming about their future and want some kind of independence and freedom. They want to choose their own lifestyles. Their friends are more important than their family members and they want to establish their own identity. At this age, the following problems may occur, which require the attention from the guidance worker:

- Adjustment with the family members and new roles in the family as well as outside
- Problems relating to academics and learning
- The emotional changes and emotional instability, physical development and physical needs
- Problems of choosing the subject for future education
- Unrealistic choices and aspirations
- New interests and curiosities

Here the responsibility of guidance worker is to help the child in developing socially desirable behaviours, to help in discovering his new self, to help him in coping with anxieties and help in developing productive habits. Individual guidance is as important as the group guidance at this stage. The child comes in contact with a number of teachers at this level. The activities of guidance may include orientation to various courses available, improvement in adjustment and social relationships, self-understanding and acceptance, looking for appropriate occupation. The guidance worker should also help the child in assessing his academic performance and the problems therein. A comprehensive guidance programme may be worked out in consultation with the teachers and principal. The guidance worker may also use the psychological tests at this stage. At secondary school stage it is important to provide information about various careers, information about the student himself and about opportunities available to pursue a career. Those who go for higher studies, vocational guidance does not end. Career options at various educational levels, information about vocational assistance and avenues for a higher study, etc., are imparted.

The Specific Functions of Guidance at this Stage

- Administer psychological tests and help children in understanding themselves. Help them in accepting their strengths and limitations
- Provide information about options available about various courses and their suitability.
- Information about tentative job openings through various educational streams
- Orient them towards the status of employment, current and future trends, requirements of skills.
- Help in dealing with their problems relating to development
- Help in assessing their academic performance and their capabilities of improving
- Help in choosing hobbies and leisure time activities
- Assist in making adjustments with self, home, peers and the school.
- Assist in developing communication skills, self-direction skills and decision-making skills.
- Organise group guidance activities.
- Assist potential dropouts with specific needs.

Guidance at Senior Secondary Level

This is the period where educational, vocational and professional guidance all become important and should be integrated. They are also interdependent.

All the objectives of guidance elaborated earlier assume importance at this level. At this stage students have a number of options. These options are going for higher studies, taking up some technical courses, preparing for competitive examinations, looking for various job opportunities on regular basis as well as on part time basis, exploring the institutions for further education suiting their finances, etc. This is a transitional period from school to college or school to world of work. They have to move out from structured and disciplined system of school education to a relatively free and independent atmosphere. While in school the progress of the students is monitored, at college level the individuals are responsible for their own performance. They are also considered as grown ups and different kind of behaviours in adjustments are expected from them. Professional assistance is especially important at this stage. The guidance worker should provide information about a wide range of educational, vocational and technical courses, list of institutions about the availability of these courses, their eligibility conditions, their preparations on one hand, the specific attitudes, aptitudes and personality characteristics of each individual on the other. The counsellor should also provide a wide range of information about the occupational fields available for students, the eligibility conditions, the entry, the remuneration and perks, progress in an occupation and information about the way of life that would be available with the choice of an occupational field. For example, if a student is opting for a medical occupation he should be guided about the life style of a doctor. There are no time limits for work in this profession and he may have to visit the patients even during the nights. On the other hand, a teacher's profession may be according to the school timings. The counsellor has to collect and collate the information about various educational courses and vocational opportunities. The collection, compilation and dissemination of information is a technical task which should be done by the counsellor in an authentic manner and the information should be updated from time to time. The counsellor has to be vigilant about the changes in the job market and should be able to guide the students accordingly. The details on how to collect and disseminate the information and also the types of information have been discussed in an other chapter of this book.

Specific Function of Guidance at Senior Secondary Level

- Help students in their transition from school to work.
- Assist students in exploring and knowing world of work.
- Help them in matching themselves with the world of work.
- Help in making right choices.
- Assist students in preparing themselves for higher education, skill development and for specific occupations.
- Assist students to excel in their field.
- Help them in exploring their personality and attitudes.
- Help them in developing desired attitudes and behaviours.
- Help them in knowing the institutions that provide financial assistance.
- Help in solving their personal-emotional and social problems.
- Help in developing a future course of action.

Role and Functions of Counsellor

The role and functions of a counsellor or guidance worker may vary according to the purpose, setting and target group. For example in a community setting where a couple has approached the counsellor, regarding a problem in their marriage. The counsellor's efforts would be to help the couple to resolve their problems in marriage. On the other hand, the role of the counsellor in a school setting would focus more about helping the individuals in choosing a right kind of career according to their capabilities, aptitudes, interests etc. The discussion in the following paragraphs would be restricted to the role of the counsellor keeping in view the school setting.

In general, the intervention by a counsellor would be remedial, preventive or developmental depending upon the need and problems of the people. It can aim at individual, some individuals, associated groups or the settings and systems that are affecting the individual behaviour. Arthur, J.J. (1941) has defined the term school counsellor in the following manner:

"The term "School Counsellor" is used to indicate the personnel or worker whose chief responsibility is to stimulate, initiate, develop and coordinate the guidance work of the entire school. He will, in many schools, also perform some or more forms of specialised guidance service; what this is will be determined by the type of organisation of the guidance activities in the school and the type of other personnel available. He must act as guidance leader and as a resource person in the school and should have superior qualifications and training for the task. In many schools he will be the only personnel worker and be directly responsible for the entire guidance programme".

Many other experts have analysed the role of a counsellor based on research studies. Bailey stated that personal advisement, planning and supervision, making community contacts; interpretation and application of tests, planning and supervision of extracurricular activities are the duties of a counsellor. Cox, on other hand, analysed the functions of 100 selected counsellors and classified the same as: (a) work with parents (b) educational-vocational-emotional guidance of pupils (c) supervision of tests – giving and interpreting test results (d) Cooperation with law-enforcing agencies (e) consultation with employers, (f) discipline (g) placement (h) coordinating the guidance programme of the school (i) home-room supervision (j) cooperation with community guidance agencies (k) teaching (l) chaperoning parties (m) follow-up of pupils who left school.

Tooker (1957) detailed the following as the functions of a counsellor.

1. First of all, he is an educator.
2. He has direct responsibility for individual counselling of students assigned to him.
3. He often has responsibility for group methods in guidance.
4. He is expected to establish relationships with great numbers of individuals, so that students will come to identify him as a person to whom they can turn for advice and help within the school setting.
5. He is expected to be familiar enough with standardised tests of intelligence, achievement, aptitude, interest and personality so that he can utilise test results in the process of counselling

6. He is often given considerable responsibility in arranging transfers of students for both academic and personal reasons.
7. He is called upon to help in such important projects as building and maintaining cumulative record systems.
8. He is often expected to conduct follow-up studies of graduates and dropouts.
9. It is not unusual for him to be asked to function as a resource person in such educational projects as the setting up of systems of reporting to parents.
10. He is usually expected to know current college admission procedures and to serve as adviser to both parents and students in this area.
11. He is expected to participate in school activities and to assume his share of extracurricular activities.
12. He is expected to maintain a knowledge of and working relationships with local business and industry so that he may be in a better position to counsel students in the area of local vocational offerings.
13. He is often expected to help in the sponsoring of guidance-related activities such as college nights, career days, and guidance committees.
14. He is frequently called upon to provide leadership in broad areas where guidance aspects may seem remote.

In practice, one counsellor may do all the activities by himself or may do some activities depending upon the objectives and needs of students.

To summarise, the role of a counsellor may be as described on the following lines.

1. Counsellor as a Consultant: In a role of a Consultant, a counsellor has to interact with teachers, parents, support groups of the individual and other systems, which are influencing the individual.
2. Counsellor as a Coordinator: A counsellor has to coordinate from time to time with the other agencies which the students may need to approach from time to time, such as the employers, the hospitals, the employment exchanges, etc.
3. Counsellor as an Orientor: As an Orientor, the role of a counsellor is to gradually inform the pupil about the world of work, to help them in developing adjustment skills and creating an environment where the pupils could have positive experience of education and learning. Orientation of guidance services is of utmost importance.
4. Counsellor as Assessor: The counsellor has to assess the individual as well as his environment. Assessment of individual includes his

academic achievements, aptitudes, interests, abilities, personality traits etc. while environment includes his family background, cultural and social roots and other factors that influence child's behaviour.

5. Counsellor as a Developer: A counsellor has to lay a strong foundation on which every pupil, specially at elementary school level, could develop himself in the desirable direction. At elementary stage, children have very little exposure to the world of work. If they have seen a teacher, milkman, or a postman at home, their choice would be to become the same in future. It is the responsibility of the counsellor to provide children a greater exposure to various avenues of work. At later stages also, his role as a developer is significant in terms of providing placement services, counselling for problems, helping the students in developing an insight to solve their problems. Career guidance becomes more important at secondary school level. The counsellor may also have to deal with adolescence problems of the students, inter-personal adjustments, etc.

Characteristics of a Counsellor

Efforts have been made to list the characteristics of the counsellors that could make them effective in carrying out the functions of guidance. Bailey listed these characteristics as:

1. A sympathetic understanding of youth
2. Emotional Stability
3. Approachability
4. Broad scope of knowledge and interests
5. Good judgement and common sense

The Committee of National Vocational Guidance Committee (1941) listed 12 characteristics:

1. A stable and well adjusted personality
2. A high degree of intellectual capacity
3. A fundamental liking for persons
4. A sympathetic and objective understanding of people
5. Facility in establishing wholesome, effective, personal and social relations, including ability to work cooperatively with other people
6. Ability to stimulate students and colleagues and to challenge their best efforts in working for ends that they come to accept as desirable
7. Perspective – ability to see and understand the total situation and the separate parts in relation to the whole

8. An understanding and appreciation of one's own limitations in dealing with certain areas of problems and with certain individuals
9. Broad general knowledge and wide interests
10. An understanding of classroom conditions, teaching responsibilities and pupil-teacher relationships
11. An understanding of working conditions and employee-employer relationships in jobs outside of educational work or in non-professional vocational life
12. Understanding of social and economic conditions and influences – general and local

Rogers, in 1942, listed five characteristics of a counsellor. They included (1) sensitivity to human relationships, (2) objective attitude and an emotionally detached attitude, (3) respect for the individual, (4) understanding of himself, and (5) knowledge of human behaviour.

Parsons stated that vocational counsellor should have

1. A practical working knowledge of the fundamental principles and methods of modern technology.
2. An experience involving sufficient human contact to give him an intimate acquaintance with human nature in a considerable number of its different phases; he must understand the dominant motives, interests, and ambitions that control the lives of men, and be able to recognise the symptoms that indicate the presence or absence of important elements of character.
3. Ability to deal with young people in a sympathetic, earnest, searching, candid, helpful and attractive way.
4. A knowledge of requirements and conditions of success, compensation, prospects, advantages, and disadvantages, etc., in the different lines of industry.
5. Information relating to courses of study and means of preparing for various callings and developing efficiency therein.
6. Scientific method – analysis and principles of investigation by which laws and causes are ascertained and facts are classified.

To sum up, a counsellor should be able to establish harmonious and trustworthy relationship with the students so that they could trust the counsellor and confide their problems. He should be accepting, listening, understanding and helping. He should be emotionally stable and mature to be able to deal the problems. He should also be intelligent enough to coordinate with various people, persons and agencies. He should also have good communication skills and knowledge of group dynamics.

Establishment of Career Resource Center

Guidance can be imparted to students in an effective manner only if the guidance worker has a proper place to sit with sufficient privacy to enable discussion in confidence, and adequate space to organise, store and display the information, and students know where and how to meet the guidance worker. Thus, there is a need for a 'career corner' or a 'Career Resource Centre'. Professional services can be provided from this Centre. In a school, such a Center should be established with the help of teachers. One room alongwith a hall may be sufficient for this purpose, where career information may be displayed, computers may be kept where students could come and explore the information. Group activities may be organised in the hall and individual counselling sessions may be held in the counsellor's room. The Career Resource Centre should be at a place, which is relatively noise-free and free from unnecessary movement of the students. For example, if it is near the canteen, too much noise or movement may interrupt the guidance activities. It is not that the guidance worker has to operate only from this Centre. He has to move out and interact with the students in the regular classes assigned for guidance activities to minimise the distance between himself and the students. Students would come to the Resource Centre only when they would feel that the guidance worker is a part of the school and their school life. Attractive display of material in the Resource Centre can catch the attention of the students. Career Resource Centre thus should be properly maintained, usable and reachable. Some times such Centre can be opened in one big school in the area that can cater to needs of other schools in the vicinity, as all the schools may not be having adequate resources.

To run a Career Resource Centre and meet the needs of the students, cooperation from Principal and teachers is imperative. They should understand the importance of these services. At many places where principals and teachers are not oriented properly, the feeling is that while teachers are given a regular time table with 20 classes a week plus other activities, the counsellor has no regular work to do. Besides orienting about the guidance activities, it is the duty of the counsellor to plan the guidance programme for the whole year with a number of activities. The programme should be shared with teachers and displayed properly.

There may be occasions where counsellor has to meet with the parents. Teachers and the individual student should be taken into confidence. Outcomes of the guidance activities performed from time to time should be shared with teachers and their assistance should be sought. Students should be asked to give their views and ideas to make the Career Resource Centre more effective and goal-oriented. In preparing posters and charts students should be involved.

Such Career Resource Centres are of utmost importance even outside the school at community level. In some Employment Exchanges, such centres have been established but due to paucity of resources and negative attitudes, these are not very effective. In schools also, sometimes counsellors are asked to take subject classes instead of guidance activities. There are also private counsellors who have started guidance activities on their own and charge high fees, which most of the students may not be able to afford.

The Budget for Guidance

Finances are required to initiate and implement a guidance programme-initially to acquire fixed assets (furniture, computer, display boards etc), to purchase psychological assessment tools and preparation of audio-visual aids, and later on for implementing the day to day guidance activities. The guidance worker should prepare a tentative budget for starting and implementing the activities for a year and communicate it to the principal. The guidance of the latter may be taken at this planning stage also. The staff required and the salaries to be paid out of the guidance budget should also be included in the guidance budget. Some indicative Heads of Expenditure in the guidance budget are discussed below;

- Staff: Besides counsellor himself at least two persons are required to assist him. The staff requirement would vary according to the number of children in the school to be attended to. In some schools, there is a prevision to train one of the subject teachers to help the counsellor in guidance activities. Such teachers are known as career masters. And they devote some of their fixed time for such activities. Special salary increments are admissible to such teachers. Staff requirements should be worked out taking into account the availability of such career masters.
- Space and Equipment: The tentative budget should provide estimates of expenditure on establishment of career resource centre, purchase of equipment like projector, lighting system, audio system, raw material for preparing audio-visual aids and furniture and arrangement for group activities. Experience indicates that school administrations normally do not have enough resources to afford a large budget for the guidance activities. Therefore, planning and budgeting of guidance activities should

be conservative with limited essentials to start with. If the programme is effective, school authorities may get motivated to invest larger sums for the purpose.

- Guidance material: Guidance material has to be collected, prepared and disseminated. The budget must provide for this. There are publications that are free of cost. Some more material can be acquired as complimentary if the guidance worker has good rapport with the agencies. Help of voluntary organisations can also be taken in the preparation of the material. Innovation can reduce the cost of guidance programme.

  Material required for the psychological assessment is costly but is essential. It is, however, one-time expenditure. Printing the answer sheets at local level can effect some saving. Record maintenance through computers may also limit the expenditure in the long run.
- Group activities: Some group activities such as organisation of career exhibitions or career conferences would require additional budget. Such activities may be planned and arranged for a cluster of schools wherever possible to optimise resources. It would be possible sometimes to get employers and voluntary agencies like Rotary clubs to sponsor such group activities.

Features of a Good Guidance Programme

A good guidance programme may be planned and executed only when the guidance worker understands the basic concepts underlying the guidance services, its principles and the processes. The objective of the guidance programme must be fully defined and understood, the target groups must be identified and accordingly a detailed programme should be drawn up. The following are the features of a good guidance programme.

1. The principle of the guidance programme is that it should be designed to serve all the people according to their needs in the process of their growth. That means, any programme, which is worked out, should have continuity and should address the needs of all. A good guidance programme will help each person to develop himself to his fullest capabilities. This full development of the individual should also be linked with the development of the society and individual should be able to help others. Here, it may be noted that some individuals might be having capabilities, which are not socially desirable. These capabilities are to be channelised in the right direction so as to be beneficial to others and not harming anyone. The benefits to the society and others are relative which

may vary according to the traditions and values of the society and culture.

2. Each person requires guidance services at some or the other time of his life. It could be during childhood, adolescence, adulthood or old age. A guidance programme should incorporate the services which may meet the needs of the individuals of all ages whenever they need them. In case the guidance programme being executed in the school is not incorporating the needs of the old people, the guidance worker should keep the information about the services available for this age group outside the school system.
3. Any guidance programme should be able to deal with varying kinds of problems. It is common to hear statements like 'he is a gone case', or 'nothing can be done for this child as he is totally mischievous' or 'he is not capable of doing anything'. In guidance services there is no scope for such statements. Each and every individual has his own strengths and limitations. Each child varies from the other in the manner of his expressions of his feelings. A guidance programme should accept each individual with his strengths and weaknesses and should be able to make an intervention programme that would lessen their weaknesses and develop their strength. The guidance worker should not keep any prejudices against any child.
4. There are cases where counsellors are in a hurry, as they have to cater to the needs of many. Group activities and guidance may not always be a substitute for individual attention. A guidance programme should be worked out in such a way that the counsellor is able to pay individual attention to the students, wherever required. The identification of needs and problems of the individuals is extremely essential. It should be a part of a good guidance programme.
5. A number of services have to be included in a good guidance programme. In most of the cases the guidance workers feel that educational and vocational guidance services is the major activity. But in the current socio-economic scenario, other services like placement, follow up, evaluation, counselling, etc., are equally important and should get a place in a good guidance programme.
6. The guidance programme should be based on the local requirements and the local resources available. The programme would vary according to the environment, the level of development and the nature of population in the local area.

7. A guidance programme should keep in mind that the services are not meant for helping the child for his immediate problem only. While providing the services, the counsellor should see the individual as a whole alongwith his background and environment, and, the aim of guidance should be the overall development of the individual. The individual should be helped in such a way that he is able to solve his future problems also.
8. The guidance work is a teamwork. The help of all the persons who could contribute in the guidance services should be taken to make the program effective.
9. Education and guidance are complementary to each other. Both go hand in hand and neither of these two should hamper the development of the individual.
10. A guidance programme should help the individuals to make their own decisions. In most of the cases parents or friends decide for children what occupation they should choose in future. Sometimes, the guidance worker also persuades the child to choose a particular kind of occupational field. This is not the correct way of guidance. The counsellor should be able to provide the detailed information to the child and the options available to him, as well as to the parents and an atmosphere should be created where the child is able to take his own line of action.
11. In a good guidance programme, the choice of a good guidance worker is important. The guidance worker should be responsible, capable and fully trained. The qualities of a good guidance worker have been discussed. However, it is pertinent to mention that the guidance worker should follow professional ethics. He becomes a role model and, therefore, he should be totally unbiased as well as competent.
12. A guidance programme can be effective only when it is conceived well and implemented well. The basic guidelines for administration of a guidance programme are:
    - To obtain and organise systematically the information about each individual, for example Cumulative Record Cards.
    - Guidance budget should be planned.
    - Time scheduling and time management should be worked out.
    - Appropriate place should be available for guidance activities.
    - Resources that can help in guidance services should be tapped and mapped.
    - There should be a liaison of the guidance programme with other community agencies.

- Appropriate material for guidance activities should be prepared and disseminated properly.
- Adequate publicity should be made so that each and all should know about the guidance activities.

Resources for Guidance and their Role in a Guidance Programme

The guidance counsellor alone cannot implement a guidance programme. The cooperation from various people in the school and the agencies outside is imperative. Even otherwise there are stakeholders who will have their impact in the guidance services directly or indirectly. For example, when a child is being counseled his parents may have to be taken in confidence for a number of purposes. A guidance programme in a school cannot be successful if the principal is not in favour of these services. There are many instances where the guidance worker could not enlist the cooperation from the principal and was asked to teach the normal subjects in the school than prepare and execute the guidance activities. Similarly, there are various services in a guidance programme which require contacts with other agencies. These could be referral services where a child has to be referred to some hospital or the doctor. For placement of the students a guidance worker needs the cooperation from employers. Again, there are mass media like newspapers, T.V, radio, etc., all of which contribute in guidance activities. These are termed as information resources. The third category of resources may be of energy resources. These may include groups, organisations or individuals who may like to spare money time or other resources available with them for the guidance activities. All these play an important role in the implementation and effectiveness of a guidance programme.

There can be two types of resources, one relating to the school and other outside—the school resources and community resources.

1. Resources Available in School

The Principal: the principal is the main administrator and is "the key person in the whole situation, and how he works will determine the success of his efforts" (Schwartz – 1953), The principal of the school needs orientation about the guidance services. The methodology of the orientation would differ according to the level and the geographical area. For example in an urban school the principal may be well versed with the guidance activity or the principal of a secondary school might be knowing the principles of a guidance services, while in case of the principal of a rural school or the principal of an elementary school the situation might be different. But in all cases their cooperation has to be sought for the proper functioning of a guidance programme. If the principal is cooperative he can provide a place to the guidance counsellor to set up a Career Resources Centre. He may provide the time to the guidance worker for organising his activities within the school time table. The principal is also responsible to provide the budget for guidance activities. The principal can also convince the teachers and the parents about the importance of the guidance activities so that the counsellor may get cooperation from the staff and the parents. A principal, who is in the school for a long time, may also help the guidance worker to make contacts with the community resources. In case the principal is busy he can depute another person to help the guidance worker as and when required.

The Teachers: The teachers directly interact with the students most of the time and therefore they can be a major source of information. The students also develop a special relationship with the teachers, specifically in the elementary school where most of the time one teacher remains in the class. The teacher is the key person who can also help the counsellor by providing the data for preparing Cumulative Record Cards. He may be mediator between the counsellor and the parents and provide information about the academic achievements of children. Teachers can be a resource for collecting information from various other sources. For example, the teachers in one school may refer the counsellor to their counterparts in other schools where guidance services are not available and the guidance worker is supposed to cater to the needs of the students in those schools also. The teachers can also assist in group guidance activities like preparation of the posters and charts. In this activity the help of art and drawing teacher may be had for hobby clubs or preparing the models. The assistance from music teacher and of the science teacher may also be taken. The teachers can also refer the students who need individual counselling for their undesirable behaviours or special problems in their school achievements. The teachers can interact with the counsellor on the issues of slow learners, first generation learners, the gifted children, the physically handicapped etc. Teachers can be helpful in evaluation of the guidance programme as well as the follow up services.

The Doctor: Generally all the schools have the services of a qualified doctor. Counsellor should maintain a good relationship with the doctor in order to refer the students who require health check up or in need of some medical help. In such cases, the advice of the school doctor may be had and the child may be referred to a clinic or hospital outside in case of need. A regular health check up programme of the students may be worked out in consultation with the doctor as many times neither the teachers nor the parents are able to identify the problems of the children relating to health. In other cases the doctor may provide the information about the health status of the children to the counsellor for health related guidance. The children with malnutrition may be identified and referred to the doctor for a diet advice. The health related information about the children in the Cumulative Record Card might be filled up with the help of the doctor.

The Librarian: A Librarian is a trained person who is well versed with the filing and dissemination of the information. His help may be taken by the counsellor for the career information services. The librarian may also help in collection of the information from various sources by writing letters to the concerned organisations, preparing the reference cards, displaying the material and preparation of career books. The school library may also be having lot of information that can be useful for the guidance worker. For example, the annual reports of the organisations which provide information about the employment trends, the apprenticeship training, the Five Year Plan documents, the reports of the committees and other literature. If the counsellor has a harmonious relationship with the librarian he can gather the information relevant for guidance activities from these documents easily. Sometimes, the space available in the library may also be utilised for guidance activities, if necessary.

The Other Personnel: The other non-teaching staff like a bus driver, canteen personnel may be helpful in providing information about the children's eating habits, the behaviour with the peer group, cooperation with others, etc.

2. Resources Available Out of School

There are a large number of resources available in the community, which can be helpful for guidance activities. A guidance worker should be able to explore these resources and should be able to ensure their cooperation. These resources are:

1. *The Parents*: The first communication of the child is with parents which continues even after the child leaves the school. Home is the place where behaviours of the child are formulated and his personality develops. The parents and the home have a lasting impact on the child's personality. Parents can be a good source about providing valuable information about the child. Parents know the various limitations of their children, their problems in the growth process and the limitations of the home. The parental involvement may be extremely helpful in identifying the problems of the children. The parent's help can also be taken to resolve these problems. There are cases

where parents need counselling to deal with their children. These areas can be over authoritativeness of the parents, lack of control, imposing their own interest on the children and so on.

The parents can also provide health-related information about the child. Moreover, when the child is referred to any clinic or hospital, parents have to be taken with the child to the hospital.

2. *Employment Exchange:* The role of Employment Exchanges has been discussed in detail in the chapter dealing with the functioning of the State agencies. Employment Exchanges not only can provide information about the registration, guidance and procedures but can also provide a lot of career literature/material. A field visit to the Employment Exchange can also orient the children to the employment market. Experts from there may be called for class talks. Some group guidance activities may be organised in collaboration with the Employment Exchanges. School visits are, in fact, a part of the guidance activities of the Employment Exchanges.

3. *The Employers*: The placement services in a guidance programme are based on the cooperation from the employers. A guidance worker should list out the employers in the vicinity, their activity, their needs for skills, the shortages, their expansion plans and future requirements of personnel. The employers can also be called to interact with the students. Field visits may be organised to the industries in case the counsellor has good rapports with the employers. During the Rozgar Melas and the career conferences, the employers may be requested to interact with the students.

4. *The Hospitals*: Interaction with the hospitals in the area is necessary for referral services in the guidance programme. For health related problems, the guidance worker may send the child to the appropriate place for health check up and advice. These can be social welfare clinics, the general hospitals and the mental health clinics.

5. *The Clubs and Other Creative Organisations:* For development of the creativity in the children and for a better use of leisure time available with the children, the counsellor should keep a track of the youth organisations, hobby clubs and other community agencies that can be helpful for the development of the children. For example, SPIC – MACAY is one organisation that motivates youth to take to classical music. Similarly, the YMCA, the YWCA, the sports clubs, the health clubs, the GYMs are some of the organisations that can be a resource for the guidance services

6. *Banks and other Vocational Institutions:* Association with banks and other institutions that can provide financial assistance to the children is also an asset. The needy children may be referred to these organisations. There are several related organisations also that provide financial assistance to the needy

children. Scholarship facilities are given to the good achievers and poor people. A guidance worker should maintain association with all such resources.

7. *The Educational Institutions and Libraries*: The information has to be collected for educational and vocational guidance from various educational institutions as they have the prospectuses on the dealing courses. Interaction should be had with all such institutions, departments, universities, and other agencies like Bureaus of Guidance, University Grants Commission and International Organisations that help for admissions outside like British Council, US Council.

Community libraries and groups also organise career activities from time to time. Moreover, a substantial literature is also available with the libraries located outside the school. All such resources should also be taken into account by a guidance worker.

8. *The Computers*: The computer and the Internet is a modern resource providing a lot of information to the guidance programme. There are several web-sites dealing with careers, and educational and job-opportunities. The guidance worker may use the computer as tool. Some of the sites which can be useful for the guidance worker have been listed in the chapter on Guidance Services in India.

Moreover, career information can be organised systematically on a computer system using 'menu-driven' approach, for easy access to the students.

Fig. 12.1: Resources for Guidance Services

- Resources in School

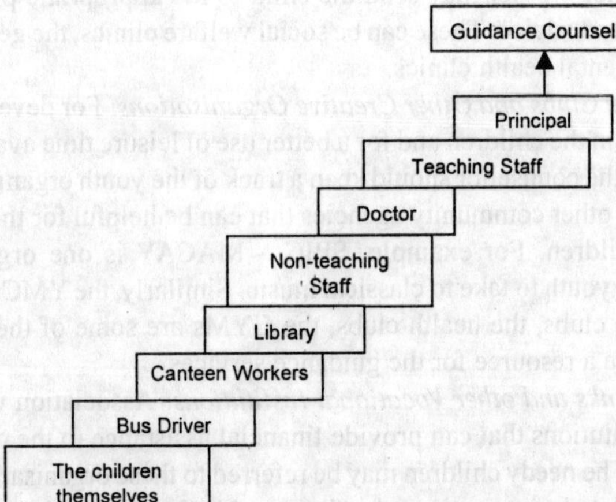

- Resources Outside School

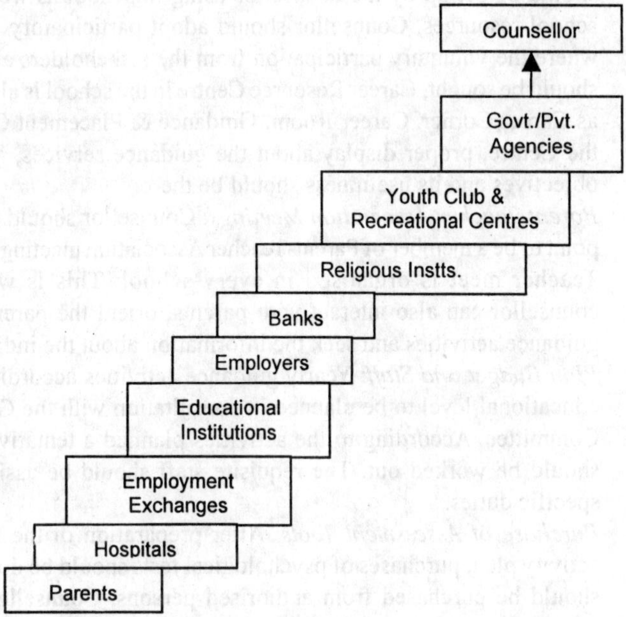

An Action Plan

A tentative action plan for guidance services in schools is proposed as below:

- *Constitution of Guidance Committee*: Counsellor should constitute a Guidance Committee consisting of some members from the school and some from outside. From the school, the Committee may have the Principal or his nominee, one teacher interested in guidance work, Officer from Employment Exchange, one or two representatives of Employers/Banks, one or two representatives from parents group, representative of students and one or two other experts from the Community. The main policy issues and guidance services should be discussed during the meetings of this Committee. The number of members in the Committee should not be very large. The ideal number may between 6 to 10. The Quarterly or half-yearly meetings may be organised. Before organising such meeting the agenda of the meeting, should be prepared and circulated to all members of the Committee in advance.

- *Setting up of a Career Resource Centre*: A Career Resource Centre should be set up by the counsellor using in-school as well as out-school resources. Counsellor should adopt participatory approach where the voluntary participation from the stakeholders and others should be sought. Career Resource Centre in the school is also named as Career Corner. Career Room, Guidance & Placement Centre. In the Centre, proper display about the guidance services, activities, objectives and its usefulness should be there.
- *Parent-Teacher Association Meetings*: Counsellor should make it a point to be a member of Parent-Teacher Association meetings. Parent-Teacher meet is organised in every school. This is where the counsellor can also interact with parents, orient the parents about guidance activities and seek the information about the individuals.
- *Plan Budget and Staff*: Yearly guidance activities according to the educational level to be planned in consultation with the Guidance-Committee. According to the activities planned a tentative budget should be worked out. The requisite staff should be assigned the specific duties.
- *Purchase of Assessment Tools*: After preparation of the guidance activity plan, purchases of psychological tests should be done. Tests should be purchased from authorised persons. Counsellor should ensure that the tests are applicable for the Indian population and norms are available for comparability and making decisions.
- *Record Maintenance*: Record maintenance is another important activity which is a must for the counsellor. Separate records should be maintained for each guidance activity/services. For example for orientation services a register may be maintained detailing the activities organised, dates, the target group, the place, the outcome and the feedback. Similarly for other services, separate files/registers should be maintained. Under counselling services detailed record of each counselling case with the dates of interviews should be kept. Such records may be maintained using Computers also.

Some Suggested Activities

1. *Elementary Level:*
   - Orientation of students with the school and guidance
   - Group activities to develop sense of cooperation and sharing, develop learning habits, adjustment with school and peers
   - Tips to give them a feel of occupations
   - Activities to develop their creativity

- Identify problems of the students and take remedial measures
- Help in developing the personalities of the students

2. *Educational Level and Activity*: Class VI:
   - Collection of information and preparation of Cumulative Record Card
   - Orientation of students about guidance activities and school
   - Orientation of parents about guidance services and school
   - Administration of Intelligence Test and preparation of results
   - Monitoring the academic progress according to the intelligence levels – Identification of slow-achievers and communicating this to teachers to organise special programmes for slow-achievers.

Some Topics for Class Talks:

- How to do Home work
- Choosing a leisure-time activity
- How to improve study habits
- Steps to improve 'Climate of learning'
- Concept of occupations
- Developing good habits

Except class talks other group activities may be chosen

- Counselling: Identified problem cases or those referred by teachers should be provided counselling.
- Meetings with teachers and parents whenever necessary

3. *Class VII and VIII* may include Orientation of new students and their parents, introduction of concepts of self-understanding, field-trips for orienting the students towards technical courses may be organised. Potential dropouts may be identified and helped. Weak students to be identified and their remedial programmes may be organised.
   Topics for Talks/Discussion
   - Training Courses after VIII
   - How to develop self-confidence
   - Hobbies and their importance
   - How to prepare for Examinations
   - How to improve academic performance
4. *Class IX and X*:
   - Orientation of students and parents
   - Preparation of Cumulative Record Card if not already available/ updating of information
   - Administration of Psychological tests, preparation and communication of results

- Identification of under-achievers and potential dropouts
- Counselling of problem cases
- Meetings with parents whenever necessary
- Discussions with teacher
- Organisation of Career Exhibition and Career Conference
- Field trips, Creativity activities
- Educational & Vocational Information

Some suggested topics for Class/Career Talks

- Educational options after X
- Vocational options after X
- Entrance Examinations
- Technical Courses after X
- Competitive examination for jobs and preparation
- Importance of choosing a right career
- How to improve decision making
- How to contact and utilise the resources available
- Financial Assistance
- Importance of Self-employment

5. *Class XI and XII:*
   - Orientation of new students and their parents
   - Cumulative Record Card and Updating of information
   - Psychological testing programme, preparation and discussion of results
   - Remedial measures for weak students
   - Information about world of work, courses, skill development programmes
   - Organisation of Career Conference, Exhibition, field trips, film shows, interaction with successful candidates
   - Financial and other Community resources
   - Understanding, accepting and development of self
   - Counselling of problem cases
   - Parents guidance
   - Organisation of interactional programmes with employees/Banks personnel etc.

Suggested topics

- Role of employment exchanges
- Banks and credit institutions
- How to match yourself with the world of work
- Educational/Technical streams after XII

- Options after XII
- How to prepare for Competitive exams
- Time Management
- Learning habits
- Importance of choosing a right career
- How to appear in interviews
- Importance of physical fitness
- How to deal with failures

Time Scheduling

Orientation activity should be started immediately after opening of the school but after settling of the students. It may be planned during the first month of the school. Preparation of CRCs and assessment of students may be started from the second month. During this time individuals with specific problems should be identified. Other activities may be planned for the whole year according to the time availability, seeing the budget constraints and needs of the students.

Follow up and evaluation of the programme should be done on concurrent basis or after 6 months of implementation. Yearly assessment of the effectiveness of the services should also be done. Some services under guidance provide immediate results while some take time. Therefore a schedule of evaluation should be decided in consultation with the guidance Committee.

13

Career Choice and Vocational Development

Ginzberg (1972) stated that the choice of vocation and development is a life long process as individuals continue to seek and get the jobs most suitable for themselves. He, however stressed on the importance of the effect of school years on career planning. Blau, Gustad, Gessor, Parnes and Wilcock (1956) also emphasised that the choices of occupations are modified continuously. They argued that there are eight factors which determine the choice of an occupation. These are demands of the occupation, technical qualifications, personal qualifications and rewards. The other four characteristics relate to the individual's information about a particular job, technical skills, social characteristics and value orientation.

The process of how children who are totally dependent on their parents during the childhood become fully independent and earn their living and become self-sufficient, attracted many researchers. Researcher were interested in knowing how this process takes place. How does a child become economically independent? How and why different people choose different working activities? Even in the same family, why is it that one child becomes a businessman while the other an engineer? To provide answers to these questions, various scholars developed their models known as approaches to or theories of vocational development.

Trait and Factor Theories

Under this group of theories, the role of individuals' traits in choosing a career has been emphasised. It is believed that an individual has some traits that have vocational salience, which commensurate with the job demands. With the help of statistical techniques, these traits can be grouped into some basic factors of personality and be measured. When a counsellor assesses the student in the school through psychological measurements, he tries to match these characteristics with those of the job demands which he collects for various jobs and provides awareness about it to the student.

These theories are based on the premise that the choice of vocation is according to one's personality. It is a process of matching of personality traits with specific occupations. Under these theories, it is assumed that job satisfaction and sense of achievement are directly related to one's personality. The main proponent of the personality theory was Holland. His exposition of the theory is based on the following four assumptions.

1. Most persons can be categorised as one of six types: realistic, intellectual, social, conventional, enterprising, and artistic.
2. There are similarly six kinds of environments: realistic, intellectual, social, conventional, enterprising, and artistic.
3. People search for environments and vocations that will permit them to exercise their skills and abilities, to express their attitudes and values, to take on agreeable problems and roles, and to avoid disagreeable ones.
4. A person's behaviour can be explained by the interaction of his personality and his environment.

This theory has been criticised on various grounds. For one, it is argued that the theory ignores the role of emotions in career choice. For example, people choose certain occupations not due to their traits but due to peer pressure, parents' demands or due to some other circumstances. Moreover, when one person is suitable for a number of jobs on the basis of traits, the theory does not explain how he chooses one from all these. It has also been seen that people with varying kinds of personalities are successful in the same job and persons of the same type of personality are choosing different kinds of jobs. Vocational choice also depends on the job opportunities. Even when a person has certain personality characteristics but if there are no jobs suiting to his personality, he has to look for some other job.

In spite of such criticisms, the theory has relevance in educational and vocational guidance as personality and traits of a person cannot be ignored.

Developmental Theories

The developmental theories consider vocational development as a part of individual's development. Super was the proponent of this theory. His theory of vocational development is based on the following:

1. People differ in their abilities, interests, and personalities.
2. They are qualified, by virtue of these circumstances, each for a number of occupations.
3. Each of these occupations requires a characteristic pattern of abilities,

interests, and personality traits, with tolerances wide enough, however, to allow both some variety of occupations for each individual and some variety of individuals in each occupation.

4. Vocational preferences and competencies, and situations in which people live and work, and hence their self-concepts, change with time and experience (although self-concepts are generally fairly stable from late adolescence until later maturity), making choice and adjustment a continuous process.
5. This process may be summed up in a series of life stages, characterised as those of growth, exploration, establishment, maintenance and decline, and these stages may in turn be subdivided into (a) fantasy, tentative, and realistic phases of the exploratory state, and (b) the trial and stable phases of the establishment stage.
6. The nature of the career pattern (that is, the occupational level attained and the sequence, frequency, and duration of trial and stable jobs) is determined by the individual's parental socio-economic level, mental ability, personality characteristics, and by the opportunities to which he is exposed.
7. Development through the life stages can be guided partly by facilitating the process of maturation of abilities and interests and partly by aiding in reality testing and in the development of the self-concept.
8. The process of vocational development is essentially that of developing and implementing a self-concept; it is a compromise process in which the self-concept is a product of the interaction of inherited aptitudes, neural and endocrine make-up, opportunity to play various roles, and evaluation of the extent to which the results of role playing meet with the approval of superiors and fellows.
9. The process of compromise between individual and social factors, between self-concept and reality, is one of role playing, whether the role is played in fantasy, in the counselling interview, or in real life activities such as school classes, clubs, part-time work, and entry jobs.
10. Work satisfaction and life satisfaction depend upon the extent to which the individual finds adequate outlets for his abilities, interests, personality traits, and values; they depend upon his establishment in a type of work, a work situation, and a way of life in which he can play the kind of role which his growth and exploratory experiences have led him to consider congenial and appropriate.

The developmental theories are also known as life-span theories.

Career Pattern or Life Stages

Super (1967) defines a career as "the sequence of occupations, jobs and positions through out a person's working life." The Dictionary of social sciences defines the term career pattern as "a series of adjustments made to the institutions, formal organisations, and informal social relationships involved in the occupation or sequence of occupations which makes up the work history of a person or the group of person".

Super *et al* (1957) defined career pattern stating that "Most commonly, an individual's career pattern describes changes in the socio-economic level of the jobs held during his work life. The focus is not on success or satisfaction but on level that on movement as shown by jobs and job changes."

It may be seen from the definitions that career pattern refers not to a single job but to a series of jobs or positions, a person has during his life time. It also refers to horizontal and or vertical mobility. The social and economic status and the job success and satisfaction are linked with one's situations.

The term career pattern originated in the sociology discipline, and is synonymous with the concept of life stages in psychology. The career pattern is the sequence of occupations in the life of an individual. This is analysed in order to ascertain the major work periods which constitute a career. In psychological terms, Buchler (1933) divided the stages of vocational life into five periods.

		Age Group
1.	Growth stage	0-14
2.	Exploration stage	15-25
3.	Establishment stage	25-45
4.	Maintenance stage	45-65
5.	Decline	65 onwards

During the exploration stages, one tries to understand himself, tries to develop right and realistic attitudes towards work, and tries to find a place in the community. It is the stage of transition from fantasy to realism and from school to work.

In the establishment stage, one tries to enter and establish oneself at the place of work, plays a role in the family, home and community, tries to progress in the job.

Maintenance stage refers to the stability in the career one has chosen and finally, in the decline stage, one tries to settle down after retirement. It devotes to lessening of energy, family responsibilities and less activity.

It may be observed that these stages not only relate to one's vocational life but to all aspects of living.

In Indian situations this career pattern may not be applicable in its true sense. For example, many men may have to continue to work due to poverty even after retirement. Some others may be under-employed or unemployed and therefore may not be able to settle down in their careers. In case of women, career patterns may be disrupted due to marriage or children, while some may not work at all. There are single women who may work after the age of 65 to earn a livelihood. Opportunities for promotions or lack of it may also affect the career patterns.

Vocational Maturity

According to Super, "Vocational maturity is used to denote the degree of development, the place reached on the continuum of vocational development from exploration to decline… . The vocational maturity quotient may thus be conceived of as the ratio of vocational maturity to chronological age. It would indicate whether or not the vocational development of an individual is appropriate of his age…". The term 'vocational maturity' thus implies a comparison of one's chronological age and his vocational development age which may not be identical. The Vocational Maturity Coefficient (VMC) which is worked out as the ratio of vocational development age to his chronological age, measures this disparity. A child of chronological age of 14 years exhibiting vocational maturity of a 16 year old will have a VMC equal to 16/14.

Super's theory emphasises the role of self-control and vocational maturity in occupational choice. Sharf (1997) conducted some studies and found that life stages explained by Super do not always apply to women, as the role of women has changed in recent years.

Chance Theories

The Chance theories propound that people enter into an occupation due to chance. The occupational choice may be directed by an unforeseen factor. Hence it is not possible to analyse the factors that are responsible for the choice of the career. The main proponents of this theory are Caplow and Herr Cramer.

Hoppock tried to combine various theories of occupational choice, which could help the school counsellors. He stated that occupational choice is need based. These needs may be sudden attractions or intellectual needs of a person. The individual tries to match the needs with the information about the occupation. The individual's information about himself as well as information about the occupations helps a person to choose an occupation. Job satisfaction relates to the fact that whether the needs one feels are met with the choice of the occupation or not. Since the occupations are based on needs, the individual continuously look forward for a better occupation that may meet his needs better.

If a guidance worker understands the human development process and also the environmental factors that influence the occupation he can help a person in better career planning.

Other Theories

Ginzberg *et al.* (1951) put forward a theory that also comes under developmental theories. Their theory identifies four factors in occupational choice. These factors are: reality testing, educational process, the emotional factors and lastly the individuals values. The theory says that the individual compromises between his wishes and possibilities. The theory refers to three periods which are 'fantasy period', 'tentative period' and 'realistic period'. During the fantasy period, a child has no knowledge of reality. He fantacises various things which are far from the reality. The tentative period is the pre-adolescent and adolescent period. Here the child tries to make vocational considerations that are more realistic according to his skills. In the realistic period the ideas and choice of a career are crystallised and specific decisions take place. The theory refers to irreversible career development.

Roe's theory of career choice is based on the childhood experiences and genetic factors. The individual tries to combine these two to fulfill his needs. This theory includes need theory, the personality theory and the childhood experiences.

Social Learning theories of decision making (Krumboltz) emphasise the relationship between biological inheritance and role of environment. The characteristics of a person come into contact with environmental forces. Self-views are formed, which influence choice of career decision.

Importance of Choosing a Career

- Choosing a career at a right time according to one's potentials is important for job success and job satisfaction.
- Entering into a career through trial and error approach may cost time, energy and money.
- By choosing an appropriate career, one can determine his life style. If a person chooses a career as tourist guide, he would know that for most of the time during his career he has to be out of home. Similarly, in a job with call centres, there may be shift duties often during the nights.
- A career determines one's status in the society. People are known by

their occupation. For example Shri Sohan Lal, IAS, or Shri Ramesh Singh, a journalist and so on.

- Choice of career also determines the pattern of upward movement as well as mobility from one place to another. Some occupations require transfers to different places.
- Leisure and recreational activities depend upon choice of career. How much time is available for leisure depends on the place where one is posted and the kinds of recreational facilities available there.

Factors Influencing Choice of Careers

1. *Physical Factors*: In several occupations such as defence, police, security related occupations, physical characteristics like height, weight and general physical endurance matters. In some others, like driving occupations, proper eyesight is required. The factors relating to general physique like height, weight, eyesight, hearing, speech, general health, any handicap—all have a place in choosing a career.
2. *Psychological Factors*: These factors are interests, attitudes, aptitudes. general intelligence and personality characteristics. Wherever parents insist upon their children to take up a particular job in which the child himself is not interested, non-adjustment takes place. Many jobs also require particular types of personality traits. For example, for public relations job, a person should be outgoing and should have good communication skills. In the absence of these, one should not aspire for such occupation.
3. *Economic Factors*: These factors include the economic status of the family, and whether the family can afford the training and the education for the child to pursue a particular career. On the demand side, scope for employment, and self-employment future trends of economy, technical advancements, legislation, all have their influence.
4. *Social Factors*: Traditions and cultural influences, social obligations, social needs and demands make an impact on the choice of career.
5. *Family Factors*: Parents outlook towards various jobs and their influence on the child, family status, parental aspirations, obligations towards family, needs of the family, family circumstances for taking up occupations outside city or country where family is residing, are some of the factors that are responsible in career choice.
6. *Individual's Demands and Values*: These factors relate to the individual's demands from occupations. These include the monetary benefits, other perks, the social security, like pension etc., status of

the job, profits, independence to take decisions, outlets for self-expressions, etc.

7. *Other Factors*: Other factors such as who would take decision for the child, availability of information about various jobs, chance factors etc. also effect career choice.

Fig. 13.1: Factors of Carrer Choice

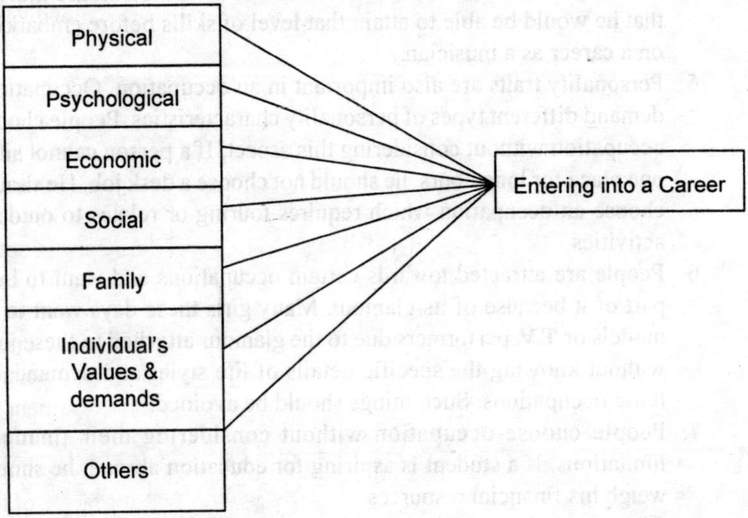

Mistakes in Choosing a Career

As has been discussed earlier, right choice of a career is important, as it determines the whole life pattern of an individual. A right choice leads to job satisfaction and ultimately satisfaction and happiness in life, while a wrong choice of career may put people in unending problems leading to frustrations and conflicts. Humphreys and Traxler have discussed about 10 general mistakes that people make in choosing a career. There are:

1. Individual chooses the occupation for which he does not have mental capabilities. Therefore, choice of career should be based upon one's capabilities.
2. People choose occupations which have limited employment potential. One should see that occupation he wants to take up has ample job opportunities.
3. People choose careers for which they are weak in its tool subject or

basic subject. A boy who is weak in spellings, comprehension, grammar, etc., should not choose a career in journalism or literature.

4. All occupations require a certain level of skills. Persons who cannot attain that level of performing skills sometimes choose those occupations. For example, to be a classical musician and performer one requires long duration of practice and a high level of skills. Even when a student is good in music, he should have extra-ordinary skills to be a performer in this field. Therefore, he should assure himself that he would be able to attain that level of skills before embarking on a career as a musician.
5. Personality traits are also important in an occupation. Occupations demand different types of personality characteristics. People choose occupation without considering this aspect. If a person cannot sit at one place for long hours, he should not choose a desk job. He should choose an occupation which requires touring or relates to outdoor activities.
6. People are attracted towards certain occupations and want to be a part of it because of its glamour. Many girls these days want to be models or T.V. performers due to the glamour attached to these jobs without knowing the specific details of life styles and demands of these occupations. Such things should be avoided.
7. People choose occupation without considering their financial limitations. If a student is aspiring for education abroad, he should weigh his financial resources.
8. Of late, everyone wants to go for computer related jobs without considering if there is a saturation of jobs in that field. There may be occupational fields where a lot of people with desired qualifications are already available.
9. Occupations are chosen by people without considering their physical strengths and capacities. For example, defense forces require good physique as well endurance and strength. One should weigh his own physical attributes before choosing such occupations.
10. Choice of career especially in India, depends upon the choice of parents. Children choose the occupation their parents want. If the parents are doctors, they want their child also to be a doctor ignoring the job demands and child's capacities. Such decisions should be avoided.

14

Job Analysis and Survey

In the chapter on Career Information a mention has been made about the direct and secondary sources of information about available educational and vocational opportunities. The information from secondary sources, *i.e.,* through printed material has its own limitations, as the same may be obsolete, biased, or not relevant to the ever-changing educational-vocational scenario. Therefore, it is necessary to collect the information from primary sources as much as possible, for it not only provides the authentic information but also the actual work situation in the organisation, *i.e.,* organisational culture, what type of workers are working and in what circumstances and what is the nature of activity. This collection of information from primary sources uses two techniques – job analysis and survey method. It may be clarified at the outset that these two approaches are not alternatives to each other. Their objectives and approaches are different, but both are useful in obtaining educational-vocational information.

(a) Job Analysis

Job analysis is a systematic technique of studying the jobs in which people are working. Shartle stated that "Job analysis is an intensive direct method of obtaining the pertinent facts about jobs." John A. Shibim said that "Job analysis is the methodical compilation and study of work data in order to define and characterise each occupation in such a manner as to distinguish it from all others."

These above definitions imply that the technique of job analysis involves collection of detailed information on aspects such as the detailed step by step operations involved in performing the job, the nature of duties and levels of responsibilities, and the levels of skills required. Further, aspects like remuneration, prospects of advancement and social security may also be covered in a job analysis.

Purposes of Job Analysis

The basic purposes of conducting the job analysis are as follows:

- To know the specifications of each job
- To identify the skills requirement of various jobs
- To make use of the above information to match the people according to their ability and skills with the jobs
- To plan training programmes for the people according to the job requirements
- To help the students to understand the nature of jobs
- To evaluate and collate the career information collected from various sources

How to Conduct Job Analysis

Job analysis requires prior preparation on the part of job analyser. The following steps may be followed.

1. A list of the jobs, which are to be studied, may be prepared.
2. The specific content and items, on which the information has to be collected, must be decided upon.
3. The sources of information are to be identified. The informants may include the incharge of organisation, the personnel managers, the employees, the supervisors, the trade unions, consumers of the product services and others who are in association with the organisation.
4. The methodology for job analysis should be worked out. This may include taking observations, information on questionnaire, discussion with those on the job in the organisation, interviews with some of the sampled employees and asking them to write about the jobs they are performing or other aspects as may be specified. No single method may be sufficient and more than one methods may have to be adopted. Methods recently developed include job psychographic method, individual psychographic method and motion study method. In the individual psychographic method, person successful on a job is tested and his mental capabilities are observed in a particular job, which he performs. This provides the information for assessing the requirement of the job because the qualities, which the successful person has, may be needed in future also. In the job psychographic method, three essential processes, *i.e.,* accurate classification of mental qualifies, valid method of evaluation and direct examination or analysis by trained examiners are included. In this technique, a specialist conducts the

job study and prepares the requirements of skills for the job. A graph is prepared which may be used to select the candidates in future. In the motion study method, observations are made on the operations performed in a job, speed of the worker and time taken to perform different operations. This is done on various individuals, norms are developed, and the workers are classified according to this study. Job analysis can also be done through using various tests and good performance qualities may be observed.

5. A job description schedule should be prepared on which the information collected may be recorded. A sample of the schedule is annexed.
6. Collect information through mailed schedules, organising interviews and other methods decided upon.
7. Scrutinise the collected information and collate the information collected from various sources.
8. Prepare the job specifications according to the collected information.
9. The report prepared may be discussed with the organisation for any amendment they consider necessary (a sample report is given for reference).

List of Items to be Covered in a Job Analysis

1. Job Name or title: It is always necessary to determine the correct title of a job. The title must be specific enough to differentiate the job from others and it should be specific enough to differentiate the job from others; it should be a title that has a common usage.
2. Classification title: Job names/titles may be different in different organisations. A classification title is one, which is a part of some standardised grouping of jobs or occupations. It should be included if one wishes to relate his analysis by a system of job or occupational classification.
3. Industry, Plant, department, division, section: These items identify where the job is found.
4. Number employed: Number employed on the job in each shift (and the number of women employed) should also be stated. This information is usually necessary, for the importance of the job depends in part on the number employed in it.
5. Hires, quits, job absences: A listing of the quits and the absences and the reasons for them has many uses. An estimate of the number of hires for the next three months or 6 months gives an indication of

future recruiting, selection and training problems and the possibilities of transfer within the plant.

6. Work performed: Is what the worker does, how he does (not why he does it) and with what tools and implements he does it.
7. The sequence of operations involved
8. Supervision given and received
9. Levels of difficulty: Indicates how complex the job is, what it takes on the part of workers in terms of responsibility, knowledge, initiative, mental alertness, judgment, accuracy, experience and education, etc., to perform the job.
10. Pay: rate and how it is determined. Other benefits, deduction and bonus, increment, etc.
11. House and shifts of work: The length of the work day and the work week and the hours for each shift.
12. Output standards: The standards of production for the job, and how these standards were devised and errors permitted.
13. Job combination and breakdown
14. Job relationship: How a job is related to others in the organisation. From which jobs inputs are received and to which jobs this job supplies inputs in each operation of the job.
15. Machine, Tools, equipment, material used.
16. Working conditions (physical).
17. Social environment: The nature of contacts with associates, customers, clinics, and the principal/pattern of relationship required, and the extent to which job proficiency depends upon team work.
18. Physical demands, hazards involved
19. Workers' characteristics
20. Previous experience required
21. Training required
22. Employment methods
23. Links with other jobs: Promotions from which jobs and promotions to which jobs.

How to Use the Information from Job Analysis

The information collected through job analysis may be utilised in the following manner:

- The results of job analysis will help improving the working methods and processes in a job, if required.

- Job analysis provides information on help and security measures available in the organisation for various jobs. These may be reviewed and feedback may be given to employers to modify the safety measures, if necessary.
- Job development programmes, *i.e.,* to match the skills available and skills required the training programmes may be worked out and job development activities may be organised.
- The information may be used for education and vocational guidance for the students to provide them a real picture of specific jobs and needs of the organisation.
- The information may be utilised for personnel selection and placement as the job analysis may be helpful in preparing the criteria for selection and placement of people.
- Technological development may be undertaken in the organisation on the basis of job analysis so as to reduce the time in performing the activities and reduce the drudgery.
- Non-productive activities of the organisation may be reduced.
- Wherever the job specifications are not available, organisations may be helped to specify the nature of jobs and duties.
- The information may be utilised for job evaluation to determine the relative utility of jobs. Accordingly, the wages, the salaries, social security measure, etc., may be fixed.
- Job analysis provides the data, which can help in preparing the standards of performance for each job. The performance of methods may be evaluated and accordingly the standards may be fixed.
- The job analysis is helpful in manpower planning—development and utilisation on one hand and organisational development on the other.
- Job analysis provides the essential input for developing a standard occupational classification.

Job Description

Job description is a part of total job analysis process. It has been defined as "the sum total of the facts relating to what is being done on the job and what type of employees are needed," (Dale Yoder). Pigores and Myres says, "Job description is a pertinent picture (in writing) of the organisational relationship, responsibilities and specific duties that constitute a given job or position. It defines a scope of responsibility and continuing work assignment that are sufficiently different from those of other jobs to warrant a specific title."

Thus, the job description provides detailed information about specific jobs. Jobs are divided into sub-jobs and the nature of duties of each is defined.

A job description should contain the following:

- The title of the job
- Job sub-titles
- Nature of duties of each sub-job
- Job location
- The responsibilities
- Amount of control
- Technology used
- Working conditions
- Promotions, rotations on the job
- Summary

These job descriptions should be prepared for each job. These descriptions should be short and to the point. These may be maintained as reference cards and be shared by counsellor with the students. The information contained in job description should be updated from time to time and factual information should be given. The analyst should not provide his own views during preparation of job description.

Job Specification

Flippo has defined job specification as a "statement of minimum acceptable human qualities necessary to perform a job properly." While job description provides detailed information about the job, job specification provides the information regarding the type of people required to perform the specific jobs. The job specification provides the following information:

- Qualification needed
- Experience required
- The specific skills needed to perform the job
- The personal qualities needed
- The aptitude and attitude to work in specified working conditions
- Other physical requirements

The job specifications can be prepared from the information collected through Job Analysis. It may be utilised to prepare students for specific jobs as well as to help employers to use as a tool for recruitment and placement.

A Sample of Job Study Schedule

Place:
Dated:

1. Name of the employee:
2. Name of Job (Designation):
3. Description of Job.
   (Whether Administrative/Executive/Managerial/Clerical/Supervisory/Selling/Servicing/etc. Mention some specific functions-for example maintaining Accounts/Auditing/Publicity/Public Relations, etc.
4. Name of the Employer:
   (Central Government/State Government/Autonomous Body/Government Undertaking/Local Body/Self-employment/Private
5. Name of the Department/Concern/Factory/Industry/Mill Office, etc. where working.
6. Place of Duty:
7. Nature of Job:
   (a) Whether Temp./Permanent/Part-time/Daily Wages/Seasonal
   (b) Whether Transferable/Non-transferable
   (c) Whether Touring/Non-touring/within the State/all over country/outside the country/Partly India/Partly outsider
   (d) On piece rate – wage rate
8. Duty hours & Holidays:
   (a) Duty hours: (Day/Night/Shift-Duty along with timings
   (b) No. of working hours: per day/per week
   (c) Holidays: (Week-end Holidays, other Holidays such as Vocations, Gazetted, Local)
9. Activity Analysis of Functions:

S. No.	*Exact Duty Performed*	*Time Spent*	*Education Required*	*Experience Required*	*Skills Required*	*Operations performed in the duty*
1.						
2.						
3.						

9(a) Technology, Machines/Raw Materials used in performing the job.

9(b) Relation with other jobs in the organisation:

(i) Work
   1. List of jobs whose outputs are inputs to the employee's job
   2. List of jobs to which the output of the employee is input.

(ii) Hierarchy: Jobs from which workers can be promoted/transferred to and from this job.

10. Working conditions:
   (a) Is the work place Dark/Damp/Drab/Stuffy/Hot/Cold/?
   (b) Is the work itself Heavy/Dirty/Unvaried/Dangerous/Solitary/?
   (c) Does it offer companionship/Teamwork/Independence/Rivalry/Prestige

11. Entry into the job, conditions for eligibility and mode of selection
    (a) Nationality/Domicile/Caste/Language
    (b) Age Limits
    (c) Minimum Qualifications Required/Training & Experience Possessed.
        (i) Academic Qualification
        (ii) Professional Qualification
        (iii) Training
        (iv) Experience:
    (d) Physical Standards:
        (i) Height
        (ii) Weight
        (iii) Chest
        (iv) Vision
        (v) Colour Vision
        (vi) Hearing
12. Personal Qualities: Required/Possesses
    (i) Physical: (a) Appearance (b) Physical Strength
    (ii) Mental: (a) Emotional Stability (b) Sense of Humour (c) Intelligence (d) Memory
    (iii) Behavioural: (a) Ability to get along with others (b) Leadership (c) Resourcefulness (d) Regularity (e) Punctuality (f) Tactfulness
13. Human Relations of the interviewee with his:
    (i) Superiors
    (ii) Juniors
    (iii) Colleagues
    (iv) Public/outsiders/Best/Good/Bad
    (v) Students/Trainees
14. Terms & Conditions of Service:
    (a) Pay Scale
    (b) Other benefits
        (i) Health Scheme
        (ii) Housing
        (iii) Children's Education Allowance
        (iv) Pension, P.F. Gratuity, Bonus, Insurance, D.A., HRA, CCA, Over-time Allowance, etc.
        (v) Leave & Leave Travel Concession
        (vi) Facilities for further education/training
    (c) Termination of service by employer/employee
    (d) Age of Retirement
15. Security of Service: (Whether secure or insecure)
16. Promotions:
    (a) Channel of promotions: Designations
    (b) Chances of Promotion: Automatic/Interview/Test
    (c) Attainments of the interviewee: Promotions obtained.
17. Responsibilities: (For safety of office Records, Equipment, Money & Building for the welfare of workers, etc.).
18. Occupational Hazards: (Danger to life/honour)
19. Job satisfaction of the interviewee: (Satisfied/dissatisfied)

20. Achievements & Failures of the interviewee:
21. Hobbies that are beneficial for the job
22. Yearly intake/Employment outlook:
23. Any other information not covered above.
24. Remarks

Signature of Interviewer

(b) Survey Method

Survey method is another technique, which helps in knowing about jobs in the vicinity. A number of jobs may be available in the area, which neither the students know nor the counsellor may be aware of. There may be new industries, new establishments and new employers who might be looking for prospective job seekers. Survey method is useful to identify the local job opportunities and the emerging occupations.. The survey may be got conducted with the help of teams of students. It not only provides the information about various jobs in the area but also helps students to have first hand experience about specific establishment or a number of establishments.

How to Conduct Survey

- Decide the area which has to be surveyed
- Prepare the teams of students who would cover the specified territories.

The area should be located near the school or the residence of the students or it should be the market area, industrial area or wherever there is possibilities of emerging occupations.

- Two persons may be included in each team
- A map of the area may be given to each student
- A small checklist of items to be surveyed may be prepared in advance. It should be short. The basic purpose of this survey is not to study a single occupation but to list out the upcoming industries and occupations and their requirements.
- Interviews may be had with the employers about their requirements and future expansion plans.
- Survey schedule may be prepared after the brainstorming sessions with the students and other expert.
- Students should be provided training in how to conduct interviews. Some mock-sessions may be organised to facilitate students in meeting with the employers with confidence. They should be guided as to what they should not do, like giving value judgment or their opinions to the employers.

- A preliminary survey may be conducted first to list out the industries, employers and the establishments. Detailed interviews may be conducted later on with each or some depending on the requirement and resources.
- After identification of the employers, a letter should be written to the employer indicating the purpose of survey and communicating him the names of the team members who would visit him for the interview. A convenient date and time may be fixed.
- After the survey, information collected by various teams should be discussed in a group meeting. Teams should be encouraged to share their observations and experience.
- A final report may be prepared with the help of the students.

Surveys are less time consuming and realistic information may be obtained. It is a primary source of data collection. Students also get an insight to the world of work, which helps them to make realistic career choices.

15

Guidance for Women

Women constitute half of the world's population but their share in the fruits of development in the society is not commensurate with that ratio. Male-female disparities may be observed in every sphere of life, *i.e.,* education, employment, remuneration, access to social assets, etc. In 43 countries of the world, male literacy rates are higher than the female rates by at least 15 percentage points. Such disparities lead to situations where 544 million of the world's estimated 854 million illiterate adults are women and 60 per cent of the estimated 113 million children out of school are girls. Half a million women die every year due to pregnancy and child birth. There are about one billion people in the world who are absolutely poor, 70 per cent out of them are women. One half of the women in Asia and Africa are malnourished.

The Indian Scene

The situation in India, in spite of various efforts at national and regional level to achieve gender parity, is not very encouraging. Societal attitudes hardened over ages do not change easily. Even if change *per se* is accepted, the deep-rooted prejudices do die-hard. A majority of people, men and women alike, still have preference for a son, and pay relatively less attention to the girl child in the matters of education, health, etc. Education even when provided to girls generally, does not aim at their mainstreaming in the society but only to find a suitable match at a lower dowry. Lopsided sex ratio of 933 females per 1000 men has been the result of such favours for the male child. More worrisome is the fact that instead of showing improvement the sex ratio has been declining steadily during the last century. Some hard facts about the situation of girls and women in India are as follows:

- Half of the female population is illiterate in the country (although gender gaps have narrowed and absolute number of female illiterates has come down from about 200 million in 1991 to about 189 million in 2001).

- Gender disparities in the enrolment ratios at different stages and drop-out rates are a matter of concern.
- Female work participation rate (25.7 per cent in 2001) is much lower than that of male work participation rate. Rural urban disparities are also there.
- There are disparities in the incomes of men and women for similar kind of work.
- Representation of women in political affairs and other decision-making bodies is almost negligible (about 7 to 8 per cent in the last 30 years in Lok Sabha and around 10 per cent in Rajya Sabha). Same is the case with All-India Services.
- India ranks even behind Bangladesh in GER. (Gender Empowerment Rate)
- Crimes against women are on the rise.

In the above scenario, it is evident that needs of guidance in respect of females would vary as compared to males. The deep-rooted traditional mindsets and cultural barriers to equality are to be addressed. Some special needs of the women are:

- The parents need counselling to send their girl children to school.
- Girls are to be motivated to go to schools and understand the importance of education.
- At present girls are allowed to develop stereotypic attitudes like they are supposed to develop feminine characteristics and are subordinate to males. Such orientation of girls needs to be changed.
- Girls are to be encouraged to choose all types of educational streams.
- The problems of girl children, specially in rural areas and poor families are peculiar. Where both mother and father go for work, girl child is supposed to take care of home and siblings. Need for proper guidance for these children and parents is more acute.
- There is a need to develop self-confidence and high levels of self-esteem among women to come out of their shells and be participants in the societal matters.
- There is a demarcation in the labour market. Women are found suitable for only those occupations that are being done by women since long, like nursing or teaching. Other occupations where women are found suitable involve drudgery and manual labour. Where some technology is introduced, women are removed and men are employed. Such a system needs change and guidance can help in changing such demarcation in the labour market.

- Not only men, women also feel that they are not fit for certain jobs. They accept jobs where low skills are required and involve long hours of work. They also accept less pay than males. Need for guidance in such situation is self-evident.
- Women depend on males for all the decisions, be it education, employment, family and so on. They accept whatever comes their way. Even when they are sent for education, it is mostly for finding a suitable match. Their careers, even in urban areas, depend upon the attitudes of the husband and in laws. Guidance can help in developing decision-making abilities in them and make them self-dependent.
- Females are not aware about their rights. They are also not aware of the importance of health and nutrition. Such awareness has to be created among women and guidance can play an important role.
- Even when the girl children are sent to schools, their retention in the school is a big issue. Most of these children do not continue their studies after elementary school. In rural areas, if school is far off from the village, parents do not send their girl children to schools.

Objectives of Guidance for Women

- To make them aware of their rights.
- To help them in knowing the importance of education, good health and nutrition and facilities available for them.
- To assist them in developing self-confidence to come out of their shells.
- To help them in developing decision-making abilities and be self-dependent.
- To help them in raising their voice against all kinds of discriminations and violence against them and make them aware of the institutional support available.
- To help them in changing their mindsets and stereotypic attitudes that they have only a secondary role.
- To assist them in empowering themselves by assessing themselves and develop according to their abilities.
- To help them in increasing their employability.
- To help them in starting income generation activities and have control on their incomes.
- To assist them in overall development of their personality.
- To help them in knowing about re-productive health care and child care.

- To help them in dealing with social evils like early marriage, dowry, rapes, social violence, etc. and familiarise them with the support systems available to them.

How to Organise Guidance for Women

1. In Schools

(i) Identify girls who are first generation learners and prepare individual case studies. This group would be potential dropout group.

(ii) Identify girls with personal, emotional and educational problems and prepare remedial measures.

(iii) Identify girls with poor health and malnutrition and refer them for health check ups and health improvement programme.

(iv) Survey the girl children who are not enrolled in the school. Organise interaction sessions with their parents to motivate them to send their children to school.

(v) Identify girls who are coming from poor families and plan a programme for retaining them in the school.

(vi) Organise personality development programmes for girl children to develop confidence in themselves and change the mindset.

(vii) Organise Community Awareness Campaign to motivate the society against discrimination against girl child.

2. Outside School

Guidance programmes for girls and women have to be organised according to the target group. There would be women who are talented but do not come out due to family pressures and shyness. Another group may be of the women who are employed but are facing role stress or work related problem. They might be having tensions due to dual roles, *i.e.*, at home and at work place. In rural areas, women might be needing guidance about income generation activities near their homes. Guidance has to be planned according to the target group. For example, women in rural setting who want to start income generating activity may be helped in forming a Self Help Group so that they can start some group activity. The concept of Self Help Group is becoming popular in rural areas these days.

A summary of the type of women's group and their needs may be as follows:

Table 15.1: Developmental Needs of Women

Target Group (1)	*Development Need* (2)
I. Presently out of Labour Force	
(a) girl children in school	Continuation of general/vocational education or technical training leading to productive employment/self-employment
(b) girl children not in school	Formal/non-formal education to bring them into the regular educational streams; vocational education or technical training leading to productive employment/self-employment; self-development
(c) adult females (not educated), neither working nor seeking work	Adult education and functional literacy; awareness generation; self-development; motivation to work, employment counseling; technical training leading to productive employment/self-employment;
(d) adult females (educated), neither working nor seeking work	Awareness generation; motivation to work, counseling; self-development; technical training leading to productive employment/self-employment;;
II. Presently in Labour Force, Unemployed	
(a) uneducated, without skills	Functional literacy; self-development; short-term employment-oriented skill training as per market needs to improve employability; organisation into SHGs where necessary for income-generating activities; credit and related services
(b) uneducated with skills	Functional literacy; self-development; short-term employment-oriented skill training as per market needs to upgrade skills and improve employability; organisation into SHGs where necessary for income-generating activities; credit and related services
(c) educated without skills	Employment counseling; technical training (institutional or on-the-job); soft skills like communication and inter-personal relations; self-development; entrepreneurial development; organisation into SHGs where necessary for income generating activities; credit and related services
(d) educated with skills	Employment counseling; up-gradation of skills to suit market demand; soft skills; self-development; entrepreneurial development; organisation into SHGs where necessary for income generating activities; credit and related services
III. Presently Employed in Un organised Sector	
(a) uneducated, without skills	Functional literacy; self-development to enhance aspirations; short duration training in simple skills and soft skills to improve productivity
(b) uneducated with skills	Functional literacy; self-development to enhance aspirations; retraining to update skills and training in supplementary skills to improve productivity; motivation to take up income-generating activities
(c) educated without skills	Self-development to enhance aspirations; short duration training to impart vocational/technical skills; soft skills; entrepreneurial development to promote self-employment

(Contd.)

Target Group (1)	Development Need (2)
(d) educated with skills	Self-development to enhance aspirations; retraining to update skills and training in supplementary skills to improve productivity; soft skills; entrepreneurial development to promote self-employment
IV. Presently Employed in Organised Sector	
(a) uneducated, without skills	Functional literacy; awareness generation; self-development; short duration training in simple skills and soft skills to enhance productivity
(b) uneducated with skills	Functional literacy; awareness generation; self-development; retraining to update skills and training in supplementary skills to improve productivity; motivation to take up income-generating activities
(c) educated without skills	Self-development to enhance aspirations; short duration training to impart vocational/technical skills; soft skills; entrepreneurial development to promote self-employment
(d) educated with skills	Self-development to enhance aspirations; retraining to update skills and training in supplementary skills to improve productivity; soft skills; entrepreneurial development to promote self-employment

To meet the developmental needs of the above target group, guidance workers should map the organisations that can help in the implementation of the programme. For example, in rural areas, a number of Non-Governmental Organisations (NGOs) are functioning at grass-root level. Some are functioning specially for the women. These organisations should be involved in organising guidance services.

Empowerment of women is a pre-requisite for development of women. This empowerment could be facilitated through implementing the programmes by Government as well as by developing the abilities and positive self-concept in women. Community mobilisation is extremely essential. Multi-faceted approach can be followed for mainstreaming of women in the society. For example, only outside help and legislation may not give the desired results till these are synthesised with self-development of women, creating awareness, change in attitudes etc. An example is the fact that with the 73rd/74th amendments of the Constitution women have been given powers of heading the local bodies. But in practice, at most of these places where women are functioning as sarpanches, only their husbands are doing the work. Here, self-development programmes linked with training in office administration, social skills, budgeting, etc. are to be organised. Guidance may facilitate such programme.

Table 15.2: Personality Assessment and Development of Rural Uneducated—Some Examples

Objectives	*Technique*	*Outcomes and Inferences*
(1)	*(2)*	*(3)*
(a) Self-awareness	Ask the individuals to - Mention five good points about yourself - Mention five negative points about yourself - Name two activities you cannot perform - Tell five things you like most *If they are not able to tell, assist them in the process.* *Give them tasks like putting thread in the needle and tell the persons completing quickly that they could do it* *Give an exercise like* - Name five colours you can see immediately. *The tendency is to look outside to locate the colours and not towards themselves and mention the colors of their dresses*	Indicates level of self-belief of the individual
(b) Awareness of others	*Ask the individual to* - Tell about the strengths of each of the other members of the group	Indicates the perception of the individual about others
(c) Problem solving and getting along with others	*Give an exercise like* - Comb hair without taking your hands behind yourself - Distribute among yourselves these matchstick flowers/stones/any other item (keep the total number indivisible by the number of person in the group and observe how they distribute).	it is expected that they would comb hair of each other indicating ability to think of a solution to the problem and inclination for mutual cooperation In the second exercise, if after even distribution, the remaining are kept apart, it may be used to introduce concept of saving
(d) Risk taking	*Ask the individuals to play*	Indicates the extent to which the individual can commit himself to goals in the face of risks involved.

(Contd.)

(1)	(2)	(3)
	- *Ring toss game* *Place several objects in front of the individual at gradually increasing distances and ask the individual to throw a ring around one of the objects, with appropriate costs and rewards depending on the distance to which the ring is aimed at and successfully thrown* - *Paper Boats game* *Teach the group how to make paper boats and ask them to make as many boats as possible within a specified time. The number of boats a person can make within the time limit should be announced in advance by the individual. Successful completion will earn rewards*	
(e) Leadership	*Ask the group to* - Discuss about the problems of the village - Perform a group task relating to the village *Show how a leader emerges during the discussion*	Indicates extent of shyness, leadership qualities, initiative, public speaking
(f) Development of creating thinking	*Give an exercise like* - A lion, a goat and a bundle of grass have to be taken across arive in the only boat available by a boatman. Only one of the three can be taken at a time. The lion eats goat and the goat eats grass, if left alone by the boatman. (The lion does not eat the boatman!). How can they cross?	Indicates creative thinking in solving problems

(Contd.)

(1)	*(2)*	*(3)*
(g) Development of positive thinking	*Ask the individuals to prepare a story from words like* - Snake, child and pot	Some possible stories are (a) the child went to the post to take out rice from it. There was a snake nearby which attacked and killed the child; (b) The child saw a snake near the post and called out to a man who caught hold of the snake and left it in the forest. The stories may be analysed for attitudes. The first story indicates a negative attitude while the second a positive attitude.
(h) Business skills	*Ask the individuals to* - Solve a simple profit and loss problem - Select a venture prevalent in the village, list activities involved and indicate how to organise *Guide them with suggestions*	Indicates entrepreneurial skills
(i) Development of social skills and overcoming shyness	*Ask the individuals to* - Tell about the strengths of the other members of the group - Role-play one as the leader of the group presenting their problems/credit needs to the other as Sarpanch/bank officer. *The exercise may be made more interesting by putting a turban on the person playing Sarpanch. The roles can be reserved in the second attempt.* - Pass a ring or any suitable object to the neighbours while music goes on. As soon as the music stops the person who has an object has to do what she is told to do – sing, dance, laugh loudly, act like someone, etc. Ask the group to come one by one to the dais, and Speak on a specific problem of the village or any subject of her choice	Observe how the Sarpanch refuses to listen or the bank manager refuses to give loan and how the leader tries to convince.

16

Guidance for Children with Special Needs

Children in the school come from varying cultures, traditions and socio-economic background. Their educational, emotional and adjustment needs may differ. A uniform educational programme or a uniform system of dealing with the children may not meet the needs of all the children. A system has to be evolved in the school that may cater to the needs of children. Guidance plays an important role to deal with children with special needs. How can the children with special needs be defined? Children with special needs are those children who do things differently than the average normal children. If a child is not able to understand what is being taught in the class while all other children can, obviously that child has some special problem. Another child who sits in the back of the classroom but comes to the front whenever something is written on the blackboard needs to be taken care of. May be his eyesight is weak and he requires a seat in the front. There may be a number of other problem cases. On the other hand, there may be children with extra energy and are always hyperactive. They feel whatever is being taught is very boring. Such children require a special curriculum where provisions are there for extra activities. These hyperactive children are generally ignored otherwise.

About 500 million disabled persons live in the world. Out of these 100 million are Indians. About 12.60 million such children are school children. It is also to be mentioned here that this does not include those with a number of disabilities such as cerebral plasy, learning disabilities, epilepsy etc. as these are not covered under the definition of Disability Act.

Types of Children with Special Needs

Children with Learning Disabilities: Children with learning disabilities are known as 'slow-learners'. Generally these children are considered as mentally retarded by the teachers. But that is not a correct assumption. These slow learners are not necessarily mentally retarded children but suffer from some other problem. These problems could be due to difficulty in memorising, writing, concentrating. Some children may have difficulty in reading or they may lack motor coordination. These children with learning difficulty are to be identified. Generally these children have normal or sometimes even above average intelligence. Golick (1970) has classified learning disabilities in the following categories.

1. Poor body awareness: child cannot locate various body parts, difficulty in telling right or left
2. Poor ability to combine vision and movement: poor eye-hand coordination.
3. Visual inefficiency: Even after normal vision, child may not be able to give selective vision.
4. Poor listening ability: easily distracted towards notice.
5. Poor integration of information from sensory channels – child is not able to integrate the alphabets with their sounds.
6. Poor grasp of sequence: child is not able to remember the sequence of things like counting 1 to 10 he will not narrate in order.
7. Poor sense of rhythm: difficulty in narrating a poem.
8. Problems with concepts: child has difficulty in identifying the similarities and variations in various objects. Poor concepts of time or number.
9. Problems in learning: like difficulty in arithmetic, remembering numbers or names, difficulty specially in memorising
10. Poor general knowledge: child has difficulty in learning general information like home address, occupation of parents, names of friends, etc.

How to Deal With Learning Disabled Children

As a first step, it is important to identify children with learning disability and to identify their specific problem. Some might be facing problems in reading or understanding, others in writing. Some children may have problem with solving mathematical problems. Apart from learning difficulties, learning disabled children may face difficulty in having inter-personal relations or social interactions. There may be various categories of learning disability ranging from mild to extremely severe. Severely learning disabled children require intensive intervention, may need special schools or constant supervision or continuous tutorials. In the regular classroom, special tutorials with direct instructions would be helpful. Social skill training, use of equipment to overcome learning problems, practice in speaking and writing, adapted curriculum should be provided. Behaviour management is another area which should be given due attention. Patience is required to deal with such students. They should be encouraged for appropriate behaviours. Simple assignments should be given and those students should not be punished because of their slow pace of learning. The special assistance should be reduced in a phased manner.

Mentally Retarded Children: Another category may be of the children whose intelligence level is lower than the desired. There are four categories of mentally retarded – profoundly retarded, severely retarded, trainable and educable retarded. Profoundly retarded children have very low levels of intelligence and may suffer from more than one handicap. Such children need support of special institutions. Severely retarded category children also have very low levels of intelligence and constantly require supervision or care in special homes. The trainable retarded children can be trained to take care of themselves in routine and repetitive jobs. However, they have difficulty in reading or doing mathematics. Some such children have some other special ability like that of singing. They are capable of performing some activities in sheltered workshops such as candle making, sorting jobs etc. Special training facilities are required for such children.

The educable mentally retarded children are those children who are borderline cases so far as intelligence levels are concerned. The physical appearance of these children is generally normal. These are termed as mildly retarded children. They require special programmes and extra classes to handle school curriculum. They are generally aggressive and need special and individual attention. They can learn to do simple routine jobs and study up to a certain level. Some of these children are very good in languages, physical activities, making craft items. Teachers need special training to deal with such students.

Categories of Mental Retardation and IQ Level

Category	*IQ*
1. Profound mental retardation	below 20
2. Severe mental retardation	20 – 34
3. Moderate mental retardation	35 – 49
4. Mild mental retardation	50 – 69
5. Borderline deficiency	70 – 79

These borderline retarded children can be taught to manage their daily routine activities and also to pursue academics upto a certain level. These children should be provided some vocational training alongwith the educational syllabus. This vocational training should involve repetitive work. Such children should be treated with care and concern. Sometimes a mentally retarded child acts in such a way that is not considered normal. He may make different poses or may be aggressive without any valid reason. Other students generally laugh at such activities of a mentally retarded child. The guidance worker has to organise community awareness programmes so that others may know about the status of the child and could deal with him with empathetic attitude.

Teaching for mentally retarded has to be extremely gentle as such children take a long time in learning an activity. Specific and continued training with patience may be helpful. The concept of gentle teaching has emerged from the Psychology of Interdependence. The Psychology of Interdependence is based on the assumption that each individual wishes to have a feeling of companionship which can modify the behaviours in the desired direction.

The parents and other family members have to play an important role in the development of a retarded child. Most of the times, parents scold the child for not learning or behaving in the desirable manner. Counsellor should help the parents in understanding the needs of the child. Parents may take professional or institutional help on a life long basis for such children.

The syllabus has to be adapted according to the needs of the child in the school. For example, generally, the retarded child is unable to do mathematical problems. Extra tutorials may also be arranged in the school so that the needs of the children could be met.

The Gifted Children: There are always some children in the class who are more capable than others. They have high IQ, can do more than one activity at a time do not take much interest in doing simple things. They feel happy undertaking extra and complex work. They can finish their tasks in a lesser time than others. They may have special innate abilities such as aptitude for music or other performing arts, aptitude for doing finer things, aptitude for doing mechanical things etc. These are the gifted children. Some special curriculum with extra and creative activities is required for such children. Special training opportunities are needed to nurture their special talents.

Various methods have been adopted to deal with the gifted children. Ability groups are made and they are kept in a separate section. Sometimes they are promoted a class higher. Having a separate section for the gifted sometimes makes them alien from the others. The other alternative is to organise enrichment programmes to enable the gifted develop their potentials and utilise the special talent they have. During the regular classes, special creative assignments are given to such students. Such children are restless in the class, cannot sit for a longer time with one activity or if they finish their task, they start disturbing others. It is, therefore, essential that they are kept busy where they can utilise their extra intelligence.

Parents are also to be guided about such children. Parents should be encouraged to provide such opportunities in the home environment where the gifted child may be able to nurture his talent.

The First-generation Learners: Another category of children, which is very common in schools especially in government run schools, is of first generation learners. Due to the special schemes initiated by the government, emphasis is on the education for each child. Parents, in the changed scenario are also aware of the importance of education and are sending their children to schools. These children are the first in their families to attend the school. No body from the family is educated. These children have peculiar problems of making adjustments in the school, learning discipline, and understanding the importance of education. There is also nobody at home to help them in doing their homework. Teachers often scold them for not bringing the relevant textbooks or notebooks to the school or for not doing the homework. Their special needs are to be understood and taken care of.

Children with physical handicaps: They may be children in a class who have some physical deformity like polio, lack of hand coordination, visual handicap, hearing disability. Or they might be suffering from severe allergies like allergy from dust, perfumes, smoke or some eating things. They might be having chronic disease like arthritis, diabetes, heart ailments, etc. Some children may suffer from epilepsy. A common problem in the students may be observed in speech. Children may not be good articulates, they may omit some words or may stammer. Sometimes speech problems occur due to emotional disturbances. Some such handicaps have been detailed below:

The Hearing Impairment

The deaf child can be of various categories. There are children who are both deaf and dumb, others can speak but cannot hear and some others are hard of hearing. The hard-of-hearing children can use the hearing device. The children of the other two categories are to be taught through sight and touch and using the sign language. Researches show that such children can do extremely well in the activities involving manual dexterity, athletics, artistic abilities and creativity. A balanced and well designed curriculum is needed for such children keeping in mind their specific abilities. All India Federation of Deaf, Deaf and Dumb Society, Delhi Association of Deaf, are some of the organisations that help deaf and dumb persons in getting employment. The most important aspect to rehabilitate the deaf child is early identification of the disability, arrangement for well-fitted hearing aids and early training in 'lip reading'.

A number of facilities and equipments are available these days which make the life of hearing impaired children easy and smooth. Deaf persons can use Telecommunication devices for communicating through telephone. Mobile text-phone equipments have come in the market. In developed countries like U.K and USA telephone relay services are available. A deaf person can communicate through a human translator. Other equipments available are the flashing lights to signal events, for example, a fire alarm or doorbell.

The Orthopaedically Handicapped

The orthopaedically children generally use artificial limbs. It is felt by the society that due to loss of hand, or leg, one is not capable of competing in normal society. There are people who are born disabled, while some others become handicapped due to some accident or injury. The latter category feels a drastic change in their lives. They feel more depressed and anxious than the persons who are born handicapped. One need of such persons is that the society understands them properly and helps them in coming out of their trauma.

Orthopaedically handicapped children require a suitable accommodation, a proper sitting arrangement and hindrance free architecture, specially the children who are using a wheel chair. Proper transportation to suit their disability is also necessary. Medical facilities should be available in the school or nearby school. Library facilities should be accessible to these children.

Visually Impaired Children

Specific needs and programmes for the visually impaired children:

- Orientation of these children for school, facilities available and how to be mobile.
- Provide them technical support and orient them towards the technology like tape recorders, computers.
- Provide information about Braill books and help in reading them.
- Develop confidence in themselves and learn inter personal skills.
- Orient the other students of the class to have a positive attitude towards the children with special needs.
- Support of a person during examinations to write the answers.
- Special curriculum and alternative questions where one is required to draw a graph etc.
- Use of actual objects for learning.
- All the written material on the black-board should be orally explained.
- Information about safety, use of electrical equipment etc.

Some Major Problems of Disabled

1. *Architectural Hindrance*: Architecture of the school building or the working place is one of the major barriers for the disabled. For example, if the building is multi-storied and one is supposed to use lift, there should be a provision of announcement about the floors, numbers should be written in Braille, the children confined to a wheel chairs should have the accessibility of lift. Children affected with polio or using a wheel chair should have proper facilities of toilets.
2. *The Attitudes*: Generally, the disabled are neglected by the society or if some people do not neglect them, they pity them. Such attitudes give negative signals to the disabled. They develop a sense of self-pity and feel as if they do not have a place in the society. They are not able to develop a sense of belonging. Sometimes even parents do not want to accompany disabled children as they feel embarrassed, specially in case of children with mental retardation. Some measures have been initiated for mainstreaming of disabled children by keeping them in the normal school alongwith other normal children. There is a need to make the fellow students aware. Acceptance in the society is extremely necessary.
3. *Jobs and Disabled*: Although there is 3% reservation for the physically handicapped in the jobs, employers are apathetic towards employing them. Even if they employ the disabled due to compulsion, they do not have a positive attitude towards them. The capabilities of disabled are not given due respect; jobs are not assigned to them. The disabled are treated as a liability and not as an asset, while it has been seen that certain jobs can be done better by the disabled. Physically handicapped are not occupationally handicapped. There is a need to identify suitable jobs for various categories of handicapped. Success stories may be helpful in changing the misconceptions on the part of employers. In the activities where lot of noise is involved, the deaf and dumb can do excellent job.
4. *Education System*: The education system in the country is yet to be made disabled friendly. It has to be employment-oriented. More academic education would not help them in their future quest for livelihood. Jobs should be identified for them and proper training, including the mental readiness for a particular job, should be given from the very beginning. For example, the work of call centres is flourishing. Visually impaired can be prepared for such jobs.
5. *The Inferiority Complex*: Another major problem which most of the

disabled suffer from the feeling of inferiority and low levels of self-esteem. Due to the handicap, they feel that they are not like other normal children. It affects their performance. There is a need to develop their personalities in the areas where they can excel. School has to provide such opportunities to the disabled students.

How to Identify Children with Special Needs

The first step to meet the needs of different categories of children is to identify them and their special needs in the class. They can be helped as early as they are identified. Teachers should be able to spot the special-needs-children for example, children suffering with physical handicap; mental retardation may be discovered through administering IQ tests. Doctors may help in identifying physical ailments. Psychologists also administer diagnostic tests for identifying learning disabilities. Parents can help in telling about the child's difficulties, for example, late development of speech of the child, any emotional problem the child has suffered from, etc. The detailed information about the child's health and dreams and other background may be had from Cumulative Record Card, if the child has come from some other school. Psychological tests can also identify the children with special talents. Sometimes other classmates and friends tell about the child's problems and exceptional abilities.

Role of Guidance Worker

A guidance counsellor has a very important role in providing services to the children with special needs. He has to perform the following functions:

- Identify the children with special needs.
- Assess their capabilities and weakness.
- Identify what these children can do and what they cannot do.
- Ascertain what specific facilities these children require in the school and outside.
- Discuss and make the teachers, parents, principal, peer group aware about the special needs of these children.
- Map the resources available inside and outside the school to help these children.
- Collect, collate and disseminate the information that may be required for the children with special needs.
- Provide counselling to such children wherever required.
- Prepare a plan for various activities in consultation with teachers which various categories of special-needs-children may require.
- Help the teachers and school in implementation of the plan.

- Provide referral services. For example, the child who has problem in speech should be referred to speech correctionist or a physically handicapped child may be referred to occupational therapist. Referral services may also be had to assess the residual capacities of children with special needs.
- Preventive measures can be taken to curtail incidence of disability. Guidance worker should make the students and community aware of the importance of immunisation against various diseases, adopt a safe life style, follow traffic rules while on road, use safety measures while working in school laboratories.
- One of the most important function of the counsellor is mainstreaming of disabled children in the school and community with providing awareness about various disabilities.

17

Evaluation of Guidance Programme

To make any programme effective it is essential that its functioning should be evaluated from time to time. The evaluation of guidance services is necessary to see what kind of services are being rendered; whether these services are beneficial to the students or not and what are the areas where modifications are required?

The evaluation of the programme may be done in terms of its objectives, *i.e.,* whether the programme is meating its objectives or not. The programme can also be evaluated in terms of the budget allocated for the services to see whether the services rendered are cost effective. Another basis of evaluation of the programme may be a time activity-planning schedule. whether the services planned during the specific period, and for the specific target groups have been rendered or not. Another basis could the outcomes of the programmes. In a guidance programme the outcome may be a number of students placed in jobs, the number of persons helped in solving their problems or the number of persons who could get educational streams of their choice, the number of persons who could be helped in assessing themselves and so on. The evaluation may be done having two groups – one group which was provided guidance and the other which was not given any services and the two groups may be compared.

It may be seen from the above that selection of criteria is an important element in the evaluation of guidance. Various criteria were adopted to evaluate the guidance programme and assess the effectiveness of the criteria by various research scholars but no one criteria has been considered as perfect. Some researches show that presence of certain services, material and activities, etc., lead to a successful guidance programme but absence of these activities does not lead to the conclusion that services are ineffective. Some of the criteria used relate to the ultimate vocational success and satisfaction. The appropriateness of the vocational choice had been another criterion for researchers. Stone studied the effect of counselling and instructions on vocational choices. The student's opinion has been used to determine the effectiveness of various school services and courses upon the vocational choices. Hoppock took the opinion of graduates and dropouts to determine their opinion about guidance programme when they were in the schools. Change in client's attitude before and after guidance has been studied by a number of scholars. Williamson and Darley (1937) advocated four criteria on which the guidance services could be evaluated.

1. A case work method which involves the reading of case histories by competent counsellors, who make professional judgments of success in adjustment.
2. Scholastic adjustments in terms of both groups of students who leave college because of low scholastic aptitude, and those who are successful. The former group may achieve desirable outcomes of counselling 'by leaving,' if they become adjusted to the fact that they have little or no chance of college success (at that particular college) and act accordingly.
3. Students' satisfaction with counselling (their own judgment report).
4. Change and development of attitudes toward vocation or other problem. (As observed by the counsellor.)

Stoops and Wahlquist have given the following suggestions for giving the criteria for evaluation of the guidance programme

1. Evaluation should increase efficiency in the field appraised by determining how well the program's objectives are being achieved.
2. Measurement, research, interpretation, and analysis are indispensable.
3. The purposes of evaluation should be stated clearly in terms of desired changes.
4. Desired changes and purposes should be flexible and subject to review, re-evaluation, and restatement, as the needs of pupils and society change.
5. Final decisions should be based upon factual data or upon valid judgments.
6. Results of measuring and counting, percentages and norms are not sufficient data from which to recommend changes. Other factors of a less tangible nature are also required.
7. All persons affected by the program should assist in arriving at the decisions made concerning the evaluation goals, procedures, and purposes to be achieved.
8. Evaluation programmes for guidance should be coordinated with, and be a continuous part of, the entire educational program of the schools.
9. Unique and experimental methods of evaluation in guidance should

be encouraged, but adopted with caution.

10. All data and information submitted should be validated, studied, and weighed before they are used to effect program changes. Evaluation, wherever used, is concerned with both the means and the ends.
11. When changes in guidance have been proved desirable through evaluation, and agreed to, then all guidance workers should enthusiastically assist in revising the program.
12. Democratic procedure requires that all who are affected by a school policy, program, or decision should share both in its making and in its execution.

There can be any criterion for evaluation of the programme but the basic objectives of the evaluation are to see whether—

- The activities planned in the programme are covered.
- The needs of various kind of groups in the schools have been met.
- The programme has been successful in helping the students to solve their various problems.
- Various groups of students have been assessed adequately and results have been conveyed to the students in proper manner.
- Counselling has been effective in solving the individual problems.
- Students were able to improve their academic achievements through the guidance programme.
- Placement services have improved through guidance.
- Career information services rendered under the guidance programme have been effective.
- Guidance worker has been able to orient the principal, the teachers, the community, the parents and ultimately the students about the guidance services.
- Students feel the usefulness of guidance services rendered to them.
- Guidance helped students to prepare themselves for facing the competitive examinations, interviews, etc.

These are some of the points the guidance evaluation programme should look into.

How to Collect Information

The general method to collect the information for evaluating the services is survey method. The information may be collected from staff members, from parents, from friends of the person who has been rendered the guidance services and from the beneficiaries themselves to assess the effect of guidance upon the behaviours and adjustments in life of the beneficiaries. A follow up survey may also be done of the persons who have been provided guidance to see their activities status.

Another way of collecting the information is to conduct experimental research by having two groups controlled and experimental in which one group is provided services and the other is not. The changes in the two groups may be measured. This method has been used to study the effectiveness of counselling. To study the effectiveness of the guidance services through this experimental method, matching of the two groups on other variables, such as environmental factor, age, education, etc. is vital

The Evaluation Technique

For collection of data, the most common method employed is the use of structured questionnaire. On the basis of the objectives of the evaluation as well as criteria adopted questionnaires are developed and sent to the persons from whom the information is to be collected. Another method is the interview method where people are personally interviewed. Interview is more personal and the information may be collected through probing. The problem in sending the questionnaire is that many people may not return the questionnaire or may not give their true opinion.

Attempts have been made to use the tests for evaluating the differences. Tests may be used on the student's pre and post guidance services. Pepinsky and others utilised socio-metro devices and observation methods. Some other scholars have used the rating scales.

All the techniques have some advantages and disadvantages. If more than one technique is followed the data may be more authentic and comparable. The suggestions may also be obtained from the students themselves. The ultimate aim of evaluation of guidance services is that the beneficiaries should be well adjusted in their lives and they should perform well when they are in schools and when in jobs.

Some Success Indicators

1. To what extent does the pupil work up to his level of ability?
2. To what extent is the school aiding the pupil who should stay in school and the pupil who should seek training and experiences outside the school? Again the criterion is based upon individual needs.
3. To what extent does the pupil learn to participate in group activities, such as expressing himself easily to others, tolerance toward the ideas of others, or willingness to help others in the group?
4. To what extent does a pupil learn to plan for himself?

5. To what extent does each pupil make educational and vocational plans that are compatible with reasonable expectations?
6. To what extent does the pupil learn to make friends and get along with others?
7. To what extent is the pupil able to establish heterosexual relationships?
8. To what extent is the pupil able to accept the responsibilities of citizenship in a school community?

Who Should do the Evaluation?

Evaluation is a specialised work involving orientation for research; the schools may not be equipped with professional persons, who can evaluate the services. It is better to take the help from outside agencies or a cluster of the schools where services are available. An evaluation committee can be constituted comprising guidance professionals, experts in the field, schools, administrators, etc.

18

Employment and Skill Scenario in India

An educational and vocational guidance practitioner, to be an effective counsellor, must have a clear background of the employment market and the skill requirements in the country. He should be able to provide answers to questions like

- What is the number of workers in the country?
- How many of them are men and how many women?
- Are they employed in rural areas or urban areas?
- In what industries are they employed?
- Is there any change in the pattern of employment across industries?
- In what occupations are they employed?
- What is the more prevalent form of employment (wage/salaried employment or self-employment)?
- What is the educational level of workers?
- To what extent is the employment in organised sector of the economy?
- What are the levels of unemployment?
- Is unemployment increasing?
- How many people are registered with employment exchanges?
- What is the employment policy of the government?
- What are the important schemes for providing wage and self-employment?
- How skilled is the Indian workforce?
- Are any changes taking place in the skill requirements?
- If so, what are the new emerging skills?

The following paragraphs attempt to provide some idea about the current employment situation in India.

According to the 2001 Population Census, the total population of the country was 1028 million, comprising about 532 million males and 496 million females. About 72 per cent of the population (742 million in 2001) lived in the rural areas and the remaining 28 per cent (286 million) in the urban areas. Nearly 42 per cent of the population comprised of children below the age of

15 years and persons above the age of 60 years. Only two-thirds of the population (65 per cent) aged 7 years or more was literate, *i.e.,* could read and write a simple letter in their own language. While 74 per cent of men were literate, only just above half of the women were literate.

About half of the men (52 per cent) and one-fourth of women (26 per cent) participated in economic activities. The total number of workers, thus, was 403 million (in 2001), of which the number of women workers was 127 million. About three-fourths of the workforce was in the rural areas (301 million in the rural and 92 million in urban areas).

In the rural areas, about three-fourths (73 per cent in 2001)[1] worked in agriculture and allied activities like forestry, fishing, hunting and animal husbandry. Only about 9 per cent of the workers were engaged in manufacturing activities, 6 per cent in trade and hotels and restaurants and 5 per cent in services. In the urban areas, on the other hand, a quarter (25 per cent) of the workforce each was engaged in manufacturing activities, trade, hotels and restaurants, and in services, while and 8 to 9 per cent each in agriculture and allied activities, construction and transport and communications. Over the years, the share of workers in agriculture and allied activities has been going down both in rural as well as urban areas, while that in rural areas manufacturing, construction, trade and transport and communications has been increasing.

Occupation-wise, as may be expected, about three-fourths[2] of the workers in the rural areas farmers, fishermen, hunters, loggers, animal husbandry workers, etc. About 14 per cent were production and related workers, transport equipment operators and labourers and 4 per cent were sales workers. In the urban areas, the occupational distribution was more diversified, with 39 per cent being production workers and transport equipment operators, 17 per cent were sales workers, 8 to 9 per cent each were administrative and managerial and professional and technical workers.

More than half of the workers (55 per cent of male and 57 per cent of female workers in 2000-01) were engaged in self-employment activities. Regular salaried employees constituted only 17.5 per cent of male and 7 per cent of female workers, the remaining workers being casual labour. There were, however, significant differences in these proportions between rural and urban areas. In the rural areas, the proportion of the self-employed workers (59 per cent) was higher than in the urban areas (41 among males and 44 among female workers). Regular employees formed less than 10 per cent of the rural workforce, while in urban areas about 41 per cent of males and 31 per cent of females were in regular employment. Over the years, the proportion of regular employees has been increasing among female workers and decreasing among male workers.

In the rural areas, three-fourths of the workforce was illiterate and only one in six was educated up to primary level. Only about 10 per cent of the workers had education beyond the primary level. In the urban areas, on the other hand, illiterates constituted less than half (44 per cent) of the workforce, 18 per cent were educated up to primary level, 9 per cent up to middle level, 14 per cent to secondary level and another 15 per cent were graduates or above.

Less than 7 per cent of the workers (6.8 per cent in 2001) were employed in the organised sector of the economy, *i.e.*, public sector and the bigger (employing 10 or more workers) private sector establishments. This share of the organised sector has been coming down in recent years, having fallen from about 8 per cent during the seventies and eighties. Globalisation and economic liberalisation initiated during the nineties has been a cause. Two-thirds of the employment in the organised sector (18.8 million out of 27.3 million in 2002) is in public sector – central and state governments and their undertakings, other quasi-government organisations and local bodies. Only 18 to 19 per cent of the employees in the organised sector were women, but their proportion has been constantly increasing over the years. In the public sector, the bulk of the employees are in community, social and personal services, financial services, and transport and communications. About 4 million workers were employed in central government offices, mainly in railways, posts and telegraph offices and defence. In the private sector, the bulk of the employment was in manufacturing and to a lesser extent in community, social and personal services. The banking sector employed (in 2000) over a million workers, the railways over a million and a half, the plantations nearly 2 million and shops and commercial establishments about 7 million workers.

Only about 2 per cent of the rural labour force[3] and 5 per cent of the urban labour force was unemployed in 1999-2000. Thus, if one considers open unemployment, the overall unemployment problem does not appear to be serious. A more serious problem is one of under-employment manifested in so many ways. People do not find work for all the time they are willing to work, nor do they find work in activities commensurate with their skills and qualifications. Further, they may also not earn commensurately with the work they put in. These phenomena are manifested in less than full time employment, low productivity and incomes.

Even open unemployment is a serious enough problem for the youth entering the labour force for the first time and educated persons. For instance, the unemployment rates for urban youth (in the age group 15 to 29) were 10.8 per cent and 13.9 per cent of the labour force for males and for females respectively in 1999-2000. Among the graduates, the unemployment rates were 7 per cent among urban males and 16 per cent among urban females. The corresponding rural percentages were 11 for males and 31 for females.

There were 41 million jobseekers registered with various employment exchanges in the country, most of them without any technical or professional qualifications or previous work experience. Unfortunately, the number of vacancies that are notified to these exchanges by various employers is currently of the order of 0.2 million only, and this number has been gradually falling year by year.

Tackling unemployment and underemployment is a priority objective of developmental planning in India. The policy of the government is to promote economic growth with generation of employment. While investments in various sectors are aimed at rapid economic growth, such growth is to be accompanied by sustainable and productive employment generation. Apart from programmes of development in various sectors of the economy, special programmes for employment generation are also undertaken by the state. Some of these programmes are the Sampoorna Grameen Swarozgar Yojana and Pradhan Mantri Rozgar Yojana intended to promote self-employment and the Swarn Jayanti Grameen Rozgar Yojana to create wage employment in rural areas. The intention of the state to ensure a minimum level of employment for all those who want it has been given a legal basis recently with the enactment of National Rural Employment Guarantee Act, 2005.

To sum up, the Indian employment scene is characterised by:

- Very high levels of underemployment, particularly in the rural areas and in the urban informal sector.
- High rates of unemployment among the educated youth.
- Limited participation of women in labour force.
- Continued dependence of the bulk of rural labour force on agriculture for its livelihood.
- Dependence of the vast majority of the labour force on employment in unorganised sector.
- Low incomes and productivity.

Policies of globalisation and internal economic liberalisation that have swept the world in the last decade and a half have brought in their wake significant changes in the labour markets of several countries, India being no exception. They have unleashed forces of competitive production of goods and services leading to innovative methods of cost-efficient production processes and work organisation. Opening up to global markets and the resultant international competition, growing foreign direct investment, new business strategies and management practices, new forms of decentralised work-organisation like outsourcing, easier access to modern technology, and changes in financial markets have all had their impact on demand for labour, which has in general been to cut down costs through shedding excess manpower, particularly in the larger units. Employment in the organised sector has shrunk throwing several thousands of workers out of secure and high wage jobs to take up less secure employment in the informal/unorganised activities. Public sector, which till the eighties had been a source of stable employment to thousands, has begun to stagnate and even shrink. The changes have not just been quantitative; they have been qualitative as well. Accompanying the reduction in the overall labour intensity of growth in general there has been significant changes in the skill structure of the manpower demand, with opportunities in certain highly skilled occupations increasing rapidly at the expense of routine skills in the traditional production processes. Rapid growth of new employment opportunities in various segments of the services sector, particularly those involving application of information technology, and increasing demand for multiple skills has contributed to this phenomenon. In the process, persons with low skill endowments and unskilled workers have been adversely affected.

The emerging labour markets, thus, offer scope for employment and income to those with skills, often with more than one skill. This is not only true of the organised sector, but even large areas of the unorganised sector that are either connected to the organised sector or are involved in export-oriented production or in service activities. Unfortunately, the educational and skill content of the Indian labour force is extremely low even in comparison with some of the developing countries. The educational structure of the workforce is such that about 44 per cent of the workforce is illiterate in the country as a whole. Another 23 per cent is either just literate or has education only up to primary level. Thus, only a third of the work force is educated up to the middle level or beyond. These overall proportions conceal wide variations between rural and urban areas and between women and men, the former being substantially disadvantaged than the latter in either case. The situation has no doubt been improving with the youth who comprise the fresh entrants to the labour force being better educated. However, the pace of change is too slow to have a significant impact on the overall educational attainments of the labour force for years to come.

Further, in a situation where demand for workforce with high quality skills and even multiple skills is increasing, only 20 percent of the Indian population has some marketable skills (according to NSSO's 1993-94 survey) even among the urban males. In the case of rural males and urban females it is only around 10 per cent, while only 6 per cent of the rural females possess any such skill. In many cases, the skills so possessed are traditional in nature, being in the areas of weaving, cutting and tailoring, building trades and motor vehicle driving[4]. Only the urban males exhibited some diversity in their skill endowments. Moreover, only 5 per cent of the population in the age group 20-24 is vocationally trained compared to 96 per cent in South Korea and lagging behind even some developing countries – 28 per cent in Mexico, 22 per cent in Botswana and 36 per cent in Mauritius. With this kind of literacy levels and low technical abilities, it is not surprising that productivity and incomes are low.

The Existing System of Skill Development

In India, skill acquisition takes place through two basic structural streams-a small formal one and a large informal one. The formal structure includes (a) higher technical education imparted through professional colleges, (b) vocational education in schools at the post-secondary stage, (c) technical training in specialised institutions and (d) apprenticeship training. A number of agencies such as, the Ministry of Human Resource Development, the Ministry of Labour, the Ministry of Rural Development, the Ministry of Urban Areas and Employment, the Khadi and Village Industries Commission, the Development Commissioner of Small Scale Industries and the Indian Council for Agricultural Research—each with a network of its own, impart vocational education/training at various levels. Some of these are short-term programmes to augment productivity and to diversify sources to earn supplementary income.

Higher professional and technical education, primarily in the areas of agriculture, education, engineering and technology and in medicine, is imparted through various professional institutions. Expansion of the capacities of these institutions is often supply-driven and lopsided as, for instance, the growth of engineering degree colleges vis-à-vis polytechnics, or the neglect of nursing education. Nevertheless, such shortages as might have developed in these higher technical and professional fields are generally more of quality, and have not posed any major quantitative constraints in the process of meeting the manpower needs of the unorganised or informal sector. Suffice it to say, there is a need for redressing the balance in the growth pattern of various levels of technical education and room for substantial qualitative improvement. The rest of this chapter will be confined to the skills at a lower level which require educational qualifications of up to secondary education.

The major low end skill building activity is confined to two major systems – at +2 level of school education operated by the Ministry of Human Resources Development through its counterpart departments in the States and the Craftsmen Training Scheme and Apprentices Training Scheme run by the

Ministry of Labour with its counterpart departments in the States. Vocationalisation of education at secondary level was introduced in 1988 under Ministry of Human Resource Development with a view to enhance individual employability and to provide an alternative to those who did not want to or cannot pursue higher general education. A scheme of pre-vocational education at lower secondary level was also started from 1993-94 to impart training in simple marketable skills and to develop vocational interests. There are now about 6,800 schools offering about 150 vocational courses of two years duration in the broad areas of agriculture, business and commerce, engineering and technology, health and paramedical, home science, and science and technology at +2 stage with a sanctioned capacity of 9.73 lakhs. Those passing out of this vocational stream are eligible for undergoing apprenticeship training up to one year under the Apprentices Act. About 20 thousand apprenticeship positions have so far been located for such apprentices[5]. A scheme for vocationalisation at the first degree level was introduced from 1994-95 to develop capabilities of students to become entrepreneurs. There are also over 1,200 polytechnics with a capacity of over 1.88 lakhs approved by All India Council of Technical Education offering three-year diploma courses in various branches of engineering with an entry qualification of 10th Pass. There are 675 Community Polytechnics, which are wings attached to the regular polytechnics, performing functions like rural technical manpower development, transfer of technology and technical support services to the community. They provide training to about 4.5 lakh persons annually. Appendix I shows the State-wise picture of various training programmes operated by the Ministry of Human Resource Development.

The Ministry of Labour is responsible for vocational training. Under the Craftsmen Training Scheme, training in 43 engineering and 24 non-engineering trades is imparted through a network of about 4,600 Industrial Training Institutes (ITIs) run both by the respective State Governments as well as those in the private sector affiliated to the scheme for recognition and certification. These courses are open to those who have passed either 8th or 10th class depending on the trade chosen and are of one or two years' duration, again depending on the course. The Ministry of Labour also runs Advanced Training Institutes and National and Regional Vocational Training Centres for Women. The Apprenticeship Training Scheme provides on-the-job training in industrial establishments and the programme is dovetailed to some extent with the institutional training in ITIs.

The training programmes for the development of manpower in information technology present another model of vocational training. The training is imparted by grassroots level institutions and the Ministry of Information Technology is merely involved along with the Computer Society of India in setting standards, testing and certification of skills. There are a number of other government departments that are imparting formal and informal training in a wide variety of areas like hotel management (Ministry of Tourism), self-employment schemes (Department of Rural Development, Department of Social Justice and Empowerment, Department of Tribal Welfare, Department of Urban Employment and Poverty Alleviation, etc.), Department of Science and Technology, Export Promotion Councils, various commodity Boards, KVIC, Universities, ICAR, NGOs, professional Bodies, Private institutions, etc. conduct a large number of formal and informal training programmes.

These formal streams of skill formation cater only to a small segment of the population. By and large skill formation takes place through informal channels like family occupations, on-the-job training under master craftsmen with no linkages to formal education, training and certification. Even though some of them are highly skilled, their skills are not recognised for employment purposes. The large workforce in the unorganised sector also has hardly any structured system of acquiring or upgrading the skills.

Table 18.1: Estimated Number of School Leavers (from Class VIII to Class XII) and Training Capacity

Year	*Estimated School Leavers (thousand)*	*Vocational training capacities (lakhs)*	*Percentage of Training Capacities to School Leavers*
(1)	*(2)*	*(3)*	*(4)*
2002	6,926	30.25	43.7
2007	10,544	30.25	28.7
2012	10,595	30.25	28.6
2017	10,617	30.25	28.5

Source: Data for 2002 from Ministry of HRD, projections for later years made in IAMR

The existing training capacity of about 3 million can, therefore, cater to at most about 40 per cent of the school leavers now and, if the capacity is not expanded, to about 30 per cent by the end of the Tenth Plan. This indicates the magnitude of the quantitative deficiency at the national level.

Skill Mismatches

Installation of facilities to the required degree by itself does not ensure that skill mismatches do not occur. These skill shortages and surpluses arise for various reasons like values attached by the society to various lines of learning, inadequate quality of training, absence of efficient labour market signaling system and absence of the training system to respond quickly to changes in the demand patterns. Creation of training capacities is one thing and it is quite another to ensure that the school-leavers pursue vocational courses instead of general education streams. With the pattern of social demand being what it is, the accent is primarily on higher education and there are relatively few takers for vocational education in schools. Students go in for vocational training only when all attempts to go on for higher education fail.

Indian Vocational Training System

Informal

- Within family
- From master craftsmen
- Informal on the job training

Formal

- Vocational education in school
- Professional & technical education
- Training in ITIs & other training institutes
- Formal apprenticeship
- Formal training for skills in labour market, e.g. KVIC,
- Various Ministries, NGOs, etc.

Problems in the Existing Training System

The problems, to a substantial degree, are outcome of the structural deficiencies in the training system. The vocational training system in the country as it evolved, for historical reasons, has generally been geared to the needs of the organised sector, though for reasons of inadequate absorption in that sector, the trainees sometimes have to find employment in the unorganised or self-employment segments of the economy. Programmes in ITIs are straight-jacketed and without strong linkages either with industries or with polytechnics or with informal streams of skill development. Rigid entry qualifications prescribed do not allow persons from informal streams to avail of ITI training and more importantly children from deprived sections. Similarly, There is considerable variation in the quality of ITI training across the country. For example, the National and Regional Vocational Training Institutes for Women run by the Central Government are of a superior class in comparison to the ordinary ITIs for women across the country, though there is no need for the variation to exist. Inadequacy of resources at the command of the State governments is a primary cause for such variations. The rapid expansion of the network of training institutions is not always accompanied by provision of adequate resources or the full complement of infrastructure necessary. Obsolescence of trades, equipment and curriculum has been a problem with craftsmen training scheme. Though an effort was made during the Eighth Plan to remedy the situation through a World bank assisted scheme, it has been somewhat of a one-time effort. Industry linkages are sought to be achieved through National, State levels and local councils and committees but active participation of the industry with a sense of stakeholders is missing. The lack of enthusiasm on the part of the private sector industry to actively participate in skill building is reflected in the lukewarm compliance with the programme of apprenticeship training. Some efforts are now being made to increase the industry's participation and responsibility in improving training through industrial committees attached to the training institutions at the local level. These linkages between institutions and industry have to be more extensive as well as intensive. This will also help in removing the common perception in the industry circles that the skills acquired under the scheme are not up to the mark.

Vocational education in schools too suffers from lack of infrastructure, inadequate equipments, lack of trained vocational teachers working full time, persistence with obsolete trades and lack of weightage given to students from this stream in admissions to higher technical education. Though district level vocational surveys determining the trades in demand are supposed to be the basis of introducing vocational courses, mismatch between demand and supply develops due to inflexibility or delays in altering either the courses or the course content. Absence of practical training is another drawback. There is now a scheme of continuing the training of those completing the +2 vocational courses through apprenticeship under the Apprentices Act, but the coverage is rather restricted. Full time teachers trained in teaching vocational subjects are also not in place. The States, who implement educational programmes, are rather lukewarm in their approach to vocational component of education, possibly due to lack of popular demand for it, and unwillingness to make a long term commitment of resources to a centrally sponsored scheme.

There are organisational problems too. Organisational responsibility for skill development in the country is, as has already been seen, scattered over a number of agencies, often without adequate coordination. This leads to avoidable wastage of resources, duplication of effort and lack of uniformity in certification of quality of skills attained. For instance, there is a good deal of overlap between the vocational courses in engineering trades (such as fitter) offered in the schools at the +2 stage and those provided in the Industrial Training Institutes. It is not certain that the levels of skills attained after completion of the courses in the two modes are equivalent. While, there is no uniformity in skill certification even in the formal training systems, there is no skill certifications system at all for the skills acquired informally.

There is no doubt a formal employment market information system at the national, State and local levels is operated by the Ministry of Labour through the State labour departments and the employment exchanges at the grassroots level. The information system is again geared to the needs of the organised sector and does not offer anything worthwhile for the unorganised labour market. Even in the case of organised sector, the system has gradually been losing its utility over years, again due to rigidity, lack of commitment and skills in interpreting labour market signals and the indifference on the part of the training institutions to quickly respond to these signals. The interaction with industrial circles necessary to capture signals about changing patterns of demand for skills that needs to be the basis of a successful labour market information system is lacking.

To sum up, the following are the problems in the skill development programmes in India.

Table 18.2: Problems in Skill Development

Vocational education in schools	Inadequate demand Lack of infrastructure Lack of equipment Lack of trained teachers Lack of linkages with market Lack of linkages with higher technical courses
Industrial Training Institutes	Outdated courses and equipment Inadequate linkages with industry Rigidity in eligibility qualifications Rigidity in trades, course content and duration Lack of area-based approach
Formal apprenticeship	State organised and forced on employers Lack of enthusiasm from employers
Labour market training	Responsibility spread thinly over several agencies No formal recognition of skills acquired Skills short-living
General problems	Inadequate labour market information Rigidity in training systems Inadequate vocational counselling Inadequate market-training linkages Lack of movement between training and employment Lack of linkages between formal and informal training Tailor-made programmes Lack of focussed approach and compatibility with change in labour market demands

What is Needed

- Converting the goal of universal primary education into a reality.
- Guidance should help in diverting students from general education to vocational and technical training.
- Establishing a sound labour market information system that would enable identification of marketable skills as per local area needs.
- Establishing a flexible training system tuned to Indian conditions.
- Link formal and informal training through accreditation and up gradation.
- Emphasise multi-skilling.
- Mapping the training institutions and other organisations providing training and converge their efforts for optimum utilisation of resources.
- Encourage the concept of training at door step.
- Strengthen industry-institution linkages for continuous modification of courses according to market needs.

NOTES

1. National Sample Survey Organisation: Report No. 476, *Employment and Unemployment Situation in India*, July 2000-June 200, 56th Round
2. National Sample Survey Organisation: Report No. 458, *Employment and Unemployment in India*, July 1999 to June 2000, 55th Round
3. Labour force comprises all persons currently working as well as those looking for work. It is the sum of all economically active persons – the workers and the unemployed.
4. NSSO's Report No. 409 on Results of 50th Round (1993-94) survey on Employment and Unemployment quoted in the Report of the Task force on Employment Opportunities, Planning commission, 2001
5. Excluding positions for graduate and technician apprentices requiring higher entry qualifications

19

Self-employment Promotion

Job seekers are generally attracted towards salaried and wage employment but such opportunities are shrinking. These job seekers are not aware of their potentials in setting up their own enterprises. They also do not have enough information about self-employment opportunities available to them. Therefore, they have to be motivated to take up self-employment. The need for promoting self-employment is because of the following reasons:

- Self-employment is more productive
- Generates more employment as when a person starts some work, he employees more people creating jobs for others
- Opportunities are more
- Inadequate wage/salaried jobs
- One can implement his ideas
- Master of his own

Characteristics of Self-employment

Self-employment can be had in a large number of activities. It can be started in manufacturing sector or business sector or service sector. The activities may range from large enterprises to small roadside activities, like selling. There are certain common features of self-employment:

- Risks: Risk of success and failure has to be borne by the entrepreneur himself in self employment
- Market uncertainties are there as sometimes there is a demand of product in the market; sometimes there is no demand
- Resources are to be arranged by the entrepreneur
- Competition is tough and one has to decide how to survive in the market
- Requires certain personality traits
- Choice of avenues is available. One can take up the work of his own choice.

- Higher incomes can be had than the wage employment
- Best use of one's skills
- Own master
- Scope for speedy development

Traits Required

Self-employed person has to manage all by himself as he has to put all the resources in the venture at start. Obviously it requires certain specific traits in the personality so that he can run the activity successfully. Some of these traits are:

- Self-confidence
- Ability to foresee and plan
- Ability to risk taking and decision making
- Managerial abilities
- Creativity and innovation
- Ability to seize opportunities
- Marketing skills
- Determination
- Salesmanship
- Ability to cope with failures or difficulties
- Proper education, training and experience in the field one is choosing

Barriers to Self-employment Promotion

People want wage employment as it ensures regular and certain income. In self-employment activity certainty is not there. One day one may earn a high income by selling his products. On an other day he may not be able to sell. In these circumstances he would not be sure of his earnings. Other barriers that hinder promotion of self-employment are:

- Social and psychological attitudes, bias towards salaried employment Every body wants a Government job.
- Educational/training systems leading to no or non-marketable skills
- Lack of awareness about advantages and facilities available
- Lack of resources
- Institutional problems (procedures, delays, corruption, official attitudes, etc.)

How to Overcome Barriers: The above barriers can be overcome by

- Imparting relevant skills

- Generation of awareness
- Motivating to take up self-employment
- Providing support services
- Providing policy environment
- Assessing aptitudes and personality and guide for developing proper attitudes and personality characteristics

Guidance worker can play a major role in overcoming the barriers.

Steps in Self-employment Promotion

The major question is how to promote self-employment among people who are looking for salaried employment. The steps in promoting self-employment are:

- Identify Job Seekers with Potential
- Motivate them to take up self-employment
- Development of entrepreneurship, where needed
- Provide information on possible avenues
- Inform about the providers of various services
- Arrange skill training
- Introduce them to service providers
- Provide any other information and advice
- Provide follow-up advisory services

Generation of Awareness and Motivation

Important elements in effectively conveying the message are

- Media (oral/mass/cultural/etc.)
- Technique (play, talk, discussions, counselling, demonstration, etc.
- Content

The medium of generation of awareness and motivation maybe person to person oral communication, mass communication through newspapers, radio, TV, etc. The technique could be a direct communication, a play panel discussions, counselling, demonstration, etc. The content of efforts to motivate should:

- Inform about the labour market conditions
- Inform about the opportunities in self-employment
- Inform about the schemes and facilities
- Indicate the relative advantages of self-employment over wage-employment

- Use audio-visual aids and success stories.
- It is important that the client is not presented a one-sided picture only giving the positive aspects of pursuing self-employment.

After Motivation

Once an individual or group of individuals is sufficiently motivated towards self-employment, the guidance worker should provide him information on:

- Possible lines of self-employment
- Rules and regulations such as registration, license, etc.
- Special schemes of assistance, such as the employment promotion fund
- Agencies providing various forms of assistance and services like finance, raw materials, training, technical advice, marketing, etc.
- Procedures for availing of the assistance and requirements to be met

Based on the information, the individual should be helped in making use of the advice of a suitable line of self-employment.

- Can he/she/they take it up? (skills, resources, etc.)
- Is the product consistent with needs, resources and acceptability?
- Can tastes be changed to accept new product?
- Can various inputs be acquired with ease?
- Is the demand sufficient in the face of competition?
- What are the marketing strategies?
- How much profit be earned and how soon?
- What would be the contingency plans?

Referral Services

After the individual makes a choice of the line of self-employment to pursue, the guidance activity would comprise the following steps:

- Assisting in preparing the necessary documentation such as the project proposal,
- Introducing to the various service providers like banks, raw material providers, technical experts in the line chosen, etc.
- Arranging entrepreneurial or skill training where necessary
- Following up with the service providers in getting the assistance required.

Post-launch Services

The guidance services will have to continue even after a self-employment activity has been initiated by the individual or group. It is necessary to organise periodic follow up to see that the activity is going on along the expected lines or if it is encountering any problems. In case of any problems, proper counselling should be provided to overcome the same. The person who wants to take up self-employment should think about the following aspects:

Some Emerging Areas in Rural Sector

Here is a list of some emerging areas that can be taken up for self-employment. The list would help a guidance worker in providing guidance to the students who may like to have their own venture.

- Agriculture
- Organic manures,
- horticulture,
- bio-fuel and energy plantations,
- floriculture,
- fishing,
- medicinal plants (in hill areas),
- mushrooms,
- quality cotton
- oil seeds

Agriculture and allied

- Fishing,etc
- Dairying
- Chinese fishing in coastal areas
- Poultry and egg production
- Bee-keeping
- Quality improvement

Industrial Sector

- Cut-flowers
- Food processing (cut vegetables,pickles, snacks, etc.) fruit processing, fish processing
- Handicrafts with improved designs
- Khadi & textiles, new products and designs

- Jute & other bags
- Repairs of domestic appliances, auto-and electronic goods, tractors and pump-sets
- Repair of boats and nets (coastal areas)
- Low cost housing materials (bricks, sheets,etc.)
- Parts for assembling in larger units (electronics)

Service Sector I

- Tourism related (guide services, adventure sports in coastal and hill areas, etc.)
- Restaurants and hospitality (value added services, practice of hygiene, stay services)
- Transportation
- Storage of agricultural products
- Packaging of foods
- Yoga, indigenous health practices

Service Sector II

- Communication services (e-mail, fax)
- Data related services (data entry, internet, electronic marketing, etc.)
- Financial services (shares, bonds, insurance, mutual funds etc.)
- Beauty-culture
- Domestic nursing

Emerging Areas in Urban Sector

- Finance, Banking sector and Insurance
- I.T. Sector
- Innovative Technology
- Tourism
- Infrastructure development and construction
- Outsourcing
- Fashion designing and media
- Service sector, like telecom, tourism, beauty culture, event management
- Innovative eco-friendly technology
- Adventure related jobs

Annexure I

Some Agencies Dealing with Psychological Tests

1. Mansayan, Agrawal Complex, Ist floor, S-524, School Block, Shakarpur, Delhi-110092.
2. Educational Psychology Unit, NCERT, Sri Aurbindo Marg, New Delhi-110016.
3. Manovigyan Shala, Allahabad, U.P.
4. Dr. S.D. Kappor, B-78, Amar Colony, Lajpatnagar No. 4, New Delhi.
5. Agra Psychological Research Cell (APRC), Tewari Kothi, Belanganj, Agra-282004.
6. National Psychological Corporation, Bhargav Bhawan, 4/230 Kacheri Ghat, Agra-282004.
7. Rupa Psychological Centre 819/60 B, Deoriabir Bhedupura, Varanasi-221010.
8. Ankur Psychological Agency, 22/481, Indira Nagar, Lucknow.

Annexure II

List of Agencies Publishing/Dealing with Career Literature

1. Central Institute for Research and Training in Employment Services (CIRTES) Pusa, New Delhi.
2. Association of Indian Universities, New Delhi.
3. National Council for Educational Research and Training (NCERT), Sri Aurobindo Marg, New Delhi-16.
4. Union Public Service Commission (UPSC) Dholpur House, New Delhi.
5. Directorate of Employment and Training Ministry of Labour, Shram Shakti Bhawan, New Delhi.
6. State Bureaux of Guidance.
7. State Public Service Commissions.
8. Career Magazines.
9. University Employment and Guidance Bureaux in the Country.
10. Private Publishers.

Annexure III

Websites Information

Name of the Website	*Contents*
• goidirectory.nic.in/dget/cirtes	Career information
• CollegeBoard.com	Personality assessment and suggested Career
• mentaltesting.com	
• ncert.nic.in	Aptitude Tests
• careers india.com	
• Career explorer.net	
• 3Smartcubes.com	
• jobs ahead.com	About career guidance
• queendom.com/tests	
• quincyweb.net	psychological tests
• naukri.com	ref.on jobs
• SmartHunt.com	IT jobs
• Career Age.com	jobs and career, employment, education and placement in India in different fields
• careerindia.com	ref.on jobs in different fields
• rozgar.com	jobs & resumes India & overseas
• rediff.com/jobs/computers	Jobs data base
• timesjob.com	Career information
• Jobs Ahead.com	Career information
• CampusonNet.com	Guidance, information on education, resources, courses & institutions, scholarships etc
• eSaras.com	edu.Website for undergraduate, post-graduate, question papers for engg. medical, management
• planetgyan.com	list of schools, (Statewise) Colleges (according to streams) institutes, coaching classes, test papers, studies abroad
• indianacademy.com	education facilities
• sifyeducation	A comprehensive on line resource for free on line tests for CAT, IIT, GMAT, GRE, Engg, Medical, Standard X/XII, etc.
	Free online courses for Std.X, Career counseling, school and college data bases, study abroad information, etc.

Name of the Website	*Contents*
• entrancebusters.com	Details of GMAT, GRE, SAT, TOEFL, TSE, CAT, CET,HOTEL, Bank, Post Officer Engg. IIT, NDA, AIIMS, MCA, UPSC Exams, Indian Universities, Careers
• infor masala.com	Information on education in India, studying abroad, jobs, resumes, employment opportunity, career counseling
• planetwidya	Education website for teachers, students parents

Bibliography

A.E. Traxler and R.D. North, *Techniques of Guidance*, Harper and Row Publishers, N.Y., 1966.

Aggarwal, J.C., *Educational and Vocational Guidance and Counselling*, Doaba House, New Delhi, 2006

Anastasi, Anne, *Psychological Testing*, New York, The Mac Millan Co. 1954.

Brief Counselling in Schools—Working with Young People from 11 to 18, Sage Publications, London, Thousand Oaks, New Delhi, 2002.

C.H. Miller, *Foundation of Guidance*, Harper & Brothers, New York, 1961.

D. Smith, *Measurement and Evaluation in Elementary Schools*, Commonwealth Publisher, 2005.

D.C. Dinkmeyer Holt, Rinehart and Winston (Ed.),*Guidance and Counselling in the Elementary School—Readings in Theory and Practice*, New York, 1964.

D.G. Mortenosen, A.M. Schumuller, *Guidance in Today's Schools*, John Wiley *et.al.* Inc, New York, London, Sydney, 1966.

D.W. Le Fever, L.M. Turrell, H.I. Weitzel, *Principles and Techniques of Guidance*, The Ronald Press Company, New York, 1950.

Donald E. Super, A Theory of Vocational Development, *American Psychologist*, 8: 189-190 (American Psychological Association, 1953). The Psychology of Careers, (New York: Harper & Row, Publishers, 1975).

E. Stoops and G.L. Walhquist, *Principles and Practices in Guidance*, McGraw Hill Book Comp, INC. N.Y., 1958.

E.F. Lindquist Ed., *Educational Measurement*, American Council on Education, Washington D.C., 1963.

E.G. Williamson Ed., *Vocational Counselling*, McGraw Hill Book Comp, N.Y., 1965.

E.W. Detjen and M.F. Detgen, *Elementary School Guidance*, Mc Graw Hill Book Co.Inc. New York, 1963.

G. Arulmani and S.N. Arulmani, *Career Counselling*, Tata McGraw Hill Publishing Comp.Ltd., N.D., 2004.

G.E. Smith, *Principles and Practices of the Guidance Progam*, The Macmillan Company, New York, 1951.

H. Weitz, *Behaviour Change Through Guidance*, JohnWiley & Sons Inc. New York, London, Sydney, 1964.

H.A. Greene et.al., *Measurement and Evaluation in the Sec. Schools*, Longmans Green & Comp., 1954.

Hahn, M.E. & MacLean, M.S., *Counselling Psychology*, McGraw Hill Book Company, IMC, 1955.

Hoppoch—Robert, *Occupational Information*, McGraw Hill Book Company, New York, 1967.

J. Warters, *Techniques of Counselling*, McGraw Hill Book Company Inc. New York, 1954.

Jane Walters, *Group Guidance—Principles and Practices*, McGraw Hill Book Comp, INC. N.Y., 1960.

John L. Holland, *The Psychology of Vocational Choice* (Lexington, Mass.: Blaisdell-Ginn and Company, 1966), pp. 8-12. Also *Making Vocational Choices: A Theory of Careers* (Englewood Cliffs, N.J.: Prentice-Hall, Inc., 1973).

John-Hayes, B.Hopson, P.P. Daws, *Career Guidance—The Role of School in Vocational Guidance*, Heinemanu Educational Books, 1971.

L.E. Tyler, *The Work of the Counsellor*, Appleton—Century, Crafts, INC. N.Y., 1961.

L.F. Moser, R.S. Moser, *Counselling and Guidance : An Exploration*, Prentice Hall. INC, NJ, 1963.

L.J. Kramel, *Testing in Our Schools*, The Macmillan Company, New York, 1966.

M.F. Baer and E.C. Roeber, *Occupational Information*, Prentice Research Associates Inc. Chicago, 1951.

P.M. Blau, J.W. Gustad, R. Jessor, H.S. Parnes, and R.G. Wilcock, Occupational Choice: A Conception Framework, *Industrial and Labor Relations Review*, (July 1956), p. 531.

P.M. Hughes, *Guidance and Counselling in Schools*, Pergamon Press, Oxford, 1971.

Psipow S.M., *Theories of Career Development*, Prentice-Hall-Inc, Englewood Cliffs, New Jersey-07632, 1983.

R.N. Sharma and Rachna Sharma, *Guidance and Counselling in India*, Atlantic Pub. and Dist., N.D., 2004.

Robert Hoppock, *Occupational Information*, 4th ed.(New York: McGraw-Hill Book Company, 1976).

S.H. Osipow, *Theories of Career Development*, Prentice Hall. Inc. Jersey, 1983 Englewood Cliffs.

S.S. Marzolf, *Psychological Diagnosis and Counselling in the Schools*, Henry Holt and Company, New York, 1956.

Swadesh Mohan Ed., *Career Development in India—Through Research and Development*, Vikas Publishing House Pvt. Ltd., 1999.

V.P. Bansal, *Organising Guidance Services in Schools*, Indian Press Pvt. Ltd., Allahabad, 1963.

W. Little, A.L. Chapman, *Development Guidance in Secondary Schools*, McGraw Hill Book Company Inc., New York, Toranto, London, 1953.

W.M. Williams, *Occupational Choice*, George Allen & Unwin Ltd., London, 1974.

Index